W9-DBQ-298

GENERATION CHEF

GENERATION
≡ CHEF ≡

RISKING IT ALL FOR
A NEW AMERICAN DREAM

KAREN STABINER

AVERY
an imprint of Penguin Random House
New York

Fitchburg Public Library
5530 Lacy Road
Fitchburg, WI 53711
WITHDRAWN

AVERY

an imprint of Penguin Random House LLC
375 Hudson Street
New York, New York 10014

Copyright © 2016 by Karen Stabiner
Penguin supports copyright. Copyright fuels creativity, encourages diverse voices,
promotes free speech, and creates a vibrant culture. Thank you for buying an authorized
edition of this book and for complying with copyright laws by not reproducing, scanning,
or distributing any part of it in any form without permission. You are supporting
writers and allowing Penguin to continue to publish books for every reader.

Most Avery books are available at special quantity discounts for bulk purchase
for sales promotions, premiums, fund-raising, and educational needs. Special books
or book excerpts also can be created to fit specific needs. For details,
write SpecialMarkets@penguinrandomhouse.com.

Library of Congress Cataloging-in-Publication Data
Names: Stabiner, Karen, author.
Title: Generation chef : risking it all for a new American dream / Karen Stabiner.
Description: New York : Avery, an imprint of Penguin Random House, LLC, [2016]
Identifiers: LCCN 2016026428 | ISBN 9781583335802
Subjects: LCSH: Miller, Jonah. | Cooks—United States—Biography. | Huertas (Restaurant)
Classification: LCC TX649.M56 S73 2016 | DDC 641.5092 [B]—dc23
LC record available at https://lccn.loc.gov/2016026428
p.   cm.

Printed in the United States of America
1   3   5   7   9   10   8   6   4   2

BOOK DESIGN BY MEIGHAN CAVANAUGH

*Penguin is committed to publishing works of quality and integrity.
In that spirit, we are proud to offer this book to our readers;
however, the story, the experiences, and the words
are the author's alone.*

For Sarah Ivria

CONTENTS

1

OPENING NIGHT

Jonah Miller bounded up the steep narrow stairs, each tread worn at the center from more than a century of use, the only reminder that this place had ever been anything but his. In fifteen minutes, when the doors opened for the first time, it would be Huertas, a Spanish restaurant that had the twenty-six-year-old chef almost $700,000 in debt before he sold his first beer—on paper, at least, as restaurant investors knew how bad the odds were of repayment, let alone profit, anytime soon. Everything but the stairs was new, a practical compromise between the dream Jonah had carried in his head since he was sixteen and the realities of building codes and water lines and oven vents and his partners' input and, always, the budget. He had managed to erase the storefront's past as a pizza place that simply stopped paying rent and gave the keys back to the landlord, a Korean place that preceded it in failure, and before all that, a vague something else. Now all he had to do was not fail as his predecessors had, in a business where it happened all the time.

Jonah was ten pounds lighter than usual on an already beanpole frame, skinny enough to catch his mother's attention and inspire his fiancée to make sure there was always takeout in the refrigerator for a late-night meal. His professional kitchen philosophy boiled down to "keep your head down and do the work," and he wasn't a screamer like some chefs, so the stress of opening his first restaurant turned inward, instead, and eroded his appetite. He referred to the space that way, as his first restaurant, because there was no chance he'd stop at one.

At six foot two, he'd developed a slouch in deference to kitchen soffits that might want to knock him in the forehead or coworkers who preferred eye contact to staring at his chin. He was, he said, too tall to be a chef—which made him laugh, because he had never really wanted to be anything else. The slump was part of an overall concession to the fact that cooking always came first. Jonah had gone to the same East Village barbershop for the last five years for a $15 adult version of a kid's buzz cut, because it spared him having to make aesthetic decisions or to engage in mindless conversation with someone who considered himself not a barber but a stylist. He had no tattoos, even though they were as ubiquitous as clogs in a restaurant kitchen. He wore anonymous dark cotton pants that were baggy enough to be comfortable on a fifteen-hour shift, and equally nondescript T-shirts and hoodies; no outlier colors or styles that required him to devote conscious thought to what he put on in the morning. His shoes were broken in and built for comfort.

What stood out was his new chef's shirt, blindingly white, its creased short sleeves not yet softened into shape by repeated washings. Jonah could have worn a more formal and more expensive double-breasted chef's coat, embroidered with "Huertas" and "Executive Chef Jonah Miller," but he chose the same shirt that the cooks and dishwasher and porter wore, and told them not to call him "Chef." Better to lead by example, he figured, than to insist on respect before he'd shown them what he could do. Hierarchy didn't mean anything. He was going to earn their admiration.

He took his place at the pass, a marble counter at the front of the nar-row open kitchen and a particular source of pride—six old pieces of mar-ble set into a steel frame, held in place with some adhesive, twelve and a half square feet of work space for $200, the price of a single square foot if he'd insisted on a pristine new slab. He checked the inanimate objects that hadn't budged since the last time he looked, because he had to have something to do: a large Spanish ham on a metal skewer set into a wooden frame; little mismatched vintage dishes, one of Maldon salt and one of lemon wedges; a canister of tasting spoons; a metal spindle to hold com-pleted order tickets; a jury-rigged rail that wouldn't last the week, to hold tickets that were still in play. He checked the fill level on his squirt bottle of olive oil, retied his long apron, and refolded and retucked a towel at exactly the right position on that apron tie, just behind his left arm.

He walked back past the roast and sauté station and the fry station, peered inside the refrigerated drawers at the mixed greens and por-tioned proteins, and headed up to the wood-burning oven to survey the prep work of the one cook Jonah couldn't see. The oven had been there when he leased the space and he wasn't about to spend money to move it, so they'd ended up with a bathroom between it and the kitchen. Until everything was running smoothly, he'd shuttle back and forth to keep an eye on things. While he was up there, he reviewed the glass jars of citrus wedges that sat on the bar, to make sure they looked good enough to suit him.

Jonah had played high school baseball, starting out as a pitcher until a chipped bone in his shoulder exiled him to shortstop and third base, and the pitcher's habit of minuscule last-minute adjustments—once the microscopic repositioning of fingers on the ball, now the equally fine placement of a knife on a cutting board—had stayed with him. It was a nice, familiar way to dissipate some of the tension.

If Jonah was right—and he had bet his professional future that he was—Huertas was exactly what a healthy range of people were looking for, from the East Village millennial crowd that cruised First Avenue to serious diners old enough to be their parents, to neighborhood residents looking for a regular haunt. He was going to serve them Basque food because he loved it and because it had newness going for it, offered in two distinct formats that gave people a range of choices, from a drink and a snack to a multicourse meal.

In the front room, where he expected the younger crowd to gather, he'd serve pintxos, little one-bite appetizers that would fly by on trays like dim sum, an endless array of impulse purchases served with Spanish beers and wines and traditional drinks like the kalimotxo, which was red wine and Coca-Cola. The pintxo list led off with the gilda, named for Rita Hayworth's character in the 1946 film *Gilda*, a skewered white anchovy curved around a manzanilla green olive at one end and a guindilla pepper at the other. There would be some type of croqueta, jamón or mushroom or fish, depending on what he had on hand, and a slice of bread topped with egg salad and a single shrimp—which might not sound as good as it tasted but was going to look alluring enough to get people to take a chance. He could build a pintxo around a chunk of octopus or some homemade sausage; the point was to have a half dozen every day, and to change the list frequently, so that repeat customers had to start all over again once they got past the gilda, which would always be on the menu, no matter what else he made.

He would offer conservas, tins of Spanish seafood—Spain put its best seafood into tins—and serve them with bread, aioli or lemon or pickled peppers, and homemade potato chips. There would be a few raciones, midsized plates, but for the most part the front room was a place to drink and snack and chat, either at the bar or at a table or standing up, which was what people did in Spain.

The dining room at the back was for what he called the menu del dia, four courses, pintxos through dessert, with choices for the entrée and dessert. Jonah planned to change some portion of that menu every week, at least, to keep people coming back for what qualified as a fine-dining bargain by New York City standards—a $52 fixed-price menu, with wine pairings at $28.

His signature dining-room dish was the egg course, huevos rotos, or "broken eggs," which summed up what he was trying to do—have fun with refined, reconsidered versions of Spanish classics. He'd tried the original at a Basque place in Madrid, a fried egg plopped on top of a batch of fried potatoes with a side of chorizo or chistorra sausage or jamón. Jonah's version had only the basic ingredients in common with the original. He used a hand-crank machine to spin an impaled russet potato into strands as slender as spaghetti, which he flash-fried, dressed with a chorizo vinaigrette, and topped with a slow-poached egg and slivers of fresh scallions. As soon as the soft egg broke, it turned the vinaigrette into a richer sauce.

It was "carbonara with potatoes, like al dente pasta with chorizo Bolognese," he told the food writers who had already started to hover, because more of their readers understood Italian references than Spanish ones. It was also about a dime's worth of Idaho potatoes and a quarter's worth of chorizo, total cost per serving about $2. Jonah prided himself on his ability to wrangle food costs below the stiff 28 percent industry standard in New York City, which was lower than the national figure of 30 percent because other costs in the city were so high. He knew how to be frugal without sacrificing flavor or quality, and he'd already explained his philosophy to his sous chef, Jenni Cianci: "If there's something left over, use it." The chefs he'd worked for had taught him not to waste food long before it became a politically correct stance, so he repurposed things that a more wanton kitchen might discard. Duck trims landed in the croquetas, and cod skin became crispy chips he could use instead of a cracker as the base of a pintxo.

His version of migas, which meant "crumbs," was another mix of style and economy. In Spain, people made migas to use up old bread, toasting coarse bread crumbs and mixing them with an egg or sausage and some greens. Jonah mixed his homemade crumbs with a slow-poached egg and bent the rules from there—he planned to add whatever vegetables were in season along with whatever protein felt like a good match.

If he splurged, it was with a specific purpose. For the opening he indulged in an order of percebes, stubby little sheathed gooseneck barnacles that clung to the rocks in Galicia, in northern Spain, and were harvested by divers who had to cut them off with knives, still attached to the smaller rocks that sustained them—$20 a pound, probably twice that if he subtracted the weight of the rocks, but "a cool experience," said Jonah. "If you want to talk wild, this is wild." He steamed a small batch in water and white wine and showed the dining-room servers how they worked, amid jokes about how they resembled little penises wearing little condoms; he snapped the soft part of the barnacle from its base, removed the sheath, and ate what was inside, which was supposed to be an aphrodisiac, or at least that was the legend. It was a good story to tell about something people weren't going to find all over town. He planned to offer them to some of the back tables, but only if he had the time to go back there and eat one with the guests.

He had thought about it all, and rethought, endlessly, in the twenty months since he walked away from a sous chef job rather than bide his time waiting for a promotion to executive sous. He still had little idea of what to expect. The big variable at Huertas was experience, or the lack of it. No one, not Jonah or his two general manager partners or his sous chef, had ever done their jobs before—each of them had leapfrogged over a step or two on the career trajectory to be here, skipped jobs that might have given them a more seasoned perspective. Jonah had been a sous chef for just over a year when he left Maialino, the Roman restaurant owned by Danny Meyer's Union Square Hospitality Group, where he had worked since he graduated from NYU; he had never been an executive sous, never managed a kitchen team. Luke Momo had worked both front and back of house at the elegant forty-year-old Le Cirque, and Nate Adler had been a beverage director at USHG's popular group of barbecue restaurants, briefly, but neither of them had ever run a front-of-house operation. Now they were general managers—and partners, because they'd wagered on Jonah's ability to pull this off, a $10,000 investment from Luke and more than $20,000 from Nate, in exchange for small chunks of equity. His sous chef, Jenni, was a line cook only three years out of culinary school when he offered her the job. Still, the four of them had in common an impressive set of skills, given that their average age was barely twenty-six, and an impatient ambition. Jonah reassured himself: The people who were opening Huertas were green but smart.

If they were a little insecure, maybe that was a good thing, since they would be motivated to work that much harder. Luke took every detail seriously, and at the moment had three servers with him in the dining room debating the proper seat-number rotation, which had plagued him for days. Identifying diners by number enabled servers to put each dish in front of the person who ordered it, and to avoid messy tableside queries like "Who has the duck?," but any system required consensus about how to number. Luke placed diner one at the southeast corner of a table and counted the rest clockwise, which left everyone confused about whether the two tables at the far side of the room should work the same way or be a mirror image of the others.

It wasn't an idle concern. In the worst-case scenario, the diner in seat three, who was allergic to shellfish, mistakenly got the plate intended for seat two, took a carefree bite, and ended the evening in the emergency room. As more people wandered in with an opinion, though, it became a lightning rod for anxiety. Nate listened just long enough to be exasperated, worried that he and Luke weren't exuding a suitably managerial air.

"We'll figure it out," he said, signaling that the conversation was over. "For tonight it's the southeast corner for everyone." That resolved, he went back to his own way of coping with opening-night nerves, which involved never standing still. He checked the bar, he looked at the reservation list that was Luke's responsibility, he adjusted the music level up and then circled back a moment later to adjust it down.

Jenni had nothing to do until an order came in, because her way of coping was to get ahead. She took pride in her exacting mise en place, the double row of small steel containers that held every seasoning and garnish and sauce she needed for the night's menu, a setup worthy of a sous and an example to anyone who worked for her. It was almost enough to make her feel ready. She stepped over to review the line cooks' setups, and that helped, too. To bridge the rest of the gap between her experience and her new job, she chattered. She couldn't help it, and in between commenting on almost everything she apologized for doing so. No one seemed to mind, as her running commentary balanced out Jonah, who tended to get even quieter when he felt stressed.

The need to keep busy was contagious, so there was a flurry of nervous hygiene right before the doors opened. Jenni made sure that her long ponytail was tucked out of the way, even though it already was, and the line cook took notice and pulled her ponytail into an even more disciplined braid. Nate, whose downtown style involved a fitted button-down shirt and narrow chinos with hems rolled to expose his ankle boots, darted into the bathroom to brush his teeth and then continued to prowl the space. Luke put on a sport coat and used his electric razor to eliminate any shadow that might have appeared since he shaved that morning.

Jonah watched a server make wipe towels, a precise ritual that seemed tonight to be two-thirds necessity and one-third superstition. First she trimmed a small edge off a set of paper hand towels, and then she moistened the slightly shorter towels so that they were neither too dry nor too drippy. Satisfied with the moisture content, she rolled them as tightly as possible and stacked them in a dish so that Jonah could wipe the rim of a plate before it went out. On opening night, this chore required an experienced front-of-house staffer, not some kid doing it for the first time. A properly rolled towel was a totem that said, This is a professional kitchen. A loose or uneven towel could be a sign that the whole place was about to unravel.

The last minutes before five thirty were somehow very long and very short all at once, and Jonah had an extended moment, right before the first customers came in, when he let himself reflect on what was about to happen, unspooled the future like a kite on a breeze. Someday he'd split his time between Huertas and his other places—plural—with a system that enabled him to develop new concepts while his dependable kitchen staffs handled the day-to-day operations. Someday his restaurants would be an incubator for talented cooks who moved on to open their own places.

He dreamed of creating the kind of kitchen that people in the industry talked about with admiration—venerable ones like those at Meyer's USHG restaurants; kitchens run by chefs just a half-generation older than Jonah, like David Chang and April Bloomfield, who served pork buns and cheeseburgers and dismissed the need for tablecloths and distinct courses and even reservations; anyplace that the three principals of Major Food Group decided to open, after four successes in as many years. The usually fickle opening crowds didn't move on from these places, unless it was to check out what the owners were doing next.

There were a handful of such companies in New York City, groups that grew exponentially, their openings always mobbed, the crowds never dissipating. At the moment Jonah might be rolling trays of cod croquetas like some first-year line cook, but it was all in the service of his long-term plan. Some young chef with an irresistible menu was going to be the next phenomenon, and he had to believe he had as good a chance as any to be the one.

Nate broke the spell to give Jonah the latest news. Ryan Sutton, just named the lead New York City restaurant critic at Eater.com after a stint at Bloomberg, had tweeted about Huertas's opening.

"That means he's coming," Nate told Jonah, assuming that a critic wouldn't bother mentioning a restaurant he intended to ignore.

He was hardly the only one paying attention. In the days leading up to the opening there had been announcements on Zagat, Tasting Table, UrbanDaddy, and Gothamist. On April 18, Huertas showed up as number ten on Grub Street's weekly Restaurant Power Rankings, *New York* magazine's list of the city's hottest restaurants—based on nothing but advance noise, since the restaurant wasn't yet officially open. The phone was ringing like mad, and a third of the opening-night reservations were for people Jonah didn't know, "which would have been more if family and friends hadn't booked earlier," he said. He'd had to post a sign on the front door on the final two nights of the five-night soft opening, a friends-and-family trial run, saying that Huertas was closed for a private party, because strangers who tracked openings came by hoping for an early glimpse.

It was exactly what Jonah had hoped for, despite the occasional twinge of anxiety about living up to the advance press, because the alternative was to be one of those chefs with little neighborhood places nobody discovered for six months, if at all, and nobody reviewed, ever. He'd much rather get noticed.

Nate tried to achieve a similar enthusiasm, and failed. He was fixated on the fact that this was the first critic to weigh in.

"It would be nice," he muttered, "if somebody would let us open before they blew us up."

An hour into service, Jonah had decided that the homemade potato chips for the boquerones plate needed more salt, that his homemade setup for order tickets was a mess, and that the people at seats three and four at the bar should get their papas bravioli for free because they'd waited too long, which meant that the fryer wasn't hot enough. He riffled through the cooler drawer of micro-greens to replenish the small tray at the pass with the specific varieties he needed, and in between orders he picked flecks of Super Glue off his fingers. He'd successfully repaired the food processor earlier in the day, but now he couldn't feel the food to make sure that crisp was crisp enough or that a piece of protein was cooked through.

He checked every plate that went out, even as he kept an eye on the big digital clock on the wall and waited for reinforcements to arrive. Jonah had set up an insurance policy for himself, three guys to help out at the start who had more experience than the rest of his kitchen staff combined. He stopped holding his breath when the first one walked in at seven, after a day that had begun at five thirty in the morning with a catered breakfast for four hundred. Dan Dilworth shrugged off his exhaustion, carved out a little space for himself at the end of Jonah's pass, and began peeling lemons at warp speed, so that slivers of peel could be candied and used as a garnish for the rice pudding.

By eight the bar stools were full, people were standing at the counter across from the bar just as Jonah had imagined they would, the three booths across from the kitchen were full, and a steady stream of people walked by the kitchen on the way to the dining room. It was gratifying, but it was an illusion, and Jonah knew it. The opening crowd, most of it, was a fickle bunch that prized new over good, and a percentage of the bar crowd would likely never come back because they were on their way to the next new place, loyal only to being current.

It was easy to spot them—funereal chic on the women, whose cut-out clothing had a mysterious chicken-and-egg relationship to their tattoos, and big shirts over little pants on the men. Silver studs on their shoes, belts, backpacks, and in their earlobes, unless they had a day job where it was acceptable to wear gauges, the earrings that opened a hole in the lobe. Anyone who was that committed to a look was not going to stick around to become a regular, because the whole point of their existence was to be wherever the next scene was.

The customers who walked past the kitchen to the dining room were older, probably more likely to settle in, potential regulars—and if this worked the way it was supposed to, regulars who came in more than once a week, because sometimes they opted for a lighter meal at the bar. But there would be attrition there, too, diners who decided that they wanted more choice on the menu or less of something Jonah couldn't even speculate on.

There was no time to dwell, because the dominant noise, in Jonah's world, was the mechanical bleat of the little gray order printer that sat on the counter to his right. Jonah and Dan danced the experienced dance of cooks who'd worked the line in a crunch, somehow managing to do what they needed to do, fast, without colliding, and with an urgency that made everyone else try to stay out of their way rather than break up the choreography. Jonah reached up to a top shelf next to the combi oven for a bag of almonds as Dan dipped out of his way and dove for a quart container of chocolate pieces from the cooler drawer. Without a word, they set out two little saucers of almonds and chocolate chunks for bar seats three and four, with the chef's compliments, a final apology for their late potatoes.

As the pace in the back room picked up, Dan silently stepped over next to Jonah and started plating cod entrées. This was how a kitchen was supposed to work, how Jonah hoped the Huertas kitchen would work once everyone got used to the rhythm and traffic patterns. Jonah had always loved working the hot line and had nothing but admiration for Dan and the other members of his special crew, one an executive sous chef and one a sous, who had some free time between jobs and would arrive in mid-May and early June, respectively. "To be able to show up in the middle of service, help out, not be in the way, roll right in without even knowing what's on the menu is a unique talent," he said. In his kitchen, a great cook was the one who got the work done without taking up a lot of psychic space.

When Nate came over to ask how it was going, the question barely registered.

"Great," said Jonah, preoccupied with what was on the plate in front of him.

"Doesn't sound convincing."

Jonah shot him a distracted but managerial smile; he had to remember that people looked to him to set the tone. "It's great," he repeated, more loudly. "Dining room pacing's good."

The bar was moving a little too fast, but that was a good thing. The pintxo runner skidded toward the pass and asked for any pintxos at all, because he had a slew of new customers, including people who were drinking and eating in the middle of the front room, balancing their drinks and little plates in their hands because there was no space at the bar or the standing counter against the wall.

"Ten chorizo, eight shrimp, eight scallops," called Jonah over his shoulder, without stopping to turn around.

. . .

The final order of the night meant that housecleaning could begin, as much a daily ritual as the preparations that preceded service. Jonah wanted his kitchen as clean at the end of the day as it had been on the day they connected the kitchen appliances; it was a matter of self-respect as well as a smart habit, given the constant threat of a surprise city health inspection. Breaking down the kitchen was hardly a glamorous aspect of his job, not the kind of thing people saw when they watched food shows on television, and someday he'd graduate from having to participate. For now, he intended to work as hard as everyone else did, to establish a baseline standard that would survive when he took his two days off.

Food went into plastic pint or quart containers, the date and contents written on a piece of blue masking tape. Cheeses and ham and half-sheets of pintxos were covered with food-grade plastic wrap as tight as a trampoline. Cooks ran up and down the narrow stairs at an angle, one with a half-sheet held overhead, another carrying a hunk of cheese tucked close like a football, to store bigger items in the basement walk-in refrigerator. The bartender decided whether the citrus wedges would last another day, stashed what could be stashed, and wiped down every surface.

The dishwasher sprinted back and forth as though he were being timed on relay legs, darting from each cook's station to the sink at the rear of the kitchen and back again to return clean plates and platters and equipment to their rightful spot. Lance Hester-Bay had informed Jonah during his job interview that he would take a dishwashing job only if there were a chance for him to move on to the line someday. In the meantime he made sure that his new boss saw how hardworking he was, no matter how menial the task.

Once the food was put away, the kitchen staff started to clean up— leaned hard against a cooking surface and scrubbed, balanced on a counter to reach the exhaust fan, got on their hands and knees to soap down every surface. The smell of cleansers quickly smothered the smells of cheese and ham and wood-oven char, and after a half hour the space approximated a kitchen that had never been used. The front-of-house staff, like any good dinner-party hosts, bused the last tables, adjusted vases, and wiped every surface clean. Well after midnight, the last exhausted staffer left for home, or for a nearby bar to decompress.

Jonah slumped into a booth with Nate and Luke to try to make sense of what had just happened. They had sold so many pintxos that the servers had lost track of the numbers, which meant that they needed a better tally system right away. Runners were supposed to circulate with a tray until it was empty and then come back to the pass to record who took what, but things had been too frantic and they forgot how many they served and to whom, which meant that the restaurant lost sales. The dining-room menu worked, though they all knew, without saying, that Dan's speed and efficiency had kept them from falling behind. The kitchen staff had tackled the nightly kitchen breakdown with inappropriate good cheer, emptying and cleaning every drawer and cabinet and surface, something to be grateful for until the novelty wore off.

Jenni had found her rhythm and recovered from her opening-night jitters, and the cook at the wood-burning oven burned her arm only once. They'd used up all of the prepped ingredients except for a cup or two of pre-sliced potatoes, which Jonah took as a very good sign. The better his volume estimates, the fewer the leftovers, the less money he threw away on unused product.

But before the partners went home, they had to address the missteps. They needed a "soigné" list to alert the staff to VIP customers and their preferences. They needed the food runners to keep an eye on the pass and grab hot plates as soon as they appeared rather than wait to be called over. The bartender had to stay off his cell phone.

Most important, in terms of building a decent total check, they had to bus pintxo plates as soon as they were empty. If plates sat on the table, customers felt that they'd eaten enough. If they disappeared, customers stared at the empty space in front of them and were likelier to order from the next circulating tray.

They analyzed the particulars and listed the next day's tasks as though to compensate for a rising elation. It would be so easy to relax—and after all, a small moment of celebration was called for, given how long they'd waited for this moment and how hard they'd worked. Jonah, who had been a line cook at four previous openings, was the most experienced member of the trio, in addition to being the majority owner. It seemed appropriate for him to provide a little happy context. This was, he told his partners, the smoothest opening he'd ever worked on, and he wasn't saying that because of any bias.

"I know stuff's going to go wrong, but I know we're going to fix it," he said. "And I think we're going to make money."

He and Nate and Luke started to laugh, with relief as much as anything. He regaled them with a story a friend had just told him of a much bigger opening, twelve cooks to Huertas's four, eighty covers to tonight's fifty, where the cooks had lost their synchronized rhythm and never got it back. "They went down in flames," was how the friend described it.

And Huertas hadn't. For all their inexperience, they'd pulled it off.

It was two in the morning before Jonah had a moment to himself, and more time until the adrenaline subsided and he could even think of sleep. He'd be back in the kitchen the next morning before ten to make his own stocks and prep for dinner. Eater was sending a photographer over at noon to shoot the restaurant's interior.

2

THE DREAM

When Jonah was thirteen, his best friend got a bar mitzvah gift certificate for dinner for two at Chanterelle, one of the first fine-dining restaurants to colonize downtown Manhattan when it opened in 1979, and for years a member of a short and exclusive list of restaurants that had received four-star reviews from the *New York Times*. Ten years later Chanterelle moved to a slightly larger location and lost a star along the way, only to win it back in 1993. It was a required destination for anyone who cared about restaurants, run by chef David Waltuck, who had gone into business when he was only twenty-four, and his wife, Karen, who handled the front of house.

Karen slipped into the kitchen to tell her husband about the two boys in suits and ties who seemed to consider themselves as serious as anyone else. When they were done with dinner, a server offered to escort them to the kitchen, if they'd like to have a tour.

They would.

When they were done, Waltuck asked the boys if they had any questions.

They were too tongue-tied to ask right then, but Jonah quickly wrote a thank-you note that posed the only question that mattered: Could he and his friend work at Chanterelle over the summer? Nobody had to pay them. They just wanted to learn.

Waltuck spent his Bronx adolescence reading French cookbooks and trying out recipes on his family, but had gone to college to major in oceanography before the lure of being a chef finally tugged him away from the life he expected to lead. He traveled to France to experience the food he'd been reading about, enrolled at the Culinary Institute of America when he returned, and ended up taking a restaurant job rather than stick around long enough to graduate. When a friend suggested that he ought to have a place of his own, he and Karen found an unlikely but cheap location, one that would make it easier to take chances.

Chanterelle was its own small-scale revolution: a shrine to French nouvelle cuisine with some Asian flavors added in, housed in what had been a bodega, a restaurant that emphasized local ingredients at a time when the city's first farmers market was three years old and included only a handful of vendors. The Waltucks hired female servers, a radical move when serious French restaurants hired only men. They promoted the then-subversive notion that an American chef could compete in terms of quality without mimicking the previous generation's methods, both in the kitchen and in the dining room, altering the definition of fine dining in ways that seemed radical at the time but were just a glimpse of what was coming.

It was the kind of story that fed the dreams of a kid like Jonah, who was about the same age David had been when he started reading cookbooks in his free time. Jonah had helped his parents cook for as long as anyone could remember, and by the time he ate at Chanterelle he had taken over as head chef at home. He might like to be a chef, assuming that professional baseball didn't work out—a reasonable assumption, given that he was good but probably not that good—and it was legal for teenagers to work for free as long as they had the proper paperwork, so Jonah and the bar mitzvah boy, Nat, spent what felt like two perfect summers at Chanterelle. The first year, they prepped endless tubs of garlic and onions and shallots. The second year, David showed them how to butcher meat and clean fish. In the afternoons, they played ball.

Along the way, Jonah's home-cooked meals became more ambitious; he created a multicourse feast for his grandma Ruth's birthday, enlisting his younger sister to create an illustrated menu that listed his showpiece dish, "Shellfish paella, saffron rice with onions, garlic, lobster, muscles, squid, shrimp peas," and a dessert of caramelized fruit skewers with a bourbon-coconut cream sauce.

The following summer, Jonah worked at a French bistro and took a hard look at his options. His pitching arm was not of professional caliber, but his kitchen skills might be, if he kept at it. This was his third summer in a professional kitchen, he didn't mind the hard work, and he loved the result, whether in a restaurant or at home: He liked making people happy at the table. If he were a chef, he could create the dishes they ate, not merely execute someone else's ideas. That could be his life.

In 2003, when he was sixteen, Jonah made up his mind: He was going to be a chef and open his own restaurant, and he was going to do it by the time he was twenty-three. David Waltuck had opened Chanterelle when he was twenty-four, and Jonah liked to compete, so he set his deadline a year sooner, for the heck of it.

He convinced Nat to start up a catering company during their junior year of high school, and that spring they shopped their résumés to some bigger restaurants, one of which refused even to consider them for an unpaid apprenticeship, called a stage—from the French *stagiaire*, or trainee—because clearly Jonah and Nat had faked their résumés. No seventeen-year-old had logged that kind of experience at a restaurant like Chanterelle.

The chef de cuisine at Gramercy Tavern believed them, though, and suddenly they found themselves in an environment that was a sea change from what the Waltucks referred to as their mom-and-pop restaurant: forty tables in the dining room, fifteen more in the casual bar room, seventeen seats at the bar itself, and crowds, always. Gramercy Tavern opened in 1994, when Jonah was seven, and was one of the most popular restaurants in New York City, alongside its older sibling, Union Square Café, which had opened in 1985. They were the foundation of USHG, which by the time Jonah started at Gramercy Tavern had expanded to include Eleven Madison Park, Tabla, and Blue Smoke, and would soon add The Modern at the Museum of Modern Art as well as the first Shake Shack.

The kitchen at Gramercy Tavern was "more aggressive, competitive, bigger, full of young, hungry chefs," to Jonah, and he loved it. Occasionally the chef who hired him let him spend lunch service standing at the pass, where finished plates were checked one last time before they headed into the dining room. Jonah got to wipe an errant drop from the rim of the plate, to consider the composition of each dish, to understand exactly how great food was supposed to look and smell and taste. The following summer he embarked on a new venture, a room-service operation for the residents of the apartment building where his family lived. Every day he posted the next day's menu in the elevator and took orders from neighbors who preferred Jonah's food to their own home cooking or takeout, and every day he delivered the evening meal.

He completed a dual major in food studies and restaurant management at NYU, wedged in a stint as a host and reservationist at Blue Smoke, and took an internship in the restaurant's office. And he cooked, part-time during the school year and full-time in the summers. Jonah worked the garde-manger and grill stations at Savoy, another downtown pioneer, where since 1990 chef Peter Hoffman, like David Waltuck, had offered a menu based on what he could get at the farmers market and from local suppliers. When Jonah took a semester abroad he headed for Spain—not France, which was no longer an imperative for an aspiring chef, as it had been when Waltuck was coming up, but Spain, whose food had not already been channeled onto American plates for decades.

By the time Jonah graduated, in 2009, he figured he was two steps away, three, tops, from being ready: He had to find a job as a line cook at a restaurant that would show potential investors how serious he was. He had to work hard and get promoted to sous chef. From that vantage point he could look ahead and decide if he needed to log time as an executive chef or chef de cuisine, to show that he could run a kitchen— or if he could step right into his future, straight from sous chef, in time to meet his deadline.

He was the first line cook hired at Maialino, USHG's newest restaurant, brought on six months before it opened in the winter of 2009, but he ended up having to work for two years, just past his twenty-third birthday, before he got his promotion to sous chef. The six gridlocked sous chefs above him weren't going anywhere because they'd committed to at least one year when they were hired, and he found himself eyeing them to figure out who might leave first, even as he sized up the competition among the other line cooks. One of Jonah's coworkers got the first open slot, but he assumed that he was in line for the next opening, or at worst, the one after that.

Nick Anderer, then the executive chef and since 2012 the chef and a partner, remembered Jonah "coming at me hard" for a promotion to sous, and a particular slot at that—the morning sous, who soon started to joke that Jonah and another line cook were trying to hustle him out the door. He wasn't wrong. As long as he stayed in place, he kept Jonah from moving forward. When he left, Jonah got the morning slot, which he liked because there was only one sous on that shift. From that vantage point he could consider his next step.

He wrote a business plan for Huertas in between shifts at Maialino and had a friend who was in design school turn his sketches into an early set of drawings and a logo. He took a cold look at the kitchen hierarchy and didn't see the next advantageous move. He'd already missed the chance to open a place when he was twenty-three, and while working as an executive chef might be the traditional path to having his own place, he wasn't convinced it was necessary. He could have his name on the menu at a place that someone else owned, or at his own restaurant. Cooks told one another: If you don't have a restaurant before you're thirty, you'll never have one. The only option that made sense, it seemed, was to quit and get on with his life.

After eleven months as a sous, Jonah told Nick he was thinking about leaving. Nick, who had been an executive sous at Gramercy Tavern before he opened Maialino, had been the beneficiary of what he called "a carrot" that USHG occasionally dangled to keep a talented chef around—he was promised the opportunity to run a new restaurant within the company if he'd hang around and be a little patient. Nick had just promoted two of his sous to share the previously nonexistent post of executive sous, and one of them was clearly on track to open a place for USHG, but there was no point in having that discussion with Jonah because it was clear to Nick that owning his own place mattered to him as much as running a kitchen did. Jonah gave three months' notice to give Nick enough time to find and train a replacement, and planned a quick research trip to Spain. As soon as he returned, he'd start raising money in earnest and looking for a space. It had taken a little longer than he'd hoped to get here, but now he was going to be in charge of the timetable. He revised his internal calendar and told himself he'd have his own place when he was twenty-five.

A generation earlier, when Waltuck decided to become a chef, the path was either reassuringly clear or exclusionary, depending on who was contemplating the journey. At the high end, the American restaurant kitchen was a respectful reincarnation of the French model, in terms of both how it operated and what it served, a rule-bound universe summarized by one chef who worked his way up as "white, militaristic, and male." Ambitious Americans studied in France and came home to wear toques and utter "Oui, Chef" with conviction every time an order came to their stations, which were organized according to the French brigade system developed in the late nineteenth century by chef Auguste Escoffier—garde-manger for the salads and cold appetizers, entremetier for soups and vegetable and egg dishes, saucier for sauces and, in a smaller place, for sauté, and the sous chef, plucked from the ranks of the line cooks because he had the potential to run a kitchen some day, to become a chef de cuisine. The few women who pursued a career in the kitchen usually gravitated toward pastry work, which offered more regular hours and, so, the chance to fulfill domestic obligations at dinnertime.

The early exceptions showed up in communities that preferred their own way of doing things, or among individuals inspired to step off the defined path; in both cases, much of the change started in California, which had institutionalized a certain skepticism about the way things were supposed to be done, and was audacious enough to name a cuisine after itself. In the late 1960s and 1970s, Berkeley considered hierarchy and pedigree to be suspect no matter what the field, and chef Joyce Goldstein remembers wondering why anyone would feel the need to embrace French tradition when homegrown attributes—equal parts passion, a sense of community, and commitment—worked just fine. She credits the city's "mom-and-pop culture" for a flourishing alternative model that supported the 1971 opening of Alice Waters's Chez Panisse—and enabled an outlier like Goldstein to succeed, even though she broke every rule in sight: She was a chef, not a pastry chef, and got a late start as chef at the Café at Chez Panisse, later still as the owner of her own place, Square One. Goldstein opened her business in 1984, when she was forty-nine, an age at which many chefs were already casualties of the physical rigors of the job, and in 1993 won the James Beard Award for best chef in California.

If the Southern California restaurant scene was built on a more traditional model—chef Wolfgang Puck and restaurateur Michael McCarty were both classically trained chefs—the people who worked there often had another agenda in mind. Los Angeles chef Nancy Silverton followed the prescribed steps up to a point—she studied abroad and worked her way up from pastry assistant at McCarty's Michael's restaurant to run the pastry program at Puck's Spago—but she and a handful of other women cooks ignored the part of the narrative that involved gender and a limited destiny. If she wanted to open a bakery and a restaurant with her then husband, chef Mark Peel, and years later make the transition to chef, opening three new places with partners Mario Batali and Joe Bastianich, she would do so—along the way winning James Beard Awards for both best pastry chef and outstanding chef, the only person to have won both honors.

There was still a kitchen hierarchy; a room full of hungry customers required something more reliable than anarchy. What started to change was the identity of the people standing at the stations and, with that, their attitude. They responded to orders with "Yes, Chef," or by calling back the name of the dish that had been ordered, wore little brocade skullcaps instead of toques, and created menus based on bounty rather than on received ideas of fine food. Cooks who were not willing to be left out pried the door open, not fast enough to qualify as a revolution but wide enough to make the insiders take note.

And then, whether inspired or threatened by the disruption, or both, the men who already had kitchen jobs stepped into the fray: Like the stifled children of authoritative parents, they rebelled. Jonah grew up in the shadow of the swaggering bad-boy cook, the expletive-spewing, drugs-and-alcohol-addled descendants of Anthony Bourdain. The anti-chef positioned himself as far from the austere French model as it was possible to do and still hold down a job; he might be talented, but he often showed up for a shift in an altered state and took pride in the fact that he could turn out great food while operating at a diminished capacity. Some members of the boys' club did not respond well to newcomers, behaving in ways that dared the faint of heart to walk in the kitchen door.

Change, however messy, had its benefits on the plate: A chef might be a somber man in a white coat and a tall hat who knew the classic French sauces, or a woman who knew them but was more interested in creating a dish around that week's bounty of tomatoes. In 1998 Nancy Silverton started grilled cheese night at Campanile, because she liked grilled cheese and could come up with lots of tasty variations, and suddenly that was a perfectly reasonable thing for a high-end restaurant to serve. Cooking was up for grabs, as was the notion of who got to do it—not yet a meritocracy, but not quite the closed society it had been for so long. That was the start; by the time Jonah started to look for a full-time job, chefs had turned their backs on geography and natural science as well. They might mix Asian and French ingredients, as Waltuck did, or go further afield to merge Mexican and Korean, because maps were nothing more than another set of restrictions. A chef could ignore the boundaries of solid, liquid, and gas and turn an olive into a quivering, olive-flavored bubble, because there was no reason not to.

. . .

The changes that came next, the ones that defined the landscape Jonah stepped into in 2013, had more to do with life outside the kitchen than inside. In 2003 there was no Facebook, no Twitter, no Eater or Grubstreet.com, no Instagram or Foursquare, no iPhone or Android. The debut of *Top Chef* was still three years away; Mario Batali might be gaining a following on *Molto Mario*, a dump-and-stir instructional television show, but the era of competitive cooking, with the lure of money, prizes, and national exposure for any talented comer, had not yet begun. The economy was good, so there was little need to rethink the spacious bricks-and-mortar model. The leading edge of the millennials had just hit twenty-one, most of them still too young to drive, not yet the kind of marketing force that defined trends.

Ten years later, nothing was the same: More people talked about food more often, in more ways, until the ability to make great food achieved celebrity status—which in turn increased the volume and frequency of the conversation. Cooking for a living developed cachet, and held out the double promise of profits and fame. Nick Anderer, who was only nine years older than Jonah, had been embarrassed to tell his professor father that he intended to be a chef, but shame was no longer an issue.

The Bureau of Labor Statistics reported that the number of chefs and head cooks in the New York City area more than doubled between 2003 and 2013, from just over three thousand to more than seven thousand, even as an increasing number decamped to escape the city's competitive job market. Restaurant openings were up, although closures kept pace, and Nick marveled that, as he saw it, "Anyone can have a 40-seat restaurant in the East Village." From there a chef could catapult to empire, like Momofuku's David Chang, who had spun the neighborhood's Momofuku Noodle Bar, opened in 2004, into a global network that continued to grow—five restaurants in New York City, with more in development; locations in Washington, D.C., Toronto, Canada, and Sydney, Australia; the Milk Bar bakery, involved in its own expansionist agenda; a quarterly food publication, *Lucky Peach*; an online market for products and souvenirs.

A chef might find herself at the happy intersection of effort and opportunity, a celebrity without seeking it, as April Bloomfield did when the man who would become her business partner, Ken Friedman, auditioned her to become the chef at his gastropub, The Spotted Pig. She was British and knew the food; he was already well into planning and needed a chef who could execute his idea. Suddenly Bloomfield was no longer an anonymous if well-regarded sous chef at London's River Café, but at twenty-nine the standard-bearer for a new dining concept—new to New Yorkers, at least—and in charge of a kitchen that would be the first of several they opened together.

Along the way, they upended accepted notions of time and space: Danny Meyer had waited nine years to open his second white-tablecloth restaurant, Gramercy Tavern, an eternity by current standards, and a model that chefs seemed in a hurry to leave behind. Nick Anderer, who worked in kitchens for eleven years before he got his name on a menu, created one at Maialino that was designed to bridge the gap between the dwindling number of orders for a traditional coursed meal—"composed appetizer, composed second course, composed entrée, composed dessert"—and the more fashionable shared plates. He imagined that the next place he'd open for Meyer's company, a Roman pizzeria called Marta, was the likelier model for the new age—no tablecloths, a big display kitchen, and pizza nudging entrées out of the way.

The familiar middle ground—a chef and his restaurant, a reservation, a meal—started to feel tentative if not shortsighted, an unreliable foundation for a long career.

Meyer, referred to as "the greatest restaurateur Manhattan has ever seen" by the *New York Times*, evaluated the scene as "good and bad," and he wasn't equivocating. Too much had changed, too fast, to be able to predict how all of this would resolve itself, whether the antic pace would last or correct itself into more modulated growth. In the meantime, the generation in play—cooks on the cusp of a career—were not likely to hold still long enough to find out, lest they be left behind.

It seemed impossible to reconcile the impact of everything that had happened in a single decade. Social media was good, surely, because it helped a young chef spread the word about his new place, cheaply and quickly—and bad because it sped up the conversation. Chefs used to have six months to find their feet before a review, but now critics showed up in the first six weeks, and an opening without online coverage might as well not have happened.

Competition television was good and bad for the same reason—it promised a backstage look at kitchen life, which got viewers more interested in dining out and in the chef as media personality, but it drew people to the profession who would never survive a season of dicing vegetables in a basement prep kitchen, as Jonah had at Chanterelle. Chef Tom Colicchio, the head judge of Bravo's *Top Chef* since its 2006 debut, distinguished that show, which allowed its contestants to "shine," he said, from shows that shamed contestants with challenges they'd never encounter in real life and loud, extended dressings-down, a difference seemingly lost on viewers who now watched cooks of any age cook under any circumstances. The Food Network alone had more than one hundred million viewers for what Michael Pollan, author of *The Omnivore's Dilemma*, called "gladiatorial combat" in a piece for the *New York Times*. Pollan saw food shows as sports television, and the analogy extended beyond cutthroat competition: Chefs could be rich and famous like celebrities in other fields.

Unless, of course, they failed, in an equally spectacular fashion. The economy was another element in the whiplash equation, with unexpected consequences no matter what it did. The healthy prerecession economy seemed at the time to be a gold mine—easy mortgages and plenty of places to rent—but it turned out to be a money trap when the recession hit and previously giddy chefs found themselves in over their heads. And the years of tight money rewarded ingenuity: A young chef might have trouble raising money to rent a space, but ambition couldn't wait, so he looked for an alternative, and the recession elevated the food truck from the ubiquitous ice-cream vendor to a gourmet outpost on wheels. Los Angeles's classically trained Roy Choi was the first food-truck operator to make the top ten on *Food & Wine* magazine's Best New Chef list, in 2010, with the Kogi Korean BBQ truck he'd launched two years earlier. Kimchi on a quesadilla made perfect sense, as long as people lined up to buy it.

Success started to look like anything that got people in the door, or up to the truck window, and eager candidates lined up for their shot. USHG had for the first time received two thousand unsolicited applications in a single year from aspiring cooks, unprecedented for the sheer number—and for the speculative nature of the inquiries, which were not submitted in response to a specific job posting but sent just in case a position opened up. Some of those cooks intended to be the next Jonah, and he hadn't even found a space yet.

Richard Coraine was a thirty-year industry veteran who now supervised restaurant development for USHG, and he saw a sea change in how people got to the point where Jonah now was. The straightforward path to becoming a chef, based on "competence and sanctions," was obsolete. In its place, more opportunity, and more disarray.

When Coraine started out, he said, "It was all logical, because you had come up through a very hierarchical and competence-driven format, and along the way you were sanctioned. You couldn't supervise somebody cutting up a chicken unless you had competence cutting up a chicken."

Money had changed all that. "If you have a pile of money," he said, "you can get a collection of recipes—yours, somebody else's—and open a restaurant, call yourself a chef. Chef is the label we give to anybody who's in control of the product that's coming out of the kitchen," which meant that the chef might have fewer cooking skills than the people who worked for him. It didn't matter, as long as he had a profitable concept that someone on the payroll could execute.

Meyer liked Jonah's odds in great part because he was more of an old-school model—he might seem to be in a hurry, given his age, but he'd already logged a decade of experience. And he had survived several rounds; some of those two thousand USHG applicants would never get as far as a sous chef job at a big-name restaurant, let alone strike out on their own. But there was no way to predict how far that would take him, because the criteria for high-profile success were not yet clear. Customers at *Top Chef* winner Stephanie Izard's two Chicago restaurants often inquired about her season on television when they asked to have a selfie taken with the chef, but she had yet to have a single guest mention her James Beard Award for outstanding chef, Midwest region. Fame, the adulation of strangers, had replaced renown, the more circumscribed respect of one's peers.

"A celebrity chef today can be someone who's worked for twenty years," said Anderer, "or someone who's got tattoos and worked at two places, and everything in between. Anyone can break in if they can work the loudspeaker, as it were."

Jonah had a hunch that the city needed the kind of Spanish food he wanted to make, an accessible cuisine that still had novelty going for it, and that the bar and dining room would each draw a distinct clientele and broaden his base. Those were his loudspeaker messages, if he could just get enough people to listen.

He wasn't prepared to contemplate the alternative, that somehow he'd get lost in the shuffle. He had to make Huertas work; at twenty-five, Jonah had narrowed his options to one. Being a chef, running his own restaurant, and from there a group of them, was all he wanted to do, and what he was trained to do. He wasn't going to be a "misfit asshole creative chef," who in Jonah's estimation was his own worst enemy because he didn't understand anything but the food. That kind of chef might regard food costs and staff morale as beneath his dignity, soulless concerns of the sort that kept bean counters awake, but Jonah looked around and figured that the way to break through was to be both creative and responsible—to make beautiful food and stay in business. More than that: Make beautiful food, stay in business, and grow.

At fifty-nine, David Waltuck again found himself among the hopefuls, like Jonah, about to embark for the second time on a new restaurant project, thirty-four years after he opened what became an exalted piece of the city's restaurant history. During the summer of 2009, just months before Jonah started at Maialino, the Waltucks had announced that they would close Chanterelle temporarily for much-needed renovations, to reopen in October, a few weeks before the restaurant's thirty-year anniversary on November 14. In October, they announced that Chanterelle would not reopen, ever, a victim of rising rents in a neighborhood that had gentrified around their once-isolated outpost.

Eater ran an item that attributed Chanterelle's demise to natural causes: "It's always sad to see a restaurant go down after a long run. But the times, they are a changin', and it would have been an uphill battle for them to keep the old timer alive."

For four years Waltuck consulted on other people's projects—offered his input on burgers and sports bar menus and tried to get used to having his creative suggestions politely declined. It was intolerable. He missed being in the kitchen, missed the French- and Asian-inspired dishes that he considered to be his signature; he yearned for a more active role. He needed a new strategy, though, now that there were no longer the kind of bargain rents that had enabled him to lease Chanterelle's original thirty-seat location for a monthly rent of $825. Cheap rent had meant that he and Karen could pursue their "very idealistic and very romantic" idea on the fly—which was how he saw it, looking back.

"It wasn't fraught," he said of the scene in 1979. "There weren't as many rules."

Thirty-five years later, there seemed to be nothing but rules everywhere he looked, which he tried to navigate in his usual reflective, soft-spoken way. Waltuck was determined to get back into the kitchen, although he and Karen faced a painful level of sacrifice if he was going to pull this off: They would have to rent out the West Village apartment where they had lived for thirty years and move to a far cheaper place in the Bronx, where David had grown up, to minimize expenses and bring in rental income. Karen now worked with a job placement group for people with developmental disabilities, so David needed a front-of-house partner. He spoke with Chanterelle's onetime general manager, who was as antsy as David was, and they worked up a plan for a new place to be called Élan, French for energetic style and enthusiasm, all of the things he intended to bring to a slightly more casual yet still refined menu.

Waltuck's four-star past meant that he would have less initial trouble than Jonah might with fund-raising—he was a legend, not a newcomer—

but he was going to have to spend more to get the kind of space that his regulars and their descendants would appreciate. To hedge his bets in a world tuned to the next young phenomenon, Waltuck decided to look at blocks where there were already established restaurants, where he might catch an opening crowd of diners who'd forgotten to make a reservation nearby and noticed Élan, the new place across the street. That would give him a bit of a head start this time around, even if he had to pay a premium for it.

He wanted a space that was already a restaurant. The story of how he and his wife had transformed a bodega was specific to its time, and the current equivalent, the warehouse space turned into a big, noisy restaurant, was not how he envisioned the next stage of his life. Bravado and naïveté, and not quite enough money, were enough to get started in 1979, but this time he had to take a more measured approach. If he got really lucky, he could assume the lease of a faltering business, move into the kitchen, and spend money only on the parts of the space that customers could see.

He was eager to take the chance, because as he saw it, there was no acceptable alternative. Waltuck had run a restaurant kitchen for all but the past four years of his adult life; he had not spent his days talking about other people's cooking or concepts, but had cooked, created dishes, trained a team to execute them. It was what he did. It was, after a well-intentioned stab at consulting that turned into an exercise in frustration, what he felt he had to do. He wasn't quite comfortable anywhere else.

3

THE HUNT

Someday, when he was successful, Jonah would be able to hunt for a location first, money in hand, and then figure out exactly what to do with it. Once he found a space he liked, he could install the right restaurant from a collection of ideas he already had in his head, waiting their turn like eager students hoping to be called to the front of the classroom. Investors would commit up front to be part of the next project, whatever it was, because they didn't want to miss out on a good bet, and Jonah would step into the real estate market with ample funds to compete for the good places. Someday he'd lease a vanilla box, which was what chefs called a vacant space—not the remains of a previous restaurant with a sad story to tell but a blank canvas waiting on his vision of what it ought to be.

That scenario would cost at least $1 million, too big of a wager on an unproven kid, even a talented one with a fast-rise résumé; he had no traction as a business owner. Jonah aimed for half that and so far had just over $400,000 pledged. If he lucked into a great location, he figured he could raise another $100,000, which ought to be enough.

He needed a space that satisfied a seesaw set of requirements: It should be in a neighborhood where there were already restaurants to attract customers, but not too many, on a street that drew both the drinks-after-work crowd and their older, bigger-spending siblings, one that lent itself to his design ideas but didn't require extensive repairs. One that he could afford, although cheap was pointless if it failed to meet the other criteria—low rent on a dead block was no bargain.

He assumed that he'd find such a place in Brooklyn, so he set out to look in the fall of 2012. Week after week, his fiancée went to work—Jonah joked, ruefully, that at least someone in the family was making money, aware that Marina did not want to be a corporate lawyer forever and was making her own investment in his future, one not tallied on the spreadsheets. Jonah hit the street with his backpack full of sketches and plans, to look at listings.

He spent the fall looking and got nowhere, so he hired a realtor in January and fired him four months later for not paying close enough attention to Jonah's parameters. He spent the next five months on his own again, looking at what must have been fifty sites, all the while reassuring his investors. No, he didn't need the cash yet, just the promise of it, but yes, he might need it any day, and sure, he assumed that he would find the right space, even as he went out day after day and didn't.

There was a fine line between a young chef on the brink of something big and one more unemployed sous chef, and it had been a year since Jonah had worked a restaurant shift. He did what he could to promote himself—worked catering gigs, participated in a pop-up restaurant downtown with a rotating set of chefs—but this was taking longer than he ever imagined it would.

There was a nice space in Brooklyn's Cobble Hill neighborhood, one of a string of rapidly gentrifying neighborhoods that ran south of the gold mine that was Williamsburg, where the streets were gridlocked on good-weather weekends with people either walking to or waiting outside of restaurants. That kind of business had to spread, so this might be a good time to get an advantageous lease in a less developed area, but the space he looked at had no basement, which meant not enough room for storage or prep. It was so close to right, though; he felt more inclined to take the next decent candidate in nearby Carroll Gardens. He offered less than the asking price, to buy a little time while the landlord considered the offer, and then he went to dinner at a local restaurant.

It did little to increase his enthusiasm, because there wasn't much foot traffic. He called a manager at a nearby place to get advice, a woman he'd worked with at Maialino, and she warned him that it was a family neighborhood, "not a hip, young crowd, less adventurous eaters, a quiet corner." Not the kind of place where diners might want to eat little bites standing near the bar, or clamor for charred octopus, or linger late into the night. He decided not to proceed.

He began to feel as though he'd looked at every available space in Williamsburg, the neighborhood that was still his first choice, but they were all too expensive, as Brooklyn prices started to outstrip some Manhattan neighborhoods. He added Manhattan's East Village to his map, although he was skeptical that he'd find anything he could afford, and was walking out of an unpromising space with a listing broker when Peter Hoffman rode up on his bicycle. Just like that, everything changed: Hoffman knew the realtor, vouched for Jonah, and headed off, and the realtor, suddenly more enthusiastic, wondered if Jonah might like to look at another place nearby. He'd just gotten the keys, hadn't been there himself, and while there was a for-lease sign in the window, it wasn't yet listed online. It was on the market but not really on the market.

They walked over to 107 First Avenue, a transitional space on a transitional block whose storefronts alternated between then and now. One door to the south was Empellón Cocina, the second of three restaurants owned by chef Alex Stupak, who had been a pastry chef at wd~50, Wiley Dufresne's temple to molecular gastronomy. Stupak gave up pastry to concentrate on Mexican food that was as different from traditional Mexican fare as his desserts had been from pie and cake and ice cream, and he went on to do what Jonah wanted to do, expanded from a West Village taqueria to this place, with a third on the way.

One door to the north was the Polish G.I. Delicatessen, owned by an Israeli who had bought it from the original Polish owner, whose initials were G.I.—a lineage that accounted for the hamantaschen in the display case in the spring, followed in the summer by a handwritten sign announcing that it was time for homemade cold beet borscht, place your order inside. Across the street, an entrenched fast-food row: Dunkin' Donuts, 31 Flavors, Subway, and a massive two-story McDonald's with a huge banner. Around the corner, an uncompromising espresso bar built for quality, not comfort.

Only three blocks up, a line formed daily during the short break between lunch and dinner service at David Chang's Momofuku Noodle Bar, as dozens of people, many of them consulting guidebooks and maps, gathered in the hope of getting a seat when the restaurant opened at five thirty. After that, the wait time grew in proportion to the attractiveness of the hour, and by eight o'clock it was possible to spend as much time waiting as eating. The noodle bar was the most famous destination on a strip that ran with dwindling intensity from the 14th Street L subway station at the top, past the block Jonah was looking at, to the Houston Street trains just below First Street. The neighborhood had easy access going for it, and south of Houston there was a growing number of smaller, scrappier places. Eventually, surely, the two restaurant rows would gobble up the blocks in between, and Jonah would have himself a prime location.

There was no way to know what lurked behind the plaster or under the drop ceiling, no way to anticipate plumbing or electrical problems in a building this old. But the space was the right size and had a full basement and two large wood-burning ovens, which was one more than he needed. Jonah was tired of looking. The landlord asked for a monthly rent of $15,000 and agreed to $14,000, at which point Jonah asked the realtor to get the listing taken off the market while they negotiated. He didn't want an established restaurateur coming in to overbid him, and he was prepared to pay for the privilege for thirty days. The realtor scheduled a meeting so that Jonah could meet the head of the realty office, who stood between any applicant and the landlord; once Jonah had his blessing, they could move ahead.

Jonah got there an hour early and sat on a stoop across the street from the office. He was about to play the supplicant in a drama where he, of all the people in the room, had the most at stake, not a comfortable position for someone who'd always had a plan and been able to execute it. He needed to collect himself, to retrieve the positive feelings that had made him think he'd be in business by now—his faith in himself and in his talent, a healthy ambition, even a slight sense of destiny, given that he'd spent half his life in professional kitchens. If he could just get on with things, he'd get to the part of the process he could control.

The realtor obviously thought this was a good match, or he wouldn't have wasted his boss's time on this meeting. The landlord, whom Jonah had met on one of his visits to the space, seemed to like him well enough. He had solid investors, people he knew, family and friends, because he wanted investors who spent with their hearts—eager to recoup their investments and more, someday, but equally happy to support what he did. He might have gotten closer to that $1 million if he'd gone after wealthy investors who spent money on restaurants the way they bought art, strictly business, but that made him a little nervous. He didn't want to be considered an appreciating asset.

His original plan had called for a capital budget of $500,000, but the people he shared it with—a restaurant development executive, a chef he'd once worked for, his dad—said he was cutting it too close, so at one point he had revised the figure up to $900,000. As he'd anticipated, he couldn't come close, though he was convinced he could make this location work with the $420,000 he now had, plus an extra $100,000 from the more skittish prospects. Several potential investors were holding back because Jonah didn't yet know where Huertas was going to end up—which limited his ability to look because he wasn't sure exactly how much he could spend.

"You need a certain amount of money to sign a lease," he said, "but people don't want to sign on until they know the location. And the less experienced you are, the more money you need up front to make a deal."

He refused to be demoralized. He tweaked the numbers again and told people he was going to find a way to make his place look like a million dollars on less than half that amount. That's how good a business head he had—rather than lose another six months to fund-raising, he had tightened up the plan until he could see how to make it work on what he had, which the realtor would have to admire.

He started to feel better. He was sitting across the street from the official start of his restaurant future, after all, with a preliminary set of drawings for a generic twenty-five-by-eighty-foot city storefront. This space was longer, which gave him even more options, possibly room for more seats, more nightly checks, greater profits. All he needed was a yes, and he'd hire a contractor to start demolition.

He headed across the street at ten, back to believing that this was going to work.

. . .

An hour later Jonah was on the street, fuming, blindsided by the broker's boss, who seemed only to want to know, Who the fuck does this punk kid think he is? At least that was the message Jonah got. The man didn't care how much Jonah had raised or how much more he thought he could get, and he wanted Jonah to know that he had been in construction himself and was a part owner of a restaurant, so he understood the business. No kid was going to put one over on him.

The broker had advised him not to haggle on terms, but haggling was an aspiration at this point. They were layers of credibility away from haggling. Jonah had controlled his temper and managed to ask how much more money the head realtor wanted him to have on hand to make this work, but the man didn't have a figure at first because dollars were not the issue. Jonah's inexperience was. He might know how to cook. He knew nothing, as far as the boss was concerned, about management and running a business and surviving the construction and permit process.

The proposed solution was simple: Jonah had to raise that extra $100,000—and he had to find a partner, somebody older, somebody with experience who knew how to finesse a liquor license hearing and navigate the building department with authority. If Jonah insisted on going it alone, the realtor would insist, in turn, on a three- or four-year guarantee on the fifteen-year lease to minimize the landlord's exposure. Whether Huertas stayed in business or not, Jonah would owe the $14,000 monthly rent for thirty-six or forty-eight months—$504,000 minimum, $672,000 maximum. Given the amount, the realtor wondered if Jonah had a deep-pocket investor who could act as guarantor.

That was hardly an option. Jonah could either find more money and a partner, which meant giving away a chunk of equity in his nonexistent restaurant, or he could find another location and hope that this realtor was an anomaly, that the next person in charge of the next listing would approve a lease application without making this kind of demand.

It was common enough to take on a construction partner, but Jonah had wanted to have a signed lease first to put himself in a better position to bargain, to avoid having need be part of the formula. This scenario put him at an obvious disadvantage: Asking someone to be his grown-up partner so that he could get a lease was hardly the way to launch a negotiation, because it gave the contractor too much leverage. He'd have to give a prospective partner equity, but under these circumstances, he might have to offer more.

Still, Jonah was not going to waste time being angry, not with a deal so close. The East Village location turned out to be a big selling point for the investors who were waiting to see where Jonah landed, and in eight days he raised the additional $100,000 he needed. He and his dad talked to a handful of contractors and ended up at lunch with Nick Thatos at a restaurant he had designed. They came away with a handshake deal to go into business together on Huertas. Nick and his partner would waive their contractor fees and defer their design fee—gamble, essentially, on Jonah's ability to repay them for the design work and include them in equity distribution once Huertas was profitable. They also wanted equity in any future project that used the Huertas name.

In return, Jonah would get his lease approved, a partner who understood city bureaucracies, and Nick's team of seasoned plumbers and electricians and drywall guys and painters, all of whom would work simultaneously on bigger projects. Jonah had to admit that the economics were good: The bigger jobs supplied steady paychecks, in case Jonah's cash flow lagged in a given week, and with luck and good calendar management, those jobs wouldn't get in the way of progress at Huertas.

Nick had been around restaurants long enough to know that equity might not be worth anything for years, but a more immediate reward came with the handshake: He insisted on the right to design the space, to use it as a showcase for his notions of how a restaurant ought to look. He had to support Jonah's concept on a practical level, and the look had to make the chef happy, but Nick would be in control of the aesthetics, after years of executing other people's ideas.

Nick's $133,300 design and contractor's fees would have been out of Jonah's range if he'd been paying Nick for the work—so Jonah made himself focus on the benefits, even though this felt a little bit like somebody trespassing on his turf. He was getting a bargain up front in exchange for money down the line, and once Huertas made enough profit to repay investors it wouldn't hurt quite so much. In the meantime, he could add the market value of Nick's work to his fund-raising total and tell people that he'd raised almost $700,000 because, in effect, he had. He contacted the realtor to give him the good news. Jonah was ready to set up another meeting.

The realtor told him to fax over his bank statement first.

With that, Jonah was plunged into a universe he hoped to visit as rarely as possible for the rest of his life, surrounded by realtors and lawyers and inundated with e-mails and margin notes and questions. He listened to them go back and forth and wondered, not for the last time, when he was ever going to get back to cooking.

The landlord had agreed to hold the listing off the market for thirty days, but the clock ran out without resolution, so Jonah wrote another check to keep the listing off the market for thirty days more. His lawyer and the realtor told him not to worry, that the deal was going to happen and the pace was not at all unusual. Still, they got to within days of the second deadline without a deal, and Jonah, not eager to write a check for another month of what was starting to seem like dithering, wondered loudly how they could wrap this up.

. . .

A liquor license was the last thing that stood between Jonah and a signed lease. With a restaurant's wholesale costs at between 20 and 30 percent of the menu price—a $10 glass of wine cost the restaurant $2.50—alcohol was the best insurance policy a new restaurant could have, a reliable profit center that made up for the slim margins on food and helped to reduce Jonah's risk, which in turn made the landlord happy. The bar at Huertas took up a third of the space, and the dining-room menu featured beverage pairings, so there was no question of opening without a license.

New York was an open state, which meant that there was no cap on how many liquor licenses a county or city or township might grant, as opposed to a closed state like New Jersey or Pennsylvania, which issued a finite number of licenses and required frustrated applicants to purchase from an existing business or wait for the occasional auction. New York State regulated the process not with a cap but with a tougher application process designed to weed out questionable candidates—and New York City required an applicant to navigate more of an obstacle course than anywhere else in the state. To get approval from the New York State Liquor Authority, Jonah had first to convince a local community board that he deserved a license.

There were fifty-nine community boards in the five boroughs of New York City, each with a subcommittee that had the right to grant, defer, or deny a license request—and if the license committee said no, the applicant had to appeal to the SLA, which meant weeks if not months of waiting for a second chance. Community Board 3, which ruled on applications in the bar-heavy East Village and Lower East Side, had a reputation for being either legendary or notorious, depending on who was talking. Longtime East Village residents looked to the board to protect them from the effects of gentrification—franchises that replaced mom-and-pop businesses, wealthy potential residents with gut renovation on their minds, what locals saw as a creeping upscale sameness that threatened one of the last unique neighborhoods in Manhattan. Business owners more often saw the board as obstinate, waging a futile battle against change, as though progress were an act of aggression. But board members were political appointees with no term limits, so diplomacy was essential.

Jonah knew that the board could be difficult, so he decided to ask only for a beer and wine license, not a full liquor license, because he'd been told that it would improve his odds. His predecessor in the space had a beer and wine license, and his lawyer, Joseph Levey, had warned him that an unproven chef who asked for more would have what he described as "an uphill battle." The words "dive bar" hovered ominously at the edge of any negotiation that involved alcohol, and neighbors worried that a restaurant would fail and sell all of its assets—including a provisional transfer of the liquor license—to someone whose business attracted loud, late-night drinkers. It wasn't a serious threat, because the SLA could revoke the license of someone who said they were opening a French bistro to disguise their dive-bar intentions—but it was the kind of concern that people raised at community board meetings, and it could get in the way.

If somehow the board were to grant a full license to a kid with no experience, it would likely come with too many strings attached, like an early closing time to reduce the chance of rowdiness, in case Jonah had his own secret plan for a late-night bar. Given that possibility, Jonah preferred to ask for a limited license on his terms, which included closing at midnight during the week and one a.m. on the weekends. He wasn't giving up but being strategic, playing the community board's game. Better to ask for less up front and come back for an upgrade in six months.

Jonah and his dad attended the September committee meeting to get some firsthand intelligence, which was not reassuring. The board members looked like they were north of fifty, maybe sixty, and it seemed to Jonah that they felt "assaulted" by newcomers to the neighborhood. A couple of applicants in their twenties wanted to invest their technology riches in a club and restaurant on the Lower East Side, asked for a full liquor license, and got turned down in a fast vote. The project was exactly what the board seemed to fear—people with lots of money and no experience disrupting their neighborhood.

In the weeks between that meeting and his October appearance, Jonah worked on a tailor-made pitch. "I'm a native New Yorker, very sympathetic," he intended to say. "Grew up in a building with a restaurant in it, and now I have a very, very contentious relationship with a bar next door to my building" in Williamsburg. He knew the difference between a restaurant that fit in and one that didn't, though he had to be careful not to sound like he was bragging.

"If you're too confident and composed when you speak," he told himself, "these are people who will think, 'Cocky kid.' I've got to tread the middle ground. I'm a local guy."

He never got to say so. The lawyer, who specialized in liquor licenses, made it clear: He was to introduce himself, speak very briefly about his plans for Huertas, and turn the presentation over to Nick, who was ready to impress the board with his decades of experience on completed projects.

Jonah reminded himself not to bristle if a board member took the same condescending position as the lawyer had, and dismissed him even though it was his restaurant. He was not going to get pissed off— or if he did, he was not going to let it show.

He had more of a chance than he'd anticipated to show how calm he could be. The committee had to resolve a roster of applications for upgrades or changes first, so new applicants weren't scheduled to start until eight thirty, and Huertas was at the end of the list. Levey advised him to go get coffee or a glass of wine and come back after eleven thirty, but he stayed to see what he could learn. Representatives of a pizza place popular with NYU students endured an hour's grilling over their application for a full liquor license and a four a.m. closing, as they tried to placate neighbors who complained about having to tiptoe around piles of vomit and discarded pieces of pepperoni. The first vote was a stalemate that yielded to approval only when a board member raised the specter of a worse tenant moving in if the pizza place relocated. At least these applicants promised a security and a cleanup team.

Compared to that, and facing a tired committee near midnight, Huertas looked like an easy approval. Jonah did as he was told, made a little speech and deferred to his older partner, but a board member came back around to ask him one question: Was he content with a beer and wine license, or was he going to ask for an upgrade?

Had the man read his mind? Of course he wanted an upgrade. The question was how to tell the truth without making the board feel that he was manipulating them.

"We'd like to have a full liquor license," he said, carefully, "but we understand we have to prove ourselves as good neighbors."

"That's a good answer," said a surprised committee member. "Never heard that before. Most people ask for a full liquor license right away and then balk when we say okay, but close by ten p.m."

Jonah got his beer and wine license and so, his lease: Ten years at $14,000 a month rent, the first three months free, with an option to extend for another five years at whatever the market rate was in 2024. Having an option at all was a plus, since extensions were hard to get starting out, but Jonah did not intend to wait around until the last minute and get hit with a big increase. He figured it was smarter to go back to the landlord five or six years from now, when Huertas was a solid enterprise and not the only place Jonah had going—when Jonah was no longer the punk kid without portfolio but rather a sought-after tenant—and get him to sign another long-term lease.

4

THE BUILD-OUT

Experience changed the pace immediately. Nick had pulled permits in anticipation of a signed lease and was at the site with a demolition crew even as the final set of comments flew back and forth, and the asbestos inspection was set before the question of who would pay for removal was resolved. The first of four thirty-foot Dumpsters sat in front of 107 First Avenue, and Jonah took the L subway shuttle in from Brooklyn twice a day, first thing in the morning and again at the end of the workday, to see how much progress Nick's crew had made as they took the space down to the original brick. There was nothing for him to do, but it was his space, and he wanted to be there in case there were any decisions to be made.

Nick was used to moving fast, and his goal was to have Huertas open before Jonah started writing rent checks on February 1. In the first weeks his workers filled the Dumpsters with layer upon layer of old plaster and got rid of the second wood-burning oven, working without electricity rather than waiting for Con Edison to turn the power on—

they jury-rigged a lone naked bulb on an extension cord from the basement and kept at it until it was too dark to see.

He made short work of Jonah's design, particularly the reproduc-
tions of vintage travel posters that Jonah had brought back from Spain.

"Nah," Nick said. They were too predictable. "You open Greek you put
up a Greek poster, open Italian, put up Italian." There would be no Spanish posters in this Spanish restaurant. No maps. No big octopus unless it
was part of a mural Nick envisioned, etched on zinc and mounted behind
the bar. Nothing that approached what he considered to be a design cli-
ché, but lots of decorative touches that made the place feel as though it
had been around forever without seeming run-down or old. Nick was
tired of the budget-driven minimalism he saw in too many small restaurants, blank walls, industrial design, spare rooms that weren't as welcoming or as much fun as he thought they ought to be. He wasn't going to do
what Jonah had envisioned, and he wasn't going to do what everyone else
was doing—but he didn't draw to scale, unlike most designers, so Jonah
would have to take his vision on sketches, verbal descriptions, and faith.

There was no point in arguing until he could see something, so
Jonah dug in, instead, on a few things that were more about him as a
chef than about design—or at least that was the position he took, to
keep Nick at bay. Jonah had a logo already, a pig standing on its hind
feet with one front hoof resting against an apple tree, a reference to the
symbol of Madrid, a bear leaning against a berry tree. The font for the
lettering resembled the street sign for Calle de las Huertas, where Jonah
had lived during his undergraduate semester, and evoked memories of
the late-afternoon tapas crawl through the neighborhood—a few tapas
and a short glass of beer, a caña, at one place, and then another, a move-
able feast. Jonah refused to budge on it, even though Nick had hoped to
change the image and the font. This was not a design dictatorship but a

partnership, and that required give-and-take. Jonah felt that he'd done a lot of giving since the meeting at the realty office. The logo stayed.

Dishware was not open for debate, either, because a plate was an extension of a finished dish, an element in the way the food looked. He was willing to talk to Nick about the physical relationship of the kitchen and the remaining wood oven to the bathroom and the bar, but the kitchen itself was his call.

Within weeks, they had what Jonah described as "some passive-aggressive tension boiling," balanced out, at least, by a shared commitment to speed—Jonah because he was frustrated by how much time he'd already spent to get here, Nick because he couldn't collect equity until Huertas was open and making money. Privately, Jonah worried about ideas he couldn't see, which spiraled into a larger worry that Nick wasn't used to dealing with chef-driven restaurants. "He's used to bringing projects in on time," was Jonah's analysis, "used to making executive decisions without getting approval, and he saves money by getting things done early." Collaborating with a chef like Jonah wasn't part of his résumé.

By early December they had abandoned hope of opening before Jonah had to start paying rent in February, thanks to three obstacles they could have anticipated if they hadn't been so obsessed with speed: They were done in by accrued delays, a predictable day here and a day there; by Thanksgiving, which slowed the pace before and after; and by a multilayered city bureaucracy that seemed sometimes to have inspectors inspecting other inspectors, as well as sets of overlapping requirements that made Jonah's head ache. As frustrated as he was, though, he couldn't imagine how long this might have dragged on without Nick, who was good at maneuvering through the maze.

Jonah felt a little lost. His early-morning and late-afternoon visits had

merged into full days on the job site, where he set up his office atop whatever pile of building materials was at the proper height for his laptop—a
stack of drywall, boxes of tiles, any flat space within range of a lightbulb.
Nick's crew was everywhere, framing and running gas and electric and
plumbing through the new interior, while Jonah spent too much time in
idle, surveying the scene and wondering when it was going to be done.

As far as he could tell, there was almost nothing left of his original
design, so he sat in on meetings he didn't have to attend, including one
with the muralist, to have some input on the placement of the octopus,
the pig, and a crocus flower. One morning he rode the subway two extra
stops and got off at the Union Square farmers market, to see where he
might want to buy his produce. There were people in kitchen clothes
everywhere, pushing big trolleys loaded up with produce, but most of
them were porters picking up an order, a couple of sous or executive sous,
not many chefs. Jonah intended to do his own shopping, to make sure he
got exactly what he wanted and to take advantage of any unexpected
ingredients, but he didn't introduce himself to any of the farmers. It was
way too early for that, though he wondered if any of them would open an
account for a new restaurant the way they did for established ones.

He obsessed about the kitchen, measured and remeasured the space
and tried to envision it up and running with all the equipment in place.
He got someone back at Maialino to measure the kitchen aisle, and went
over himself to take photographs and check the measurements, because
he had the sense that the Huertas kitchen was going to be too wide if they
used an existing interior wall to define it. Having to take an extra half
step for each task could slow a cook down dramatically. Jonah wanted
the right pivot width, so that a cook could work at the flat-top, pivot, land
at the opposite counter to plate the contents of a sauté pan, and turn back
before anything overcooked. On a busy night, the hot line would be a row
of cooks executing repeating half-spins, if the space was right.

Moving the wall a foot farther in would make a big difference. Moving it sixteen inches, he figured, would be perfect. Every professional kitchen he'd worked in seemed to have a built-in flaw, one the chef clearly hadn't seen coming, and Jonah kept a log of them in his head, to keep from making similar mistakes. Here was one he could avoid.

The more Jonah thought about it, the better a new wall looked. They could add six seats in the expanded dining space, which meant $150,000 to $180,000 in added annual revenue. He presented the Maialino measurements to Nick and made his case—would it be a big, expensive deal to move the wall?

They couldn't add the seats, Nick explained, because they were at the city's seventy-four-person occupancy limit, figuring sixty-five seats and nine employees. Anything more required adjustments to the existing sprinkler system, which could mean having to run an expensive new water line to the street, and a second means of egress, which they didn't have. Still, Nick was perfectly happy to move the wall, even without the promise of more customers. It was an easy fix.

Life got better from there. The wood-burning ovens did not comply with codes for venting exhaust, but Nick found a way to upgrade rather than replace the existing system, to retrofit the welding and insulate the ductwork. He would have to drop the kitchen ceiling and a section of the dining-room ceiling eighteen inches to cover it, but the plan met code specifications and cost only $4,000—a huge savings, since the cost rule for a new vertical vent system running to the roof was $10,000 per floor, and this was a four-story building.

Jonah cheered up with every sheet of drywall that went up and every decision easily made, and eventually he and Nick became partners in adversity: When the building department threatened to hold up a set of permits the plumber needed, they made a frantic dash to the permit office, and Jonah drove Nick's car around the block while Nick darted upstairs to straighten things out. When Nick got a discount price on boxes and boxes of kitchen tiles that weren't the custom sizes he wanted, he set Jonah up in the basement at a massive tile cutter, showed him how it worked, and left him there, wearing a construction mask, cutting hundreds of tiles into three different sizes and happy to do so, because it kept him occupied and saved thousands of dollars.

For the time being Jonah had a day job, which he'd never had before and would not have again once Huertas opened, and he didn't mind the normal hours or even the mindless tasks. He drafted friends to help him stain new wood to look battered and old, for wainscoting in the dining room, and when he found barely used chairs and bar stools at a bargain $20 and $30, respectively, he grabbed two more friends, rented a van, and drove out to get them. Chairs at Maialino had run $600 apiece, "but they know they're not going to be out of business in a year," he said, which was as close as he got to entertaining the possibility that he might be.

Maialino operated in a far more protected universe inside the Gramercy Hotel, which absorbed some of the operating costs, and as part of USHG, which benefited from economy of scale and decades of experience. Jonah had no such buffers, so he settled for what he could afford. The chairs and stools were the wrong color, but all he had to do was rub them down and paint them, and congratulate himself on having saved thousands more. He was able to recycle table bases from the pizza place for the dining room, which freed up money for custom tops, and Nick recut and reupholstered an existing booth so that he needed only two to be built from scratch.

Kitchen equipment was not as open to compromise. "There's a huge disparity between good and shitty things," said Jonah, and he was determined to buy as much of the good stuff as possible, starting with the ovens. He knew exactly what he wanted: a Jade range like the one he'd cooked on at Maialino, in a slightly different configuration—a six-burner model outfitted with two open burners on the right, where a right-handed chef wanted them to be, and a flat-top that took up the remaining two-thirds of the space, heated by one long burner that ran underneath it and took an hour to heat up and another to cool down. It was the kind of range he'd have forever, he said, a vote of confidence in his future. Next to it he'd put a combi oven, which let him cook three ways—convection, steam, and a combination. It was expensive, but nothing else had the range a combi had. He wanted a gas one because it was cheaper to run, but the supplier happened to have a prefabricated electric model that someone had ordered and then canceled, for $8,000 instead of $14,000. It would take three years of constant use before Jonah came close to spending the $6,000 on utility bills, at which point he could upgrade and sell this one to the next newcomer.

Jonah's ideal kitchen would be full of All-Clad skillets, which cost about $120 for a twelve-inch and $90 for an eight-inch, five or six times more than the cheap ones from China. He splurged on a couple of them, and then he searched online and found a store outside Pittsburgh that sold All-Clad irregulars, and grabbed eight more for $500. He haunted Fishs Eddy, a store that sold both vintage dishware and sturdy new patterns, and picked white dinner plates with a raised, leaf-patterned edge, $1 apiece for unused Syracuse China originals from the 1950s, before the company merged and moved its production to China, enough new reissues to fill out the order. He bought plates shaped like scallops, and mismatched vintage plates for pintxos and raciones.

He listened to pitches from local dishwashing companies that leased equipment to restaurants, from basic machines to a computerized model that gave each employee a log-in number and enabled Jonah to evaluate who used the cleaning chemicals most effectively. And he thought, We'll both be in the kitchen. Can't I just watch? He chose a cheaper option.

The big decisions made, he sat down with Nick and Nate and Luke in mid-December to see if they could pick an opening date that would stick, preferably one that would keep him from having to pay a second month's rent on a dead space. Nick predicted that the plumbing and gas work would be done before Christmas, even with the holiday slowdown. The combi oven could be there whenever Jonah said he was ready for delivery, and the Jade took two weeks to arrive once he notified the supplier. There was more done than there was yet to do. March 1 seemed like a reasonable target.

Jonah put a publicist on a full-time retainer to help with the launch, an expense that seemed as essential as rent, now that there were so many potential outlets for stories, each with a voracious hunger for copy. A single restaurant that was satisfied to be a singleton could probably assign a staffer and get good-enough coverage, but if Huertas was the first brick in a brand, he needed someone who already had contacts and knew what to send to each of them. The publicist on the pop-up project he'd participated in had generated an impressive amount of coverage, and he could always cut her back to part-time once he was under way. Together they decided to give Eater an exclusive early heads-up, as much to gauge interest as to get coverage.

On December 18, they contacted an editor at the website to say, "We wanted to let you guys know first" about an anticipated March opening.

"We'll see," came the brief reply. Nothing happened.

Jonah couldn't hire his friends any more than he could buy $600 chairs; they had as much experience as he did and their own trajectories to map, which did not include taking a cut in pay or position, not even to work alongside a friend. He would have hired any one of a number of guys he knew to be his sous chef—but they were already sous chefs at bigger places, so the next step for them was as significant as it was for him. They were looking for projects that gave them a better title or more money or both, or aiming for their own places, just like Jonah, whether as a chef-owner or in the shade of a larger group's corporate umbrella. He couldn't compete with that. He was going to have to hire people who weren't quite ready, hope that he could mentor them into shape, fast, and be grateful for the weeks here and there when he was going to have temporary help.

He couldn't hire anyone, for that matter, until he had an opening date that stuck. It turned out to be a good thing that Eater ignored the March announcement because the date evaporated over the holidays. Revised estimates ran from four to eight weeks more, which put him in a hiring bind: He couldn't ask anyone to give notice on an existing job until he could put them on payroll, but he didn't want to throw away money putting someone on payroll too many weeks before opening.

Jonah had stayed in touch with Jenni, a Maialino line cook who started there as part of the extern program at the Culinary Institute of America's Napa Valley campus in Northern California. She wasn't ready to be a sous chef—they both knew it—but she was good, and after three line-cook jobs at three restaurants in three years, she was motivated to take a chance.

Any step up in a restaurant kitchen was a game of musical chairs, and always had been, because the number of positions declined as a cook moved up the ladder; there were fewer sous than cooks on the hot line, fewer executive sous than sous, fewer chef de cuisine jobs, and, perched on top of the human pyramid, the executive chef or, definitively, the chef. The difference for this generation was that more contestants jostled for a spot at every step of the way. It had become crowded enough at the entry level for both teachers and students at CIA to voice their concern: In 2008, the teachers' union issued a no-confidence vote in the then president, citing slipping academic standards, and three years later a group of students filed a lawsuit charging that the school was accepting too many students, diluting the program in the process. There was no guarantee that someone Jenni admired would be looking for a sous, and would choose her, at the moment she decided she was ready, but there was surely the promise of plenty of competition: One national study reported that the number of culinary school graduates had increased by 25 percent between 2006 and 2010; in 2013 the number of schools offering culinary programs was up 30 percent over 2009. It might be slightly early to try her hand at a sous position, but it might not be a moment too soon.

Jonah worked on his sales pitch even as he hoped he was right about her potential. Jenni had an undergraduate degree in business because she wanted to own her own place someday, so he appealed to her entrepreneurial side. Yes, coming to Huertas was a speculative move—but if it worked, she was that much closer to her goal. She could end up running this kitchen when he opened a second place, and that was invaluable experience for a would-be owner, experience even he didn't have.

"This is different," he told her. "If you want to open your own place, honestly, this is more useful to you than working at a place someone else opens. It's a relevant learning experience. With security."

She said yes. Jonah had his sous chef—and she could start at the end of March, which gave Jonah time to work through the menu with her for what now looked like a mid-April opening.

He made one more kitchen hire, for continuity as much as anything. Juan Peña had been a porter at Maialino until Ruvi, the restaurant's master butcher, had taken him under his wing. Juan could butcher anything, which meant that he could learn to make sausage. He could also assemble pintxos, help out in a prep crisis, or fix electrical problems. When Jonah found out that he'd left Maialino because he needed more hours and had not landed well—he was working as a parking attendant—he offered Juan a job being Juan, whatever that turned out to mean at Huertas. He was Jonah's talisman; when Juan walked by the pass on his way to being capable, in one way or another, Jonah felt that much more confident.

As for the rest of the kitchen staff, he'd wait until right before the opening and save a little money by procrastinating.

Jonah had a good balance in the front of house, though he hadn't planned it that way. Luke was his first hire as general manager, another high school baseball player who might have pursued sports had he not injured his knee, once in high school and again in college, requiring him to find a new outlet for his competitive drive. He'd had a tutorial in high-end European hospitality at Le Cirque, but Jonah's restaurant offered equity and a promotion and the chance to have some less formal fun. Luke was twenty-six, too young to turn down a promising adventure.

Then Jonah heard that Nate was looking to make a move, and it made sense to talk to him as well. He was Luke's polar opposite—a twenty-four-year-old with dual degrees from the University of Pennsylvania's school of arts and sciences and from its Wharton business school. Nate had opened a take-out and delivery food service for students as part of an independent study in hospitality, started at USHG after graduation, and was blunt about his approach to his work: "I continually need to prove I'm at the top, no matter what I'm doing." He was a good fit, given his background, possibly better than Luke, so Jonah took him on as a second general manager and partner, even though that was one more than the standard model. Jonah could take advantage of their differences: Luke would focus on making sure that the front of house ran smoothly, while Nate monitored the day-to-day finances and developed the beverage program, at least for starters.

Luke and Nate were old school and new guard, respectively, which might be just the right blend for Huertas. And they were as eager as Jonah was to own something, to be in charge of their fates: On top of investing their own money, they'd each taken a cut in pay that seemed even worse than it was, at first, because of the long hours. Still, Jonah had imagined the future often enough to make them a promise that was intended to compensate for all of it: This wasn't a job but a career.

The delivery of the kitchen equipment would have been a shining moment—the day on which the emphasis shifted, appropriately, and all the design elements took a backseat to function—if the specifics of the delivery hadn't been so infuriating. Jonah glared at the shining steel Jade oven, which had the burners on the left and the flat-top on the right, the opposite of what he wanted, and was the wrong proportion as well: Instead of standard burners next to a flat-top that occupied two-thirds of the top, he got oversized burners that took up half the space and a flat-top that was smaller than what he'd envisioned. The stand for the combi oven was not the one he ordered, so it couldn't be installed. He couldn't help but wonder if suppliers made mistakes like this on orders from bigger chefs. He assumed not.

Worse, the supplier seemed singularly unconcerned about the impact of his error with the oven stand. They'd have the right one sent out. Mistakes happened. The fact that Huertas was opening in early April—absolutely—and that Jonah needed to take the kitchen out for a test drive didn't seem to concern him. The stand would go out immediately, though he wouldn't get specific about exactly when immediately was.

Jonah found the lack of empathy appalling. "I had hoped to work with them down the line," he said, "but now I hate them. I spent forty-five thousand dollars with them. I understand that's a blip on their radar, but they act like they expect thirty percent of things to go wrong."

That wasn't all. When he and Nick agreed to narrow the kitchen by sixteen inches, neither of them took into account the gas line that ran from the front to the back of the kitchen, behind the ovens and the deep fryer, a line that sat three inches out from the wall. Jonah's perfect aisle was now three inches narrower than he wanted, which made it that much harder for cooks to get past each other. He was the proud owner of a mistake that his employees would recall, as he recalled errors at places he'd worked, when they opened their own places and swore they'd get it right.

Jonah liked to say that he was good at not stressing over things he could not control, and when he did blow up—it was March; how much longer was this going to drag on?—he preferred hyperbole to a noisy explosion.

"If we fail I'm going to leave town and never come back," he said, as though he meant it. "I'm not kidding. I wouldn't be able to handle it."

When Gavin Kaysen was Jonah's age he drew up a list of life goals, and one of them was to open his own restaurant by the time he was thirty. By then he had appeared on *Food & Wine* magazine's annual list of best new chefs and won the James Beard Rising Star Chef Award, but he still didn't feel ready. He revised the list and decided to open his own place when he was thirty-five.

Kaysen was just a year younger than Nick Anderer, only eight years older than Jonah, but his experience—a classical education at what might now be considered a stately pace—more closely resembled that of his mentor, fifty-nine-year-old chef Daniel Boulud, who had built a global business on the success of two Michelin-starred restaurants, Daniel on Manhattan's Upper East Side and its more casual sibling,

Café Boulud. Anderer used "jailhouse" to describe the atmosphere in the kitchens where he had learned to cook, places where advanced degrees were rare and the early Anthony Bourdain—the confessional renegade cook, not the television host—was an object of admiration. Kaysen followed the more formal French training model: After he graduated from the New England Culinary Institute in Vermont, he worked at the restaurant at Domaine Chandon, on the grounds of the Northern California winery opened in 1973 by Moët et Chandon, and then made his pilgrimage overseas, first to L'Auberge de Lavaux in Switzerland and then to the venerable L'Escargot in London, an outpost of French cuisine since 1927. He returned to the States to become executive chef at El Bizcocho in San Diego, which landed him on the *Food & Wine* list; five years after that he moved to New York as chef de cuisine at Café Boulud, where in 2008 he won the Rising Star award.

Kaysen and his contemporaries might have knife skills and personal ambition in common, but his conversation was peppered with words like "legacy," and, like his older role models, he found freedom in kitchen discipline. His restaurant, if and when he had one, would be built on formal technique and professionalism; he was part of an effort to build a competitive team for the international Bocuse d'Or cooking competition, a biennial contest named for chef Paul Bocuse in which the United States had yet to place higher than sixth, and had created a foundation with Bocuse's son, Jerome, and Boulud and the chef-owner of The French Laundry, Thomas Keller, to support and train the team. He was at dinner with Boulud and Keller in 2010 when Keller asked Kaysen, who was about to turn thirty-one, about his plans for the future.

"What's your goal?" he recalled Keller asking him. "Do you want to have a restaurant someday, or what are you thinking? I'm not trying to get you out of Daniel's world. I'm just trying to understand."

Despite his list of life goals, Kaysen had begun to wonder if thirty-five was too late—if in fact thirty-one was too late and he'd already missed his chance.

"I feel like I might be past it," he confessed.

The two older chefs disagreed. Keller pointed out that he was forty when he opened The French Laundry. Boulud was thirty-nine when he opened Daniel. Kaysen knew it but had forgotten; it seemed so late, when he considered the ages of chefs who were opening places now.

"What's the difference between now and then?" he asked them.

"Nobody wrote about it then," said Boulud. No one had clocked his progress; there was scrutiny within the profession but not this constant, urgent level of chatter, which made maturity seem suspect even to Kaysen, who knew better. The notion of too late was a new phenomenon.

It was part of his hesitation, though—the stories he anticipated, the attendant hype or worse, the lack of it, the questions about timing that surely would surface in the narrative about him, and not with the collegial affection that informed Keller's question. And yet two of his mentors said that age was irrelevant. If Kaysen stopped pushing himself to align with some imaginary schedule, if he thought about having his own place without putting a time stamp on it, he could do it when he felt ready, and not before, a realization that allowed him to relax and wonder if he ought to look around a bit, just to see what might be available.

He did, not a concerted effort but an occasional inquiry, and then, in the summer of 2013, he stepped up the effort. Kaysen loved New York City and respected the prevailing notion that a serious chef had to make his mark there. He had a following that he could turn into investment dollars, so it would not be as much of a stretch as it would be for a younger chef—but he also had a reputation, between his work at Café Boulud and the Bocuse d'Or team, and that sense of history. He wasn't interested in a little space where he could start the next part of his career. He wanted a substantial location where he could build something that would last.

Early in the process, Kaysen found a beautiful space downtown, across the street from Mario Batali's Otto, a popular, informal place known for its pizza and pasta—but the NYU crowd was too young, too casual, too fleeting, and probably, at least some of them, constrained by an undergraduate's budget, and Kaysen lived on the Upper East Side. When he imagined his future, he walked to and from work.

It was too soon to compromise.

He devoted more energy to the search, looked at dozens of spaces in Manhattan and even a few in Southern California, and rejected each one. Then one morning, as he walked his dog, a new question came to him. Why was it so important to stay in New York City? He loved the city, but he'd started to wonder if he loved it because it was the best place for his family to be, or because he was supposed to, because success there was supposed to mean more than accomplishments anywhere else.

He had an epiphany, standing on the street with his dog: He didn't have to open a restaurant in New York. He wouldn't fall off the face of the culinary map if he did it somewhere else. He could go anywhere; in fact, he could go home and have a restaurant in Minneapolis, where he grew up. If his reputation survived the self-imposed exile, he would have a chance to distinguish himself in a way he couldn't in New York City. He'd have a higher profile the minute the doors opened, and he'd have a better family life for himself, his wife, and his two small children. Real estate was cheaper, so theoretically he'd get to spend more on food. It felt risky, but it might be a bigger opportunity.

People in the Midwest ate. "If I cook good food and deliver good service," he told himself, "they'll find me."

Kaysen announced his planned departure from Café Boulud in March 2014, a month before Huertas opened, as Jonah sat mired in inspections and delays. The news caught the New York restaurant community by surprise, and Kaysen quickly became a symbol of a threatened culinary diaspora. If he had the confidence to turn his back on the restaurant capital of the entire country, other chefs might consider doing the same. If he thought he could find reliable, enthusiastic diners in a place where the cost of doing business was far lower, where there were fewer openings each week to distract those diners, and so, less competition for media attention—if it was in fact possible to build a business from an outpost like Minneapolis—then a young chef could reasonably ask whether fighting to succeed in New York was worth all the trouble.

Early April slid too quickly into mid-April, but finally, it was time. Huertas still didn't have a front door, although it had columns of steel-rimmed horizontal windows on either side of a wooden slab that served as a temporary door, and a round table set to the left and right of the entrance. The host station was to the left as a guest entered, across from a long rough-hewn wooden bar that had been finished with a deep sheen. The mammoth zinc mural, hung behind the bar, with shelves in front of it to hold bottles of wine and, not soon enough, hard liquor. On the opposite wall, a counter for the standing crowd, and behind it, a row of high tables that ended at the service station midway through the front room.

Farther back there were three big booths, wide enough to hold six, easy, maybe eight in a pinch, the best seats in the house for diners who loved theater, because they faced the open kitchen. People there could check out the eggs being slow-poached in the immersion circulator, or consider a departing tray of pintxos, or watch the team of young cooks at work. The dining room took up the back third of the space, dark wood and gray paint, exposed original concrete floors and dark acoustic ceiling tiles that looked more like the strands of Jonah's huevos rotos than like the usual cottage cheese. The booths were trimmed in etched glass set into thin welded steel frames. The lights above the bar were custom made.

Huertas was going to open on Tuesday, April 22, after four days of friends-and-family tryouts that turned into five as the date got closer, because there was no such thing as too much rehearsal. Bad news didn't last any longer than good news did: The correct oven stand arrived, the flipped placement of the flat-top and the burners seemed less significant as time passed, and there was daily evidence of progress, from the delivery of dry goods to the first batch of chef shirts and kitchen towels. There weren't any big decisions left, of the sort that led to disagreements or large amounts of permit paperwork, and a comforting inevitability descended. The date was official; an e-mail announcement had gone out to investors. Everyone was in completion mode, though it looked like a race to the finish for the electrician, who was setting up the lights over the bar.

When an expensive midtown Spanish place closed its doors with only one day's notice to the staff, someone else's failure became Jonah's good luck, and he inherited a line cook who'd gone to culinary school in Spain as well as Stew Parlo, an experienced, unflappable bartender who would be the perfect person to develop cocktails with Nate and launch the expanded bar menu once Huertas got its upgrade to a full liquor license. Jonah and Jenni worked on the menu and figured out what they needed to order to get started; he intended to ramp up one step at a time during the soft opening, first offering drinks and a couple of pintxos, then the full bar menu, and then, on the last two nights before the official opening, the dining-room menu as well.

Jenni had watched Jonah make the staff meal at Maialino when he was a sous, so she took that on as one of her first managerial tasks, and on April 1 she set out trays of food along the kitchen counter even as Nick's crew cleaned up construction debris and remnants of their own lunches. She was going to help transform the staff into a family, and giving them a great meal before they started a shift was a smart way to start. This first meal set the tone: Huertas took care of its employees.

They were just finishing up when the Department of Health inspector arrived for a final preopening inspection. Health Department inspections were always a surprise, in terms of the exact time, but this was worse: Jonah drew an inspector who was legendary for her attention to, and criticism of, the smallest detail. On a good day, he did things that attracted an inspector's heightened scrutiny. The Health Department was nervous about sous vide because it involved cooking vacuum-packed proteins for a long time at lower-than-standard temperatures, and the fact that Jonah was one of the few chefs in town who'd taken a safety course to get certification didn't do much to offset the concern; prepared incorrectly, sous vide ingredients could harbor botulism or salmonella bacteria. He kept the jamón on display, which increased the risk that its temperature could rise above the acceptable 41 degrees Fahrenheit. As he watched her jot down notes, he wished for that predictable kind of trouble. She wasn't going to bother him about eggs or ham today, not with so many other infractions staring her in the face.

He stood by, helpless, as she took in the scene: trays of food perched on the kitchen counter, construction dust, and general disarray. She went downstairs and found mouse droppings, because the restaurant still didn't have a front door or a basement door to close off the delivery ramp that ran to the street.

She tallied the violations and let Jonah know that an inspector would have to come back before the soft opening to confirm that he had resolved what he swore to her were temporary problems. He ought to take this very seriously: She wanted to be sure he understood how much trouble he could have been in.

"If you'd already been open for business," she told him, "I would have shut you down."

One of the things that sustained Jonah was a little movie that had played in his head for years, in which he spoke to the assembled staff of his first restaurant on the first night of service, which for Huertas would be the first night of the soft opening.

He used to wonder who the staff would turn out to be, because until now they had been fantasy stand-ins for people he would meet down the line. He had arrived at down the line: His front-of-house staff, most of whom he had not known three weeks earlier, all of whom played a role in what he hoped would be his success, were folding napkins and checking glasses for water spots, while his cooks ticked off the items in their mise en place. As the chef-owner, he had to say something to them, which he did not like to do.

The place was as hectic as he expected it to be, but right before the doors opened he gathered everyone together and stood on a chair so that they could see him. "Here we are. Long time coming," he said, with an unexpected catch in his voice that made him speed up a bit to get past it. "Long time coming. Still getting to know some of you, great kitchen staff, and Luke and Nate have put together a solid team. This is my fourth time opening service. We're going to be busy, we're going to make mistakes, that's what this is for. People tonight are family, loved ones, people who want us to succeed. Make a mistake, don't hang your head— just fix it and we'll talk after. Anything you need from me, Jenni, Luke, Nate, let us know, and if I'm too busy, I'm sorry, I'll get to you later."

They waited to see if there was anything more. "I want you to be happy, to be around for a long time," he said. "So have a good service. We'll have a beer and talk it over in a few hours."

The next three nights were a parade of people who wouldn't sit down because they wanted to congratulate Jonah or one of the cooks, or had to take photographs, or saw friends across the room and detoured to say hello. Nat, the long-ago bar mitzvah boy, was there, having taken a job in restaurant development—his business card had a purposefully ragged edge, designed to look as though someone had taken a bite out of it. Other members of the original Maialino sous chef team showed up to wish Jonah well and suggest that he figure out some way to brighten up the flavor of the rotos with a bit more acid, which was what he needed them to tell him. His parents held court and shared memories of Jonah cooking at five, at ten, as a teenager.

On the fourth night they opened the dining room in back for the first of two full-service rehearsals before Tuesday's opening. For the first time in a year and a half, Jonah was going to feed people not just pintxos but dinner; for the first time, at all, in his own restaurant. He hurtled downstairs, and when he came back up he held a bouquet of skillets in one hand.

He waggled them in Jenni's direction.

"Tonight we get to cook," he said, with a weary and hopeful smile. "Pans and everything."

5

STAMPEDE

Slammed didn't begin to describe Huertas's first week of business. "Slammed" was a good word to toss around after a busy night, but not for a ninety-hour week that was a continuous loop of prep and service and cleanup, interrupted by something that barely qualified as a long nap before the cycle began again.

That single week beat Jonah's projections for the entire first month of business—$34,800 in sales for a week, compared to anticipated first-month sales of $32,200. He and Nate looked at the sales numbers every day, because they believed that vigilance made the difference between a successful restaurant and one that might seem healthy, only to slide off the rails too quickly to save. They had based their projections on losses at the start, possibly straight through the summer, because that was usually how it went; investors commonly had to wait as long as five years to see a first return on their money. Friends and family had broken even when it was supposed to lose $8,000, but that was a partisan crowd. Their first reaction to the week's numbers, to real sales, was to assume that they had made a mistake.

They had anticipated a $5,000 loss over the first two months. The way things were going, they might not lose anything at all. Best of all, they were making "sick money" in the dining room, in Jonah's giddy estimation. Pintxos were fun, and they got people in the door, but the menu del dia was his brand, his chance to show that he could refine and expand Spanish food without getting fussy about it—and by extension, that he could do the same with whatever cuisine he tried next, not Spanish necessarily, not at a Huertas sequel and so, not a partnership based on necessity. Just Jonah and Nate and Luke building their business.

The trick was to achieve great numbers without sleeping in a booth between shifts, which Jenni had jokingly mentioned as an alternative to her hour's commute to Queens, where a sous chef could afford to live. There wasn't a straightforward fix. Restaurant profit margins were notoriously slim, about ten cents on the dollar, and there were frustratingly few ways to improve them. The rent was set. There was little leeway on the other two fixed costs, labor and food, because past a certain point they couldn't trim their way to profitability. If Jonah looked for profit in even cheaper ingredients or a staff that was leaner than was practical, he ran the risk that the food wouldn't seem special enough, and the service, cursory. The better way to reduce ninety hours a week to a tolerable sixty or seventy was to make Huertas a place where people craved two more rounds of pintxos or had to try the wine pairings. An increase of a couple of dollars per check, multiplied by checks per year, could subsidize a bigger staff without putting a dent in the profit and loss statement that Nate planned to produce every month.

Check-building was the long-term answer, but the immediate challenge was to get more help, fast, because they couldn't sustain the grueling schedule. Jonah had underestimated the number of bodies he needed, figuring that he could expedite—call the orders, monitor the timing, check each plate before it went out—while Jenni handled the roast and sauté station and the line cook took care of fried foods and pintxos. One more person at the wood-burning oven, and a part-time culinary student to pick up the slack a couple of shifts a week, and he thought he had his staff.

Even that didn't last the week. The cook at the wood-burning oven, overwhelmed, announced after four days that she was leaving three days later, and Jonah, incensed that she quit without giving proper notice, had her come in the next morning to train the culinary student and then told her to pack up her stuff and get out. Joe, the student, was suddenly in charge of a station he'd never worked before, which meant that a new chunk of Jonah's day was devoted to teaching and supervision.

Jonah was pitting olives when he should have been fielding interview requests, and Jenni was asleep on her feet. He quickly installed a cousin of one of the Maialino prep cooks in the basement prep kitchen, laboring over garlic and onions and carrots and shallots the way he had at Chanterelle. Jenni got her roommate, Alyssa, to agree to work on the nights Joe was in class, in addition to her job as a private chef.

Dan didn't have many night shifts available, but Jonah's next two temporary stand-ins would arrive starting in two weeks, and they had plenty of time on their hands, stuck in a chef's purgatory between projects that didn't pan out and new jobs that might not start for months. Chad Shaner had left his job as executive sous chef at Union Square Café to pursue a project in Southern California, but it didn't turn out to be a long-term position, so he was back trying to figure out his next move. Chris McDade, who would arrive at the end of May, had worked alongside Jonah at Maialino and, like Chad, left town for a job that didn't pan out. He came back to be the executive sous chef at Marta, but the opening was delayed. They both needed a job between jobs—and while Jonah had to pay Chris more than he paid Jenni, he wanted to have both of them around for what he hoped was an extended packed house.

They would bail him out if it stayed this busy. If, on the other hand, the crowds subsided—and he had to be realistic, because openings were never the same as the day-to-day—his kitchen habits would keep him out of trouble. Jonah enjoyed the challenge of transforming what another chef might throw out, and showed off his latest effort at the afternoon lineup meeting, what he jokingly called his "garbage pintxo," made up of the fat trimmed from the jamón and the two-inch-long potato cores left over when they spun out the thin strands for the huevos rotos. He deep-fried the potato until it was slightly crisp on the outside and had absorbed flavor from the fat, and then he wrapped it in a charred ramp. The potato already earned its keep in the rotos; the jamón, on the list of meats. The only food cost was the ramp, for a pintxo that sold for $3. He couldn't get more economical than that.

Jonah tried to be reasonable about his expectations, to be prepared for whatever happened after the initial rush, but the problem with making money at the start was that it made losing money seem like failure. He reminded himself that losing money, was the norm at this point, and if it happened it didn't necessarily mean that he was doing anything wrong.

He was aware of niggling front-of-house problems—he had to be, much as he preferred to let Nate and Luke handle them—but he told himself that they were primarily a function of being new and inexperienced; nothing of any lasting concern. Nate was already getting resistance from the occasional guest who wanted a cocktail, which was going to be an issue only until they got their upgrade in six months. In the meantime, they had to make the wine and beer lists too tempting to reject. To that end, they had tasted dozens of Spanish wines, until Jonah's palate went numb, and decided to make their own vermút, which required more sampling and multiple trips to a nearby Indian spice store for inspiration. They looked for beers no one else served, or beers that were great deals, and offered traditional Spanish combinations like the kalimotxo. Jonah weighed in on all of it—no one was going to consume anything he hadn't blessed—but that would calm down with time, as they solidified the list.

Luke faced small, irksome problems that were easy to fix—they found a receptacle for wet umbrellas and would figure out what to do with coats that at the moment hung off of the bar stools onto the floor. Much of the crew was entry-level, aside from a couple of experienced servers working the dining room, because someone with a solid résumé was likelier to head for a place where the size of the tip pool and the number of shifts were more predictable. More training would help with that: One of the servers had already come in on his day off to practice busing tables, which meant that Nate and Luke had figured out how to inspire rather than demoralize the guy.

Canceled reservations were a bigger and more troubling issue, endemic to the business and less likely to resolve with time. Jonah knew, from places he'd worked and people he talked to, that no one had the perfect solution for diners who made reservations and didn't show up. They could call everyone on the list the day before, to confirm, but some people said they were coming and still didn't appear. As the new kid on the block, Huertas was getting more requests for reservations than they could accommodate—so if someone bailed, they lost money on a table they could have filled, a table that might have turned into regulars.

OpenTable, the online reservation service, tried to police users who racked up multiple no-shows, but people with commitment issues knew their way around the rules—they changed their e-mail registration and continued their last-minute defections under a new name. High-end restaurants like Per Se and Eleven Madison Park tried penalties—EMP charged $75 if a party failed to cancel forty-eight hours in advance and then didn't show up—but that could backfire, especially for an unproven, far more informal place like Huertas, because it seemed punitive to diners who were used to changing their minds without consequence. During the recession, when every reservation seemed that much more precious, overbooking had become a popular answer, even though it increased the possibility of long wait times and was tougher to calibrate at a small restaurant. The easiest solution was to hold back a number of tables for walk-ins rather than take reservations for all of them, but finding the right formula was impossible, really, until Luke had a better sense of several variables—the no-show rate, the speed with which he could turn a table, and the number of tables he could seat simultaneously without putting too much pressure on the kitchen.

"I figure a table of two needs ninety minutes to an hour and forty-five, a table of four, two hours minimum," he said. "And part of this is keeping a table in my back pocket. I need wiggle room, an emergency plan. That's part of the system. Not every table is available on OpenTable, and usually it's me or Nate answering the phone, or Jonah, who will ask me."

Luke didn't have a formula yet, but he didn't expect to, so soon. "It's a matter of understanding our space as we go on," he said. "It's a nuance I haven't figured out yet, what I can accommodate. It'll just come."

Jonah was less sanguine. The nightly percentage of cancellations took its place on the roster of numbers he kept in his head, alongside the food-cost percentages, the number of pintxos sold, the media inquiries, the wine pairings, the overtime hours, and the nightly check averages, which could always be a little higher.

He tried to set all of it aside when he was in the kitchen, because he had an ambitious agenda. Jonah wanted to make as much of the menu in-house as he could, even though it was a lot of work; he took pride in the fact that the quince paste that went with the cheeses was homemade. He wanted to change at least one dish on the menu del dia once a week, maybe more often than that—another labor-intensive exercise, because it meant that the kitchen had to master a new dish and prep a new batch of ingredients.

He figured that the best time to introduce a dish was on a Tuesday or Wednesday night, when things were marginally calmer than they were on the weekend—but he knew he was in trouble as soon as he looked at the reservation list for what should have been his second manageable Tuesday night. Luke had booked five large parties at the same time for the menu del dia, three groups of six and two of seven, using all three booths and two of the dining-room tables. It didn't matter if the kitchen was on top of things as thirty-two people took their seats at once, and he took little solace in the fact that someday they'd be able to handle this kind of rush. Two weeks in was not someday, and this wasn't one of Alyssa's shifts, which meant that Jenni would be doing more cooking than plating.

Jenni was responsible for all the back-room dishes at her station, but the only way to get fourteen egg courses out simultaneously was for the line cook to help her out, which meant that she, in turn, had to stop making pintxos. The runners could keep circulating the cold pintxos that were already prepared, but the croquetas and the homemade potato chips were on hold. As the orders hit, Nate helped run plates to the dining room, while Luke stood at the host stand to greet the guests and keep an eye on the book. No matter what they did, though, service was a nightmare that they could have avoided if only they'd staggered the reservation times.

On a night with a better rhythm, Jonah might have time to encourage a hustling cook or acknowledge a server who jumped in to run plates or clear dishes at a table that wasn't in his section. Not tonight, which made for a new problem. When the shift ended, Nate reported that some front-of-house staffers had started to complain: Jonah was difficult to approach, they weren't getting constructive feedback, he seemed so disapproving. A couple of them came up to Jonah the following day to apologize for whatever they thought they'd done wrong, a preemptive confession of failure before he got around to criticizing them.

He came to the afternoon front-of-house lineup meeting to say that apologies weren't necessary, he appreciated how seriously everyone took their work, and he wanted them to understand that a one-word reply wasn't him being curt. It was him being focused in the middle of a difficult service. As Huertas got busier, there would be more one-word replies. Everyone had to get used to it and not take it personally.

It was not yet time to pass out compliments. The worst thing they could do, he told them, would be to believe their early press.

"We haven't done anything yet," he said. "Hype is hype. We have to continue to get better."

Jonah was happier in mad-scientist mode, a paper coffee cup in one hand and a whipped cream canister in the other, huddled with Jenni in front of a microwave oven they were about to use for the first time. He wasn't satisfied with the rice pudding dessert on the menu del dia, and he had seen a recipe for an almond cake developed by Albert Adrià when he was the pastry chef at his brother Ferran's famed El Bulli on the coast of spain northeast of Barcelona, which had drawn pilgrims lucky enough to get a reservation until it closed in 2011. The cake was a good fit for Huertas because it was a spin on a more traditional cake, and it would work with a range of other flavors; if it came out well, he could put his own stamp on it. Jonah aimed for plates that looked appealing, not aggressively artful; he wasn't going to serve an aerosol-powered, microwaved almond cake unless it tasted better than a basic almond cake. Still, he liked the idea of a new technique with a weird edge. He was all for experimentation if it yielded something that was delicious, first, and fun on the plate, second.

Jenni made a batter out of sugar, egg white, ground almonds, and a little bit of flour, which Jonah spooned into the aerosol canister. He cut a slit in the bottom of the coffee cup to give any accumulated steam a vent, shook the canister, and filled the cup one-third of the way up, a cautious guess. The recipe he'd seen said halfway, but he was a little worried about how much the cake might puff up, as the batter was shot full of air. He placed the cup inside the microwave, turned the oven on, and he and Jenni leaned close to the door to watch.

"It's working," he said, as the batter poufed to more than twice its original size, a dome of batter rising above the top of the cup. After a couple of minutes he removed the cup and cut it away to expose a slightly gooey cone of almond cake. Next time he'd leave it in the microwave for a few more seconds, to make sure it set, but this was going to work. They had an almond cake that tasted good and resembled a loofah sponge, two or three portions per coffee cup. All that remained was to figure out what to do with it.

"Chocolate and goat cheese," said Jenni.

"Not goat cheese," said Jonah. "Maybe almond crumble, almond cream."

A sous chef was supposed to have opinions. "I don't like almond extract," said Jenni, a vote against almond cream, which required it.

"Almond puree," said Jonah, to acknowledge her opinion.

"Almond cream," said Jenni, backtracking. She did not want to seem obstinate; it was Jonah's menu, after all.

He was stumped. A puree might not have enough flavor or the right consistency, so he gave Jenni a new task to add to her to-do list. Between now and the start of service she had to make a puree and a cream, try them both, and figure out the answer. Almond cake in some form was going on the menu.

The more pressing task was to get someone to dash out and buy a second canister, to make sure they had enough batter ready to go.

Jonah cooked to satisfy himself, in the end, not for the six people in the first booth, not even for the critics whose arrival was the subject of constant speculation—or rather, he figured that by cooking for himself he cooked for all of them. If he cooked instead based on assumptions about what people might want, he'd pull his punches, and the food wouldn't be his anymore.

He was hard to please and felt compelled to move on as soon as he was happy with a dish. Jonah never cooked the same dish twice at home, because that was where he got to try new things, to stretch past the constraints of Spanish food, which already felt to him like a one-off. If he could make great Spanish food, he owed it to himself to master something else next time. And he balked at food truisms, which he considered a creative challenge. Nate said that they shouldn't put chicken on the menu because people didn't go to restaurants to eat chicken, which they made at home or bought to go. Jonah, always with an eye on the bottom line, figured he could make chicken work by pairing it with small amounts of more luxurious ingredients, like morel mushrooms. Nobody was going to tell him what he could or couldn't cook. He was, after all, the cook who got the *New York Times*'s attention with cow's stomach.

One of his first responsibilities at Maialino was making braised tripe, a mainstay of classic Roman cooking but not an easy sell. Jonah didn't care. He made the best tripe he could, tripe that met his exacting standards, day in and day out for months, working alongside Chris to turn out two batches every week, about seventy-five pounds of it. First he had to blanch the tripe multiple times, and then simmer it in stock and cook it down in a tomato sauce. When he got lucky, he got the one oversized pot with a spigot, which he opened to release the blanching water into the floor drain. The other big pot was too heavy to carry over to the sink, and there wasn't a strainer big enough to handle a batch, so when he got stuck with that pot he resorted to siphoning, which worked—except for the day when he sucked in on the hose for a moment too long and ended up with a mouthful of foul-tasting tripe blanching water while Chris, grateful not to be Jonah, lay on the kitchen floor and laughed.

Jonah didn't care, or he didn't care once he read the reference to it in the *Times*'s January 2010 review, which he had memorized: "Mr. Anderer's tripe is served in a tomato sauce with pecorino and mint," wrote then-critic Sam Sifton. "It's light, delicate even, slightly sweet, with a backbeat. You can dance to it."

Mr. Anderer was Nick, and the recipe was his. The execution was Jonah's, though, at least half of the time. A backbeat you can dance to. He thought about that line, sometimes, when the talk turned to Huertas and reviews.

Nate lived in a state of constant preoccupation with how to do things better, and if exhaustion overtook him in mid-thought, late at night, he woke up wherever he'd left off. He was never not thinking about Huertas. It occupied him on his bicycle ride in from Brooklyn, on the ride back home, on his day off, when he was out with friends. He was not about to let anything about the business side get by him.

Luke, in contrast, had worked for a restaurant group that defined success in terms of decades, not weeks, which suited his less antic rhythm. He kept a notebook in which he jotted down every idea he had for how to improve service, no matter how small. He talked about getting good over time, in incremental steps.

At a Friday afternoon lineup meeting, heading into what promised to be a busy weekend if the reservations showed up, Nate introduced a new moneymaking special, the "can and conserva," $12 for a can of beer, probably one that wasn't on the menu, to make it seem even more special, and a tin of seafood, which had already proved itself a popular item. The cheapest tinned seafood on the menu was $10, so Nate instructed the staff to describe this as a free beer. It was a great deal.

"It should be an easy sell," said Nate, a note of imperative in his voice.

When it was Luke's turn, he consulted his notebook and recited a list of slang phrases he'd heard the servers use, none of which he wanted to hear in the future:

"No problem."

"Hey, how you guys doing tonight?"

"What's up?"

He preferred a list that included "You're welcome" and "How are you?" without the "hey." When he looked up from his notebook at the incredulous expressions on a couple of faces—were speech patterns really the key to Huertas's success?—he did his best to explain.

"It doesn't mean that we're a formal environment," said Luke. "We want to have a friendly environment—but not be the customer's friend."

The traffic hierarchy was next on his list. Right of way in the narrow restaurant went, in order of priority, to guests, hot food, and dirty dishes. It didn't matter if a server had a set of hot plates resting on his forearm. A guest always had the right of way.

Posture mattered, too. Luke exhorted the staff to stand up straight, and on this one, Nate backed him up. If someone felt the need to stretch an aching muscle, they should slip out of the customers' line of sight into the stairwell.

"And if someone's headed to the bathroom," said Luke, "get out of their way. Don't rush, but move quickly. This is like a Broadway stage. Every movement you make gets noticed."

Nate agreed with this, too, but he was mindful that the first tenet of USHG's philosophy was to make sure that the staff was satisfied. If they didn't come to work happy, they weren't going to take good care of the customers—and this was starting to feel too much like a grown-up lecturing the kids. He wanted them to think of him and Luke as experts, but accessible ones, who not so long ago had been on the receiving end of all this information.

He decided to confess to his own set of nerves.

"Look, just think about something bad you do and work on it," he said. "I bite my nails. That's pretty gross. 'Look, a partner in a restaurant biting his nails.' That's really gross. I'm working on it." All he wanted was for everyone in the room to work as hard on whatever their equivalent bad behavior was.

"Verbiage, posture, table maintenance," he said. "That's our focus this week. We'll add more next week."

On his way into work on Saturday, Jonah stopped at a little secondhand store in Williamsburg, the Brooklyn neighborhood where he lived and couldn't afford to work, to buy a couple of dozen butter knives. It hadn't taken long to realize that people who ordered the menu del dia came in hungry, anticipating a four-course menu. They could get impatient waiting for the pintxo first course, but if Jonah gave them something to nibble on they might order a glass of wine or vermút in addition to the wine pairings with the meal. He'd decided on radishes served with flavored butter, which they'd tried for the first time the night before, precipitating a knife crisis. The dishwasher had to wash batches of them in the middle of service so that the servers could dry them for subsequent courses, which made everybody crazy. Jonah liked vintage dishes and cutlery, which contributed to the we've-been-here-forever vibe, so he bought a bunch of mismatched little knives.

He came to work feeling that he'd made progress this week. He'd survived the Tuesday service, their worst yet in his estimation, and he thought he'd done a good job of addressing his supposed snappishness without backing down about standards. He had a new, seasonal pintxo with grilled asparagus and ramps, and bunches of broccoli rabe flowers and purple chive flowers to use as garnishes. The weather report wasn't promising—threatened cloudbursts could make people skittish about going out—but there was a benefit to that, too. It'd give everyone a chance to work on the suggestions that he and Nate and Luke had made.

Chad had arrived in town and had a reservation tonight, to check out the food before he started work in the coming week. In the meantime, Alyssa had turned out to be a workhorse, efficient, precise, and fast, just what he needed until the next wave of reinforcements arrived. She had gone through the four-year program at the Culinary Institute of America's main Hyde Park campus on nothing but loans, so she had a pressing need of a paycheck; he could count on her to show up. Between her three days, and Chad, and Chris right after that, the fourth week of Huertas's life promised to be a relief, and possibly a pleasure.

The shift started on a forgiving note, able hands in the kitchen and a steady stream of customers rather than a flood. Jonah had the pintxo runner take over the job of adding garnishes to the pintxos, which made the runner that much prouder of what he was selling and saved the line cook some time. He moved the Spanish ham up to the wood-burning oven station to make more space for the order tickets. The front-room staff got better at the endless loop between the kitchen and the bar, so the food never stopped flowing. The inexperienced server who thought she should stand at the service station across from the kitchen until someone beckoned her over, rather than step up to the pass whenever she saw a plate, was encouraged to find another job.

The first hiccup was an order that sounded as though someone who knew Jonah was playing a joke, making special requests designed to drive him crazy. The server leaned over the pass and explained the order ticket in a lowered voice, as if sharing a terrible secret:

No asparagus in the migas with asparagus, which reduced it to a bowl of toasted bread crumbs and egg.

No fish or shellfish in a restaurant whose menu was built on them, requiring the kitchen to substitute a dish Jonah would have to make up on the spot.

A hard-boiled egg instead of a slow-poached egg for the huevos rotos, even though the soft egg was supposed to thicken the vinaigrette into a sauce.

One diner at the table had what the server described as "issues" with octopus and would prefer something else.

Jonah had to customize an array of dishes and somehow sync them with the regular orders at the table, and he was in the middle of it when another server appeared with a plate of lamb, minus a single bite. The customer didn't like it.

Five people studied the plate. Jonah was mystified; it looked fine to him.

"Are we telling them anything about the lamb?" he asked. "If the guy had known it was going to be this pink, he might have ordered something else."

"I told him medium rare," said the server. "He just wants it a little more done." Clearly the customer's notion of medium rare was less pink than the chef's.

"Well?"

"No. Just a little more done."

Jonah grimaced. They would have to figure out a description that better conveyed how the lamb was going to look.

"He's making a big mistake," he said quietly. "It's perfect medium-rare." He handed it off to Jenni with a request for a minute more. When the server came back to retrieve it, Jonah held the plate in his hand for a moment before he relinquished it, as though debating whether to send out something he wouldn't eat.

It was painful to turn out what was essentially the wrong food: If the migas had been a balanced dish without asparagus, if a hard-boiled egg achieved the same texture as a softer one, if overcooked lamb were any good, he would have offered the dishes that way in the first place. There was nothing he could do about taste preferences and allergies, about an aversion to shellfish or fish or octopus, but the interpretive requests grated. He was the chef. The idea was to sit down and enjoy his best efforts, not revamp them and, in doing so, throw a dish out of whack.

And yet hospitality seemed to demand accommodation, except for the few chef-owners who made a no-substitution policy part of their brand from the start, transforming the formal absolutism of the European kitchen into a T-shirted but no less definitive stance about what people should eat. David Chang and April Bloomfield hardly wanted for customers, even though he refused to make substitutions at his Momofuku restaurants, and she insisted that it was Roquefort or no cheese at all on the hamburger at The Spotted Pig in the West Village. That wasn't how Jonah wanted to operate. He'd rather a customer was happy with his meal—or at least he had thought so before this evening. Right now he wasn't so sure.

The best thing to do, he figured, was to make inside jokes to keep the cooks' spirits up. Another diner sealed her fate and credibility when she complained loudly that there was no decaf.

Nate conveyed this to Jonah with a sly grin, and Jonah replied just loud enough for Jenni and Alyssa to hear.

"Tell her to go back to the Upper West Side," he said, the neighborhood where Jonah, Nate, and Luke had grown up, known for a great number of mediocre restaurants that might not care how bad the decaf was. "We're below Fourteenth Street. We don't have decaf here." Downtown had standards and was proud of it, was the way he felt.

By nine the bar was packed and the tall front tables, full, even if several of the parties qualified as extended family—friends of Jonah and his parents, the line cook's parents, Chad. A party of three, people Jonah didn't know, sailed past the kitchen on their way out, and the man stopped just long enough to tell Jonah that he'd been looking for a pintxos place and clearly Huertas was it.

It took Jonah a moment to process the stranger's compliment. "Well," he called at the man's departing back. "Thank you."

It was after ten when a couple passed by the kitchen on the way to the dining room, but the reservation sheet said that the last table was at nine thirty. Jonah beckoned Luke over to the pass to find out why a nine thirty reservation was ordering at ten fifteen.

"Why did these people wait forty-five minutes for a table?"

"Table fifty wasn't ready," said Luke. "They sat at the bar."

Jonah's features flatlined: His eyebrows, his eyes, his mouth turned into grim horizontal lines, and he looked as though he was trying very hard not to say what he was thinking.

He pointed to the first booth, directly across from the pass, which had been empty for hours. "Why didn't we put them there?"

It was a trick question. There was no good answer, because they should have used the booth, and Luke didn't even try to respond. He'd been anxious about getting everything right, as Jonah and Nate were, but he came from a world of rules, not improvisation. At this point in Le Cirque's long history, he'd learned far more about gracious, codified hospitality than about putting out fires. The couple had a reservation for the menu del dia, which they served only in the dining room. He simply hadn't considered putting them anywhere but there.

"How many drinks did we buy them at the bar?" asked Jonah.

"They had hard cider," said Luke.

Jonah hardly considered that much of an apology for a forty-five-minute wait. Luke should have put them in the booth and comped them a glass of wine or sherry. Jonah forgot that he was in an open kitchen three feet from customers and raised his voice loud enough for anyone to hear.

"But how many fucking drinks did we *buy* them?" he asked. "Forty-five minutes is amateur hour. We ought to buy their whole fucking meal."

He turned away from Luke, asked a dining-room server what the couple had ordered to drink with their delayed dinner, and said, "Good. Comp them," without even registering what the answer was.

"They're really happy," she said, to try to calm him down.

"I suppose that's all that matters." He gave her a plate of complimentary pintxos, the special tuna quenelles on cod-skin chips, and went back to work, too angry to speak either to Luke or to Nate, who had zoomed over to quiet things down.

Luke retreated to the host station to make sure there was no more trouble brewing and came back to report that there was in fact one more reservation at ten thirty, and that another nine thirty was clearly a no-show. Jonah brushed past him without making eye contact to run dishes to someone he knew. He simmered for fifteen minutes, not talking to anyone, until a hapless new runner asked a question he should have known the answer to.

He refused to talk to the kid.

"Get me a manager."

When Nate came over, Jonah addressed him as though the runner were not standing right there, with guests as close as they'd been for the previous outburst. "This clown comes over to me," he began, pushing on the word "clown," but he was too upset to talk, and instead let himself be distracted by the final ticket of the night.

The runner darted back to the bar to make sure the problem had been resolved, and then meekly approached the pass again, to report that everything was okay. Jonah ignored him and pronounced sentence as soon as he walked back onto the floor.

"Either he wants to work here or he doesn't," Jonah told Nate, who was hovering nearby. Nate could educate the kid, fast, or fire him.

The people who'd been left at the bar for forty-five minutes were the kind of mistake that could do damage if they didn't leave happy—on a small scale, if they decided never to come back or mention Huertas to a friend, or on a viral plane, in a Yelp review that got traction and inspired other anonymous diners to exaggerate their discontent. There was no room for blunders like that.

There was no time, either, not in a world where Huertas hit the Power Rankings before it opened and the review window was much tighter than it had been. The last generation of chefs had used the early weeks at a new restaurant to fine-tune the operation, but more media outlets meant more competition, and everything had sped up accordingly. In his first three weeks, Jonah had fed food magazine editors with voracious websites to fill, television producers who wanted to check him out for a morning-show feature, and bloggers who ranged from well-informed to self-promoting, even as they prepared to move on to the next new place.

Nate was already tracking reviews; Gato, TV chef Bobby Flay's heralded return to the kitchen, got a review in *New York* magazine only six weeks after it opened, which meant that the magazine's critic, Adam Platt, had to have eaten there during the first month of business. By that count, a critic could walk in the door at Huertas tomorrow, if he hadn't already done so, unnoticed, two days earlier. Jonah and Nate and Luke always told the staff that they had to behave as though everyone were a potential critic. For all they knew, they had just offended the *New York Times*'s Pete Wells, here for an early visit to see if Huertas deserved his attention, by making him wait—or if not Wells himself, then his next-door neighbor or best friend or dentist, someone whose offhand negative comment could damage their chances of a review.

The only thing worse than an early review or a bad review—the latter a notion they refused to entertain—was no review at all, and the math there was daunting. The *Times* ran a weekly restaurant review, and *New York* magazine had switched to a biweekly publication schedule the month before Huertas opened, effectively cutting its review output in half. There would be about fifty reviews a year in the *Times* and just over two dozen in *New York* magazine, not counting special issues and lists of the best this or that. According to the *Zagat Guide*'s annual survey, 111 restaurants had opened in New York City in 2013, which meant that most of them would never get reviewed. Some got a first visit that didn't warrant a second, some got the standard three visits, and of that second group, some got reviews that drove business and some got reviews that made them yearn for benign neglect.

There was no way to affect the process, except to be as ready as possible, immediately, always. So Jonah blew up at Luke, on the chance that a ten-year-old dream had just been derailed by a couple stranded at the bar.

Nate was angry at both of them, at Luke for a silly mistake and at Jonah for a leadership gaffe, so he cornered Jonah in the basement office before they left for the night. "If you want to get angry at people," he said, "do what you have to do. But don't vilify Luke or me in front of the staff. Do it behind closed doors. I can handle it. But we have to get the most out of the staff—and if they see you belittle us, it doesn't work."

Jonah showed up at lineup again the next day, when he should have been getting ready for dinner service. He had to address what had happened without caving in—had to make the front-of-house staff feel more comfortable without yielding to some kind of feel-good compromise. He told them that several guests had complimented him on doing a good job "for only being open three weeks," which stuck in his head and had the opposite of the intended flattering effect. To him, it meant that they'd noticed mistakes they were willing to forgive because Huertas was less than one month old.

What he wanted to hear, he told the staff, was, "Amazing—and only open a couple of weeks." He did not apologize for demanding the kind of effort required, nor for blowing up at Luke.

"I'm very disappointed in what I saw," he said, "but I know we can do better."

6

THE FAVORITE

Grub Street's Restaurant Power Rankings made sure that Huertas opened to a crowd, and on May 1 Eater extended the streak by including the restaurant at number seven on the Heatmap, a monthly list of the twenty New York City restaurants that were generating the most buzz. It was the best kind of publicity, an endorsement without any of the qualifiers that might show up in a review, one based more on anticipation than on experience. Restaurant-chasers could hardly ignore a restaurant that was on both lists, even if it probably discouraged some diners from checking out Huertas until the early rush subsided—the ones who functioned at a more modulated pace, the potential regulars. A slowdown, with luck an almost imperceptible one, was inevitable and would likely happen as soon as the June Heatmap came out and the crowd that followed its recommendations moved on. In the long run, that could be a good thing: Just as the trendier customers gathered their miniature leather backpacks and shrink-brimmed fedoras and left, the next wave would muster its courage and venture out, reducing the odds of the dip in sales that the partners watched for, warily, in each day's sales totals.

For now, Huertas was on the short list. By mid-May there was a ninety-minute wait at the bar on a Friday or Saturday, and better still, people waited rather than head up the street to look for an alternative. Stew was in his element behind the bar, his eyebrow perpetually cocked in amusement, the constant patter droll enough to entertain but never a real conversation, which would disrupt his drink rhythm. People got a half-smile that said, Have a good time, but remember, I am not your best friend or confessor and I have to take care of everyone. He served the bar customers, handed off drink orders to the servers for the tables and the booths and the dining room, and did it all with enough of a flourish to make it look like fun. A passerby who hadn't seen the rankings saw a knot of people on the sidewalk, or glanced in and saw the wall-to-wall crowd, and figured that a place he'd never heard of must be worth a look. The crowd built itself.

On some weekend nights Jonah had to wait until twelve forty-five to break down the kitchen, and he kept one burner going even then, in case somebody wandered in late and hungry. The front-of-house staff started to shake itself out—one server quit before he got fired, another hurt his hand and showed up anyhow—and the kitchen kept its rhythm, with Chad and Alyssa to help. One night Antonio, a dishwasher from Empellón Cocina, wandered in to size things up and look for opportunity, told Jonah that he was using the wrong dish soap, and landed a Huertas shift from nine at night to one in the morning on top of the afternoon shift he already worked next door. Suddenly everything got that much smoother; adding Antonio was, Jonah said, "a godsend," because Lance, the original dishwasher who wanted to cook, was a first-timer whose enthusiasm outweighed his experience.

Grub Street, Eater, and Zagat ran a brief item on the percebes on their websites and caused what Jonah called a "mini-stampede," which required him to order more of them and turn what was supposed to be a small treat into a temporary big deal. The conserva-and-beer deal was more of a draw than he or Nate had anticipated. He got people who ordered the menu del dia to eat chicken, despite Nate's reservations, by piling on morel mushrooms and asparagus, as he had planned—and he got them to order a cod entrée, the economical fish equivalent of chicken, by serving it with beets and emergo beans, a large white bean with a creamy texture and sweet flavor.

He didn't get as many people in the back room as he wanted, though—occasionally a dining-room table sat empty all night, and frequently the ones that did fill failed to turn a second time. Cancellations were still a problem, so much so that Nate endorsed overbooking by 15 or 20 percent, which was about the percentage of no-shows. If they were wrong on any given night, if fewer people bailed and the tables backed up, Nate knew how to finesse a wait.

"I can get out of a sticky situation by smiling and buying them drinks and then they're impressed with the operation," he told Jonah. He wasn't going to leave a party stranded at the bar, as Luke had in the incident that so enraged Jonah, but would find a way to make the wait so enjoyable that people didn't mind. If the occasional party got irked and gave up, they'd still fill more tables than they were with the current system.

Luke, still smarting from the confrontation over the people he'd left at the bar, found himself reluctant to get in the middle of the debate—his credibility had sustained a sizable dent, or he worried that it had, although Jonah hadn't brought it up again. Jonah's silence was difficult to parse. They might be past the incident, or they might not, and Luke felt imbalanced, not knowing. The fact that the staff hadn't said much in the wake of the blow-up made things worse, somehow.

All of that aside, Luke knew that his perspective on reservations would frustrate both Jonah and Nate, should they ever ask, because it still boiled down to wait and see. Luke simply needed time to be able to figure out how many of the dining-room tables they could hold back, and he thought it foolish to rush into a new plan until they fully understood the existing one.

Jonah agreed on that point: They needed to clarify their reservation policy rather than worry about how to manage the confusion. They didn't take reservations in the front room, to encourage people to walk in on the spur of the moment. They took reservations in the back, to accommodate people who wanted a more formal dinner and didn't want to wait for it—but given the current imbalance, he wanted to seat walk-ins in the dining room when there were empty tables and let them order pintxos or raciones from the front-room menu. Jonah didn't like to see empty tables in the back, not after a party had walked through the crowded, noisy front room to get there. On an off night, the room felt like purgatory. They had to communicate that it was available to people who got discouraged by the wait in the front.

Nate had a solution that he wasn't quite prepared to share, not yet, because it required them to tinker with Jonah's basic concept. He thought they might need to blur the distinction between the front and the back menus, not emphasize it, because people just didn't get it. Other restaurants had a bar room and a dining room—Gramercy Tavern, where Jonah had spent a summer, was one wildly successful example— but when Nate thought about it, front and back at Huertas were "radically different," maybe too much so to make sense. The front and back at Gramercy Tavern were conceptual siblings, with more casual dishes served à la carte in the tavern room and a set of fixed tasting menus in a more formal setting in the dining rooms. He worried that Huertas was more like two distinct Spanish places cohabiting in a single space. A person in the front couldn't really cobble together a full meal, and a person in the back couldn't access the bustle that made the front feel like more fun. Nate was in more of a hurry than Jonah and Luke were to push the issue if the back room didn't improve, but it was too soon to insist on any kind of official change.

They spent an increasing amount of time trying to figure out how to fill tables, to be one of those places that was booked solid from five thirty until after ten. Some of the most popular restaurants in town simply didn't take reservations and had elevated the long wait into a bustling outdoor scene, when the weather was good, or a stint at the bar, or even at someone else's nearby bar, when the weather was bad. They took cell-phone numbers and contacted people when their table was ready—or if a place was too popular to require such niceties, simply took names and left it to the diners to monitor their own progress. A surprising number of people accepted the policy as part of the fun, as reassuring proof that they had made the right choice. Jonah didn't want to do that. He talked a lot about the "experience" he wanted to provide, which involved making a diner feel cared for but not smothered. A guaranteed and untended wait was not part of his welcoming formula.

Whatever they did, the priority, for now, was to get through a crowded night without any large-scale glitches and hope that momentum carried Huertas through the traditional lull between Memorial Day and Labor Day—or rather, hope that they continued to attract the kind of media attention that sustained the momentum. Opening Huertas, opening any small place that wasn't part of an existing restaurant group, was like balancing on a set of stones to cross a stream, one step, one mention, at a time. So far they were luckier than many: Just as the May Heatmap expired and Huertas fell off the list for June, Zagat notified Jonah that he'd made the dining guide's 30 Under 30 list of young industry leaders in New York City. It was a nice nod, but the official announcement wouldn't come until early July, a potentially helpful coincidence for the midsummer launch of brunch service, useless as long as it had to be kept secret. July was halfway to the other bank, the more secure footing of the post–Labor Day season; they needed coverage in June. *Food & Wine* was interested in featuring huevos rotos in their "Anatomy of a Dish" feature online, but that wouldn't run until August. Jonah appeared on a local cable show not because it would necessarily draw a big audience now but as an audition tape to show to larger outlets. He doubted that anyone saw it.

Jonah was invited to appear as one of sixteen contestants on Esquire TV's *Knife Fight*, a cable competition show among professional chefs run by Ilan Hall, the *Top Chef* winner in season two, and accepted with trepidation. If he'd felt he had a choice he would have said no, because there was nothing about it that appealed to him—he didn't see himself as a performer, winning seemed beside the point, and losing, an unnecessary humiliation. There certainly wasn't time to make anything that represented what he could do, and even if there were, mystery-box ingredients seemed chosen to stymie, not inspire. The only things the show had in common with his life were knives and raw ingredients and sources of heat, but turning it down was not an option, according to the publicist. When a cable show offered exposure to a chef with a new place, the only acceptable response seemed to be sure, thanks, even though it had the longest lead time of all the opportunities. By the time *Knife Fight* ran, Huertas would be a year old.

To get more attention now, the partners came up with two new promotional ideas for June, one authentic, the other an opportunistic nod to the popularity of sports bars. Pintxo pote was a tradition at many Spanish bars—bargain prices on nights that were otherwise too quiet— so Jonah decided to launch his own pintxo pote night on Tuesdays, every pintxo $1, when they usually cost between $2 and $4 each. And on Sundays during the World Cup they'd set up a big-screen television in the dining room to show soccer games, and serve cheap drinks and cheap food in the style of the competing countries, with a Spanish twist: beer or a wine-and-Coke for $3, and dishes like Swiss rosti potatoes with the garlic sauce from Jonah's papas braviolis for $5.

Both ideas ought to merit at least an announcement on Eater, Grub Street, and some of the smaller local food sites, and the soccer afternoons would help to ease the staff into daytime weekend shifts, in advance of brunch service. That was the far more important announcement: Brunch launched on July 5. Too late, Jonah realized that they may have overdone it, putting out three announcements in barely three weeks. There was nothing to be done—he couldn't reel it back in—but he worried that bargain pintxos and soccer might eclipse brunch coverage. It was hard to know how much news was enough and not too much.

The challenge was not to think about any of it, since it was too late to fix, but to focus on the day-to-day and the fact that he and Marina were getting married in Sonoma, California, which required him to disappear for five days. Had Huertas opened on any of the opening dates it had missed, Jonah's long-planned wedding would have taken place after the restaurant had settled in, maybe even after it had been reviewed. He might have stayed away for more than five days including travel time. He and Marina might have had a honeymoon, which was out of the question for at least six months. The best they could hope for, instead, was to be left alone long enough to have a fast good time.

Nate and Luke swore they wouldn't bother him, Chad had settled into a routine in the kitchen, and Chris was set to arrive the day Jonah left town, and both of them had cooked in far bigger kitchens for many more people, under the kind of pressure that made even a rough day at Huertas look easy. They were there to exude calm, keep the collective spirit high, and maintain standards, all the while being careful not to step on Jenni's less experienced toes.

. . .

Nate calculated the May figures before Jonah walked out the door and gave him an impressive pre-wedding present: Instead of losing $25,000, which was what they had projected for their first full month of business, they had made $20,000, a $45,000 swing in the right direction. It was exceptionally good news, and they allowed for a moment's euphoria before they forced themselves into a more sober and businesslike frame of mind. As Luke said, it was always better to under-promise and over-deliver, whether they were dealing with investors or customers. People had come in the first time because of all the media attention, but what if the press so far had been too positive? If it over-promised, if it made Huertas sound even better than it was, people might be disappointed and not come back.

Luke liked to say, "The only way to get a great review is to be great every day," but they weren't there, not yet. He also liked to talk about how important it was to be humble, and if they were being humble, they had to ignore the very coverage they were chasing. Publicity was like a business suit one size too big; they didn't quite fill out their image. It wasn't that they were making big mistakes. They were inconsistent from one shift to the next—but they were new, that was all, and it could take a while to adjust to the variable of a fresh batch of customers every night. They needed a little time, and the airspace between reality and what people said about them made them hope that the media would neglect them for a couple of days, because they'd never had to operate without Jonah around. They wanted critics to catch wind of Huertas, even as they hoped no one would bother until the chef-owner got back from California.

The first night Jonah was gone, Jacques Torres came into the restaurant with an editor from *Bon Appétit*. Torres, the French chocolatier who for years had been the pastry chef at Le Cirque, now ran his own stores as well as a Brooklyn factory. He was a welcome guest, predisposed to enjoy himself and happy to acknowledge that he had. At the end of a meal in the dining room he walked over to the kitchen with candy and cookies he'd brought for the staff.

He wanted to meet the chef.

Jenni explained, apologetically, that the chef was in California about to get married.

Then who is the sous?

Jenni said that she was. Chad and Chris might outrank her in terms of experience and pay, but Jonah had told everyone that she was in charge.

"Then if the chef is gone, you are the chef," said Torres, who instructed her to come out of the kitchen for a photograph, and to stand in the middle of the group, which was where the chef belonged.

Jenni had wanted to be a chef since she was a kid in the kitchen, like Jonah, although she had a different dream: a little place in Northern California, near her folks, or a food truck, which appealed to her because it represented less risk and more freedom. She could have a life and a family and a food truck. She would have gone straight to culinary school if not for her father's concerns about the instability of her chosen career, which translated into an attractive offer: He'd send her to college, and if she still wanted to go to culinary school when she was done, she would have had four more years to save money for it. A bachelor's degree in business sounded like an asset, so she agreed, and once she graduated she enrolled in the two-year associate degree program at CIA's Napa Valley campus.

She chose New York for her externship, a six-month stint in a professional kitchen, because it would be her one chance to work in what was still the restaurant capital of the United States, the big leagues, and she figured she'd learn more in that competitive environment than she would anywhere else. Six intense months, and she'd return to CIA to finish up her classwork.

Jenni trailed at Maialino and at one other restaurant, and both of them offered her an externship, Maialino at $7.25 an hour and the second place at $11. Her trail at Maialino had both scared her and inspired her, so she said yes to less pay, because the point of an externship was to learn, and $3.75 an hour was hardly the difference between being broke and being rich. When she was done, Nick Anderer offered her a job as a line cook at the $11 hourly rate she would have made as an extern at the other restaurant. One by one, Jonah and the other sous chefs sat her down and said the same thing: You went to CIA to get the job of your dreams. This is the job of your dreams. You could quit Maialino to go back to school to spend another $30,000 to graduate and work someplace that's not as great as this, a year from now, or you could stay put.

She had an eye for the strategic bet, even if it bore no resemblance to what she had told herself she was about to do, as though having a plan freed her up to think about something that wasn't part of it, to consider surprise from a safe vantage point. Jenni had never intended to work in New York City and had always planned to return to school, but this was too much of an opportunity to pass up. She told her skeptical parents, "If you'll pay the next $30,000, okay, but if not, I'm not paying another $30,000 to get the same kind of job I have now. I have my foot in the door at just the kind of place I'd be headed to." The second-year curriculum at CIA required stints working front of house, which she'd done in high school and college, and banquet class, pastry, and European cuisine, which had little to do with her long-term goals. She could learn more about Italian cuisine at a real job and get paid for the privilege.

Jenni flew out to California, sold her car, packed some of her furniture, flew back to New York, found an apartment, and went to work two

weeks later on the garde-manger station plating cold salads and appetizers, with the promise of a move onto the hot line when Nick decided
she was ready. Within months she was on the morning hot line, and
then morning contorno, cooking side dishes for breakfast and lunch,
and finally the evening shift on the flat-top.

The promotions were heady stuff, and they fed her natural impatience. When Jonah announced that he was leaving Maialino to open a
place of his own, she told him to keep her in mind. She let him know
every time she moved to a new job, and when she got to a tapas bar he
said he was glad she was learning about Spanish food, which was somewhere between a vague expression of interest and a job offer. She knew
she was a long shot for anything more than a line-cook position with
Jonah, but she also assumed that he couldn't pay enough or promise
enough stability to lure one of his sous chef peers into the kitchen.

Jenni had so far worked at three restaurants that were part of established empires, owned respectively by Danny Meyer, by chef-owner
Andrew Carmellini, and by chef Mario Batali and his partner, Joe Bastianich, because she was committed to building her résumé by working for what she called "known" chefs at high-profile places. "I thought
I was moving back to California," was her reasoning, "and I wanted
names they would recognize." But a promotion to sous chef in a big
operation could be tough, with so many line cooks clamoring for each
post. The smart move might be to move to a smaller place, to "a mom-
and-pop, basically," to add sous chef to her résumé.

Jenni was a bit apprehensive about the added responsibilities—
ordering, scheduling shifts, being in charge on Jonah's nights off, and
helping him with hiring and training until she was ready to take over
those tasks herself. She worried about the undoubtedly expanded
hours—but then, she always worried about something, by her own
admission. She said yes when Jonah offered her the sous chef job at a

starting salary of $38,000, not huge by the standards of the big places she'd worked at but acceptable because it meant that she was done being a line cook.

She tabled any notion of having her own brick-and-mortar restaurant or food truck, although she was careful to tell Jonah that this was a one-year commitment, in case going home proved too strong a lure. At the same time, she couldn't help but wonder what new options she might have if Huertas was a success. Sous chef to executive sous to chef de cuisine; she could run the Huertas kitchen when Jonah and Nate opened a second place. Her food truck dream might even end up a shared project. In any case, she'd be part of the story they told when they looked back: Jonah, a passionate young chef, had bet on himself and traded a safe ascent for a start-up; Nate and Luke had created a business model that enabled them to expand; Jenni had taken a chance on them and been the reliable presence who helped the company grow. She might not have the resources to invest her own money, as Nate and Luke had, but she could see equity for herself down the line, a reward for being essential. It all made sense.

Jonah had been Jenni's "go-to guy" at Maialino, the one who would always listen if she had a problem or a complaint. Now he'd hired her for a job she wasn't quite qualified for. She intended to repay that trust by being the best sous chef he could have wanted, erasing the memory of the friends he couldn't afford.

Jonah was on the flight to California when a man who might be *New York* magazine's Adam Platt walked into Huertas, alone, and took a seat at the bar. The longtime critic had abandoned his anonymity the previous December with a cover photograph and article in the magazine's annual "Where to Eat" issue, writing, "I would like readers to know what restaurateurs around town have known for years. Adam

Platt is a tall, top-heavy, round-faced gentleman who often dresses for dinner in the same dark, boxy, sauce-stained coat he bought off the rack at Rochester Big & Tall thirteen years ago."

The man at the bar wasn't wearing a jacket, but he fit the rest of the description, and he looked like the man in the cover photograph. Or maybe he didn't; in the midst of a collective anxiety spike, none of the staff trusted their senses. It was absolutely Adam Platt, unless, of course, it wasn't, a possibility they couldn't afford to consider. They had to operate on the assumption that one of the city's major critics was about to order some of the passed pintxos and might even try one of the raciones. Whatever he did, they could not acknowledge that they knew who he was, or even thought they did, because those were the rules of the game. They had to pretend that he was about to get the same level of attention they would shower on an out-of-town tourist whose opinion mattered to no one. Another man walked in and joined him; no clue there.

Among established restaurants that had already been reviewed, there might be gracious acknowledgment of a powerful guest—whether it was overt, an extra course that appeared unbidden, or covert, an obsessive attention to that guest's experience. For first-timers, obvious moves were out of the question. Nate could not walk up to the man at the bar to say how glad he was to welcome the first critic of any significance, nor could the bartender comp him a drink, lest they offend him or scare him off.

It was an odd bit of etiquette: They could and would treat him like a god, which in their universe he was, as long as they pretended he was nobody special.

None of the principles had ever been in charge when a critic walked in; not Jenni, whose eyes widened at the news, not Luke, who felt the need to text Jonah despite the communications embargo, not Nate, for whom the man at the bar was a lightning rod: Six weeks after Huertas opened, at the dawn of Nate's entrepreneurial life, a man who could nudge the restaurant toward success or failure was at the bar, and the chef wasn't here.

Nate wasn't worried about anything specific—Jenni knew what she was doing, Chris was there to enforce calm if she got rattled, and it wasn't as though Platt had booked a table for six in the back and was about to dig into the menu del dia cooked by someone other than the chef-owner. He wasn't concerned about the experience; he was overwhelmed by the simple fact of Platt's presence. Huertas had just been plucked from the pack for a shot at one of *New York* magazine's twice-monthly reviews, which could catapult them higher or put a lid on their progress. Either way, it was out of his control, and that was the killer: He couldn't change the menu, ask Jenni to add a dish or tweak a presentation, or alter the drink list. There wasn't any time.

Nate turned the corner in front of the kitchen pass so that he was out of the bar's line of sight and scrabbled his fingers against the tile wall as though he could find something to cling to on that shiny, slick surface. He leaned on the pass with his head down, looking wobbly enough that one of the servers came over to make sure he was okay. Nate shook him off. He didn't know what else they could have done, but what they could do suddenly seemed wildly insufficient. There was a very important loose cannon sitting at the bar—or a man who got great service all over town because of his striking resemblance to the critic. The probable Platt could fall in love with the place and show up in the dining room next week, or just talk about the bar menu, or decide that Huertas wasn't worth a full review, or turn out not to be Platt. They wouldn't know for sure until they saw something in print, or didn't.

Luke was 99 percent sure that the man at the bar was Adam Platt, which made it his job to ensure that everything ran smoothly—but that was always his job, so there was no need for anything beyond a degree of added vigilance. He prided himself on his perspective, developed at his fortunate first job at Le Cirque, where he'd had a short stint in the kitchen before he decided he was meant for front of house. Legendary cooks had run that kitchen, Daniel Boulud among them, and for four decades the restaurant survived everything from changing menu trends to the 1993 loss of its fourth star from the *New York Times*, when critic Ruth Reichl compared the dismissive service on an early visit to an exquisite experience on her return, once the staff knew who she was. Luke arrived late in the game, when memories contributed much of the glow, but he'd learned a methodical rhythm there, a level of service that he believed could be translated to inform any new setting, no matter how casual.

He knew that Jonah and Nate were skeptical about some of what seemed important to him, but he insisted that certain practices translated to any restaurant, no matter how downtown the vibe, and he clung to his set of priorities. Nate had already announced that there was no need for a manager to be at the host stand to welcome guests; the hosts they'd hired were able to do the job, and it felt kind of fussy to have Luke up there when he could be putting out small fires during service. Luke stayed put, because the host stand was a guest's first impression of Huertas, and he wanted it to feel important. While he was not about to suggest that an aging bastion of fine dining like Le Cirque was anything to emulate, he liked to think that he was in charge of taking the long view at Huertas. If he increased the volume of cross-country texts now that a critic was at the bar, it wasn't nerves as much as an appropriate desire to keep the chef-owner informed.

Luke figured that a modulated approach was the best way to avoid two common mistakes: the restaurant group that grew too fast, opened multiple outlets before the first one was settled, and went out of business at two out of three outposts before the principles knew what hit them, and the high-profile group whose cocky attitude translated into endless waits or imperious service, because "people don't like that, they like personal attention." Once Huertas was a success, bigger companies and investors would show up at the door with new concepts and the money to implement them, and he and Jonah and Nate had to be careful not to let a bad idea turn their heads. Hotel partnerships were big right now because the hotel absorbed some of the costs, but collaborating with a hotel from his old stomping grounds, the Upper East Side, would be foolish no matter how much money someone waved in front of them.

"That's not in line with the East Village," Luke told himself. "We're homey, not glitzy and glam. Sometimes you have to take a step back and ask yourself, Is this the right thing to do?" It was his job, he figured, to make sure that the partners were selective about the opportunities that would surely come their way.

He wasn't going to be satisfied with one restaurant any more than Jonah and Nate were. A chef couldn't work in the kitchen forever, so he needed a network of places where he could step into an advisory role as he got older. The same was true for him and Nate; it was fine to be closing up at one thirty in the morning when they were in their mid-twenties, but they didn't want to do it forever. They all agreed that Huertas was the first step, not the destination. The issue was how fast to take the next step. Luke was starting to think that it was his responsibility to make sure they didn't get ahead of themselves.

"We're in the culture of the next big thing," he said, "and worse, all the media are trying to find the next big thing. We're still racing, not pacing, ourselves."

The next day, at lineup, Nate apologized to the front-of-house staff for his behavior. He had not led by example, he had let his nerves get the best of him, and he vowed not to let it happen again—even as he exhorted the staff to be on the lookout for the next Platt visit, and to study the few photos he'd managed to find of Pete Wells, the critic at the *New York Times*.

Huertas got its needed mid-June publicity when it landed at the top of a *Village Voice* list of the ten best places to watch World Cup soccer, just as Jonah learned of a much bigger pending story: Eater wanted to send over a photographer because the site was running a review by a critic who had managed to visit unnoticed. It appeared on June 28 as the second half of a double review by Robert Sietsema, who led off with Donostia, another Spanish place a few blocks away from Huertas. Not a place to go for a full meal, he wrote, "but as a place to snack and explore the alcoholic beverages of Spain, Donostia is unparalleled."

Huertas, in his opinion, was both more and less, terrific overall, particularly in the back room, but inconsistent on a couple of dishes he felt compelled to warn the reader to avoid. He disliked "the spongy hake croquette resting in a puddle of indifferent garlic mayo," and he dismissed the percebes as an overpriced novelty act. He quibbled with the idea of a prix fixe meal in the back, which he found "faddish," having nothing to do with Spanish tradition, found the third course too small to be an entrée, and the vegetarian option "grease-sodden."

And yet the migas were "brilliant!" and the rest of the back-room menu, memorable. Huertas got two stars to Donostia's three, which rankled, but not enough to stick, because of the quote that was pulled out of the review and highlighted alongside the text.

"Lucky for us," wrote Sietsema, "the four-course feed via chef Jonah Miller verges on the superb."

7

BRUNCH

For the first time—or finally, if Jonah was being a realist—Huertas lived up to its new-restaurant budget projections and lost about $5,000 in June. It was a smaller loss than he'd estimated, and no surprise. If anything, the solid numbers for late April and all of May were the shockers. He should have reacted with a shrug and a bit of gratitude that it wasn't worse, but the good opening numbers—no, the ridiculous opening numbers—had spoiled him. Any loss at all seemed a more precipitous drop than it was because, until now, Huertas had been the exception to the start-up rule.

The competitor in him did not want to slip into a lower gear. "I want to make money all the time," he said, disappointed that he hadn't been able to sustain the numbers.

Jonah lectured himself: He knew the summer was going to be slower, and maybe that was a blessing, a chance to get used to brunch and get ready for the fall, when he planned to open seven days a week and add weekday lunch service and, at some point, a special family-style dinner on Wednesday and Sunday nights. He could see the table in his head—a big platter in the center, a whole chicken or fish, or a pork roast, with a bunch of side dishes and hard Spanish cider. Summer was for refinement and planning, and the first item on that agenda was brunch.

Spaniards might not eat brunch, but New Yorkers did, religiously, with the under-thirty crowd devoting hours each Sunday to drinks that took the edge off of Saturday night's hangover, a stabilizing plate of food, and conversation to put the previous night into focus. Brunch was an imperative debrief with a menu, and Jonah felt compelled to offer it. The challenge was to figure out a menu he could live with, one that didn't stray too far from what someone might eat midday in Spain—retooled raciones alongside dishes that put a Spanish spin on a more typical American brunch. He wasn't a purist, but there were limits, and he had a shorthand for what he wouldn't do: This was not a mimosas-and-hollandaise menu. He could walk out the door at Huertas, walk five minutes in almost any direction, and be staring at a mimosa and a plate of eggs Benedict, or a mimosa and a three-ingredient diner's choice omelette, or, for the vegetarian, a mimosa and a bowl of steel-cut oatmeal with fresh fruit.

"It's a good neighborhood for brunch," he said, taking a swipe at the competition. "Lots of mediocre places open."

A couple of days before the first brunch service, he laid out samples of his efforts for the front-of-house staff, minus the hake croqueta that Sietsema had described as spongy. Jonah wasn't so vulnerable that he'd kill a menu item because one critic didn't like it, but he wasn't taking any chances. He wasn't arrogant, either; maybe the execution had been off, or maybe it could stand a little improvement. He retired the croqueta until he could figure out which it was.

A jamón and queso sandwich was a standard in Spain, but Huertas customers weren't going to settle for plain ham and cheese, so it became a pressed sandwich on a roll ordered for that sandwich alone, the warmth to bring up the flavor and the roll to distinguish it from anything else on the menu. Spaniards ate rice pudding, too sweet for a main dish, so Jonah worked instead on a porridge that combined Calaspara Spanish short-grain rice, for a traditional element, with farro and red quinoa, a nod to current tastes, all of it cooked in milk and served with slivered almonds to bring it back to Spain.

Jonah had an instinct about where to stop, in terms of accommodations, and he explained the parameters to the staff. Sure, they would add fresh fruit to the porridge, $6 for a side order. No, that did not include fruit that might be a staple of an American brunch menu but didn't show up in Spain.

"If someone asks, 'Can I have a banana?' No. We're not a hotel," he told them. "You say, 'Every fruit we have this weekend is fresh from the greenmarket.'"

The bocadillo de calamares, battered and deep-fried squid piled on a roll, was as popular as jamón y queso in Spain, but in the East Village it posed a challenge, a double negative for the growing number of people who avoided gluten, between the white-bread roll and the battered squid. Jonah put it on the menu anyhow, because people liked fried calamari, and because anyone willing to eat eggs Benedict was likely to be unrepentant about the bocadillo.

"Tell people it's fried calamari on bread," Jonah instructed the servers. "It sounds like a po'boy. It'll work." He planned to put a mound of mixed greens on the plate as well, not that anyone in Spain ate a salad like that. New Yorkers seemed to regard a small side salad as their virtuous due, and it made the plate less beige.

One of his favorite dishes was what he called Spanish French toast, because that was the only way to convey what it was: eggy bread flavored with orange and cinnamon, deep-fried until it was crunchy on the outside but still custardy on the inside, served with whipped cream and fruit compote.

"We can sell a ton of these," said one of the runners. Crisp, sweet, topped with whipped cream and fruit; who wouldn't prefer it to hollandaise?

"It's the most kid-friendly dish we have," said Jonah. He asked only that the servers downplay the availability of maple syrup. Good maple syrup was very expensive, and frankly not part of the dish. They had to have it on hand because people expected it, but they didn't need to be aggressive about selling it.

"Doesn't need it," said Luke, supportively.

"What if someone wants it not deep-fried?" a server asked.

Jonah deflated for a moment, trying to imagine the diminished nature of the dish without the contrasting textures. It wasn't as though he could turn cream and sugar and eggs and white bread into health food simply by avoiding the fryer, and the trade-off was substantial: no crust, and just as fattening.

"I just wouldn't advertise the fried part of it," he said.

The important focus, for the servers, was the list of side dishes at the bottom of the menu—bacon that Jonah spiced and smoked in-house, homemade sausages, and slices of jamón. He wanted to change the way people ate brunch as well as what they ordered, to get away from the one-person, one-plate model. The Huertas brunch menu was built on sharing, with a main dish for each person and then, if it worked as he intended, little plates to pass around, so that the person who ordered the porridge could sample a strip of bacon, a chunk of sausage, maybe even a sliver of the tortilla that someone had ordered for the table. It wasn't the old notion of brunch, but it wasn't the current small-plate model, either, not quite. Too many small dishes could disrupt the experience, as a constant "Want some of this?" replaced conversation.

He anticipated two built-in problems that would be easy to fix as long as the servers stayed sharp. Churros with chocolate sauce came five to an order, so a server had to alert the kitchen if a party of six ordered them; an extra churro for free and everyone at the table would feel special. An expensive item like the homemade bacon or sausage meant a small extra charge, with the emphasis on small. There would always be people who wanted "one egg done this way," Jonah warned, which he'd be happy to do.

"That's why it's good to have slow brunches at first," he said, "to get used to the process."

"We don't anticipate busy," chimed in Luke. "That was the intention."

Coffee was an afterthought at dinner, when most people didn't bother, but essential at brunch, when they ordered it before they even looked at the menu. Huertas had a $4,800 espresso machine, but the cup of drip coffee they'd been pouring at night—sorry, no decaf—was not a high-quality introduction to a meal, not in the midst of a post-Starbucks third wave that saw microbrewers and local roasters popping up all over town. If Jonah cared enough to make his own quince paste and to smoke and spice his own bacon, he had to think about coffee service— or rather, he had to let a couple of front-of-house staffers who had been baristas at Maialino do so, as he was still skeptical that it mattered as much as they said it did. He couldn't argue with their logic, though: The coffee ought to be as good as the food that followed it. He wanted to encourage his staff to suggest ways to improve the restaurant, to feel that they had a personal stake in its success, so he agreed to spend another $1,000 on a drip coffee setup from the company that sold beans, sold and maintained the equipment, and trained the staff as part of the package.

Espresso drinks were handled only by the two staffers who already knew how to use the espresso machine, but drip coffee was going to be everyone's responsibility, and they had more to learn than they realized. A representative from the coffee roaster set up a Fetco coffeemaker in a nook at the bottom of the stairs, brewed a pot, and gathered the front-of-house staff around him. The standard Bunn coffee brewer was shunted off to the side, as obsolete as a landline.

For a half hour the group sipped and listened. One of the two staffers who knew what she was doing explained that the pervasive approach— "get Italian roast and load it up with milk and sugar"—was as out of fashion as the Bunn coffeemaker. Coffee had distinct flavor notes, like wine, in this case based on where it came from and how it was roasted, and it deserved the same kind of respect. Fine coffee was a beverage, not a wake-up in a cup, certainly not the result of hot water indiscriminately splashed over grounds.

There were rules:

Rinsing out the basket that held the grounds between each pot was key. "If there are grounds left in the basket it's like re-brewing coffee," said the supplier's rep, "and you wouldn't re-scramble eggs you made yesterday."

Temperature was just as important, and hot was not the goal. "Coffee tastes better as it cools."

The recipe for fine coffee was precise, exactly 105 grams of coffee per pot, which one of the experienced staffers would weigh in advance and set out in plastic quart containers.

The grind was everything, which was why the trainer was going to mark the proper setting. If the beans were ground too fine, the coffee would be weak; too coarse, and it would be strong but could be bitter. The way the ground coffee hit the basket mattered as well. "Give it a little shake to level the coffee, or the water will flow around it and not extract the flavors," the trainer said, to looks of increasing alarm from servers who had thought that pouring coffee meant just that, and were trying to figure out where, in the midst of a busy shift, they were going to find the time for all this. "And don't jam the basket in, or the coffee will shift to one side."

"Be quick," said one food runner, with a baffled grin, "but not too quick."

They had to add water in two careful stages, a "pre-wet" before the full pour to moisten the grinds, and then the rest of the water, premeasured, to make a pot. They ought to throw out any pot that was more than an hour old because the coffee started to "degrade," explained the trainer, but he understood the financial imperative. "We'll find the happy medium between what's good and what you can afford to waste."

And when brunch service ended they had to clean everything – carefully, completely, and using a food-safe cleanser instead of soap, which left a residue.

All that for a cup of coffee, and they hadn't even addressed whether to break down and offer decaf. A slow start to brunch service began to look more and more appealing.

Employees outnumbered diners for the first brunch shift on July 5, and the first table to be seated belonged to Wilson Tang, a restaurant owner who'd advised Jonah about the community board liquor license hearing, the kind of guy who brought his family to a brunch opening to show his support. Tang had left a job in finance to take over Nom Wah Tea Parlor, Chinatown's oldest dim sum restaurant, from his uncle, who had gone to work there as a teenager in 1950 and bought the restaurant in 1974. He had been spared the permit hassles, nervous investors, and limitations of a shoestring budget; although he'd had to go through the process on a second place he'd opened just months before Huertas, he operated from a relatively secure position. He did what he could to encourage a young chef like Jonah, who operated without any of the advantages Tang had inherited.

He and his family sat at one of the two round tables at the front windows, which caught some of the dwindling sunlight. The rest of the room was a cool, dark cave, and Jonah began to chafe at two things he could not change and had not considered when he was looking for a space: Huertas faced east, which meant that the sun was overhead and gone before even the earliest brunch crowd was done eating and drinking. If he'd been across the street, facing west, it wouldn't be so dim—and it wouldn't have mattered as much that First Avenue was an unappealing site for a sidewalk café, with trucks barreling north and a lot of ambient noise. Jonah hadn't even bothered to inquire about whether sidewalk seating was merely unpleasant or forbidden, because he wasn't interested. He couldn't compete. The plum locations were on Second Avenue, one block to the west, and Avenue A, one block to the east. When the weather got nice, diners headed for the sun like lizards seeking a warm rock.

It mattered more than what they ate, which was demoralizing. Jonah had hoped, even assumed, that people would defect from the open-air usual-suspect menus once they heard about the great Spanish fried toast with fruit compote, or all the new ways to consume weekend eggs, but the places with outdoor seating were jammed no matter what was on the menu. The definition of a great summer brunch seemed to include fresh air.

Or maybe the day after the Fourth of July was a bad time to start serving brunch, because everyone was away for the holiday weekend, a theory that required him to ignore the mimosa drinkers a block away. Jonah couldn't figure out exactly what the empty room meant. He thought and waffled; his rhythm was off.

"This is the longest day of my life," said Jenni, who had sent out two brunch orders and had nothing to do. She'd gone to sleep at one thirty the night before, only to wake up at five for no reason. She couldn't fall back asleep, which left her too tired to organize her morning, too tired to eat breakfast before she came to work, too tired to do anything but stay awake until brunch ended.

On a busy day, Jenni could work straight through from morning prep to the end of dinner service and not collapse until she was done. On a dead day like this, the most pressing item on her agenda was fighting fatigue. She tried to distract herself by paging through a Spanish cookbook with Joe, the extern from a local culinary school.

"This sounds delicious. We should make this. Sugar-coated fried bread," she said, tapping a page with her finger until the sound woke up a couple of brain cells. "Oh. French toast. We're making it already."

Chagrined, she allowed herself the smallest complaint aimed at anyone who might listen: She was hungry. She needed protein. Even a spoonful of peanut butter would help.

Chris, who seemed never to fade, dove into the kitchen's snack cache and produced a banana, which he deep-fried and put on a plate with a dollop of peanut butter. He plunked it down in front of Jenni, let her register how nice the presentation was, and cut it into thirds for her, Alyssa, and himself.

"Wait," he said. "I have a better way to do this." He grabbed another banana, floured it first, and dipped it into the deep fryer. Jonah wandered over as Chris started to slice it—new food drew everyone, no matter what it was—and Chris ceremoniously handed the first piece to the chef. He plated the rest as Nate and Luke joined the group.

"You can't eat it," Chris warned Nate. "It's floured."

"I can eat it," said Nate, who ate a gluten-free diet most of the time, except when desire occasionally trumped reason.

"And you don't even share," said Luke.

"Dude," said Nate, his mouth full. "There's more right there for you."

But Chris had put the remaining three slices in front of Jenni, grabbed a bottle of a sweet reduced sherry sauce, and drizzled some of it over the top. Brunch service might mean two tables of friends in an otherwise dark restaurant, but he had standards. Nobody was going to get through a shift on a glob of peanut butter on a spoon, or even on a deep-fried banana that improved with a second draft.

Richard Coraine, USHG's chief development officer, had told Jonah that the Huertas business plan was one of the best, most comprehensive proposals he'd seen—high praise from a man who had spent thirty years in the hospitality business, developing new restaurants or choosing not to pursue projects that failed to measure up. He knew every pitfall a start-up faced; he knew what was going on at Huertas without having to walk in the door. A young chef might have a notion of the food he wanted to cook and the space in which he wanted to cook it. Coraine had a fuller sense of just how much of their energy was about to be diverted from food.

"A cook cooks," said Coraine. "But a chef-owner manages."

Jonah's first management challenge was the fun part, as he looked for ways to help his staff build their skills and survive the opening rush. But their sense of mastery rose just as the number of customers dipped, and the sum of those two things was too many empty minutes. If people felt that they knew how to handle their jobs and had fewer tasks spread over the same number of hours, they skipped right past relief and hit boredom, which in turn sat next to anxiety about job security.

That was a new problem for Jonah. Traffic was still too unpredictable to consider cutting shifts, which could leave him understaffed, and free time wasn't as valuable as a paycheck. He didn't want to risk losing anyone to a more reliable job, and yet he couldn't pay people to stand around. He had to find something more than promises about the fall to keep them engaged.

"It's hard to keep people focused when it isn't busy," he said. "Much better when there's too much to do." Pintxo pote helped, some, on Tuesdays. Soccer Sundays were sketchier, but he saw another opportunity there. On one Sunday the crowd was so small that he let the servers watch the game with everyone else, so in a way they were getting paid for doing what they might have been doing if they hadn't been at work. If he couldn't increase the tip pool, he could at least let them enjoy the afternoon.

The Eater review didn't yield an immediate bounce, though Jonah blamed the dead Fourth of July weekend for that as well as for the low brunch turnout. He tried to inspire people by example—showed up even when he could have carved out a little free time for himself, and tackled any chore, no matter how small. The handle on the walk-in refrigerator broke, not for the first time, so he took it apart, found a broken spring, and went to the hardware store to buy a replacement. He fixed it himself, a nice distraction from the fact that summer was turning out to be slump season after all.

The second brunch weekend was as slow as the first, and Nate, who liked to be well ahead of trouble, started to look for explanations that he could shape into a theory and, from there, a practical solution. He commuted on his bicycle from Fort Greene, in Brooklyn, and by mid-month he'd realized that the streets were deserted no matter what time he was out, which had to be a big part of the reason for the empty tables on the weekend—and, he had to admit, the dwindling numbers at night. He wondered if the competition was suffering as much as Huertas was. It would be reassuring to know that more experienced and successful restaurateurs were in the same boat, which meant that the problem was on the street, not inside the restaurant.

He approached the owners of El Rey, a tiny, popular spot several blocks south that was only six months older than Huertas, to see if they could put things in perspective, which they could. Everyone was suffering, in great part because the people who sustained restaurants weren't, anymore. When the economy was bad, as it had been for the previous five summers, people who could no longer rationalize a weekend out of town settled instead for a long, alcohol-fueled brunch or a couple of dinners out. This year, a healthier stock market had put money back in people's bank accounts, so for the first time in a while they took that monthlong time-share at the beach.

If they kept spending when they got back, business was going to be great after Labor Day, but for now it was way too quiet.

There was nothing Nate could do about the mass exodus, but he could try to improve things on a small scale. On an empty Sunday in mid-July, he stood in the doorway ready to will people to abandon a cloudless day for the cool, dark recesses of Huertas. One woman wandered up, talking on her cell phone, and stood in the shade of Huertas's entrance, glancing at the menu posted in the window while she continued her conversation. She hung up but didn't move, as though she were confused about what to do next, so Nate wandered over to ask if he could be of any help.

"What happened to Empellón?" she asked, referring to the restaurant next door.

"Nothing," he said, "but they're not open for brunch."

He waited. Huertas was clearly open for brunch. He smiled, but she was already back on her phone, heading up the block.

A half hour later his mood had improved, based on nothing more significant than two tables of first-timers, representatives of all the people who had yet to try Huertas, some of whom would find out about it from these newcomers. "This is the best brunch in New York City," he announced to no one in particular. By mid-afternoon the window tables and three of the bar tables were full and there was one guy at the bar and a bigger party in the first booth. It wasn't good by a long shot, but it wasn't bad, and it was definitely a move in the right direction.

8

LOSS

Luke told Jonah they needed to talk, knowing that there were only two ways the conversation could go: Either Jonah would reassure him that he was making a valuable contribution, which Luke himself had begun to doubt, or he would quit, keep his small ownership stake, but lose his scheduled bonuses.

The couple who had waited at the bar for forty-five minutes back in early May had a dramatic effect on Huertas, but not the sort anyone had anticipated, no harsh online comments, nothing like that. For Luke, the incident was a sign that he was the wrong guy in the wrong place, a nagging feeling that refused to go away. The man who was always wary of the next-new-thing mentality felt out of sync, and he confessed his concerns to Nate a couple of times—who at first reassured him that everything was fine, but after a while acted more like a sounding board when he saw that Luke was getting frustrated or upset. Maybe everything wasn't fine; Jonah had yet to acknowledge that there was a problem or to reassure Luke about the value of his contributions. That was part of Luke's discomfort—he wasn't always sure that Jonah and Nate were right about what increasingly seemed like a hurried agenda.

Luke got caught in a cycle: He felt that he ought to have more input, but Jonah didn't seem as interested in what he had to say as Luke thought he should be. He started to doubt that his participation was of sufficient value, got sidetracked by insecurity, and let his work suffer by not speaking up as often as he had in the past, which gave Jonah cause to be less interested.

But Luke saw himself as an essential link between the chef and the customers, because he was the one greeting them at the door and visiting their table or bar stool to see how they were doing. What he had to say about the menu ought to count, he thought, and yet it seemed not to. At first he told himself that he had to get used to working at a chef-run restaurant after Le Cirque, where the owner was from the front of house and the chef, an employee. In the end, he felt as though neither he nor Jonah had figured it out.

"I think communication has been trying for me," he said. "For example, the development of the menu. For a chef that's incredibly personal. They put their heart and soul into it, and it can be hard for others of us to have input. But that's our responsibility, to have input. It's our job to have input. We look at the structure of the menu, and sometimes specific dishes. We try to identify problems with the business in any area. That's our job."

So he came to Jonah, to give him a chance to say that Luke had misread the signals.

"When it gets to a year," Luke began, "I don't want you to feel that I haven't earned my sweat equity," which working partners earned once they'd been at Huertas for that long. He wanted Jonah to understand that he felt hamstrung, that he could do more if only Jonah would listen.

Jonah wasn't going to argue with him about his perceptions because they were accurate. He had started to turn to Nate rather than to Luke—and had come to think that having two comanagers was not a smart idea in the first place. There was no rationale for having both of them, and of the two Nate was a better fit. Luke was a sweet guy with what Jonah thought of as a "midtown, over-the-top showmanship background." Nate was "more of a bulldog who takes things in his teeth," which was better for the business in the long run. If Jonah had known that Nate was available when he started to look, he would have stopped there.

It was a painful meeting, but Jonah could not afford to be guided by emotion. This wasn't going to get any better. He'd be more relaxed, he realized, with just one managing partner.

He didn't ask Luke to stay. Luke gave him a month's notice, and they agreed not to tell the staff until two weeks before his departure, to give them less time to feel unsettled.

For an angry moment, Luke thought about asking for his $10,000 investment back, but he didn't let himself say anything about it. He prided himself on being a glass-half-full type of person, and it would have been a stretch for Jonah to write that check right now. Besides, Luke wanted Jonah to know that he still believed in the restaurant's potential and hoped to be helpful down the line, if there was anything that he or Nate needed. Leaving was a personal decision, not a change of heart about the business.

Still, he was upset about the outcome, if not entirely surprised. His priority now was to figure out how to present this as his decision, not as an indication that he couldn't hack it. He had talked about this opportunity nonstop since he first got involved—and it wasn't like he had a great next job lined up. People might think that he was giving up, or worse, that he'd been encouraged to leave.

"Lots of my friends know this place," he said, "and they were excited for me. How do I explain it to friends, and professionally?"

More and more, Luke thought about the question he'd asked Jonah before he decided to become a partner: Did Jonah worry at all about starting a business without having any management experience? At the time, Luke had said that it seemed an unusual step to take—most would-be owners waited until they'd worked as an executive sous or chef de cuisine before heading out on their own. In his distress at Jonah's attitude, now, he decided that the skipped step, not his own performance, accounted in great part for what had happened.

He, Nate, and Jonah had plenty of energy and passion, but they were making it up as they went along, their ideas based too often on borrowed memories of places they'd worked or on philosophies of people they admired. It wasn't their own knowledge or experience, though it made him feel like an old fogey to think that way.

They didn't yet have a strategy. They had reactions, and Luke wasn't comfortable operating on the fly like that, or on what felt like the fly to someone who was used to a more considered pace.

"That middle step might've helped," he said. "And neither Nate nor I have been the top guy. We took a chance. Chefs have unique personalities; they think they can do everything. We have all this confidence because we have nothing to tell us otherwise. We're in our twenties. There's no nuanced perspective. We think we can do anything. We operate on confidence and emotion."

"We don't have perspective on anything," he said. "We're too young."

Nate was not the sort to dwell—not when Huertas was "bleeding money," in his urgent estimate, as losses increased in the first two weeks of July. Nobody was going to come out and say that it had been a mistake to have three partners when the usual arrangement was two, one in the kitchen and one out front, but it had been an odd fit regardless of the personalities involved. He felt that he'd learned a lot from Jonah already, about technical proficiency and precision, and that the two of them operated on a similar high-speed wavelength. While he was sorry that Luke felt uncomfortable enough to leave, he had to admit that he was excited about the new arrangement, and hopeful that he and Jonah could start to turn things around.

"In the long run it's sort of what I always wanted, so I'm okay with it," he said, his mind already a jumble of plans he wanted to discuss with Jonah, everything from menu changes to cocktail dreams to new promotions. If Luke was the most cautious of the three, Nate was the one who figured they had to take chances. He was aware that the transition wasn't going to be easy—as it was, he spent his two days off answering questions via text or phone call, and even that was about to evaporate. It was going to be a siege, at least temporarily. It was also his chance, two months shy of twenty-five, to be in charge of everything at Huertas outside the confines of the kitchen, which made him more excited than scared.

Luke saw the partners' youth and inexperience as a drawback, while Nate saw it as a plus: They were flexible, while an older restaurateur might be stuck in his ways. They were fast on their feet and open to suggestion. Nate networked like crazy, ate at restaurants he admired, took mental notes throughout the meal, and met more experienced restaurateurs for lunch or drinks to ask for advice.

"I want to say to Jonah, You go back to the kitchen," he said. "Let me run the business."

First, they had to resuscitate it. The first brunch shift brought in $550 instead of the thousands they'd projected; revenue for the first week of July was $11,000, when an average summer week should bring in $23,000. Yes, it was a short week because of the holiday—but no, a single day would not have made enough of a difference. It was the worst week so far, and all the rationales in the world couldn't erase the fact that they were down from almost $35,000 per week in May. He and Jonah agreed: In retrospect, it was probably a mistake to launch brunch so quickly, over a holiday weekend in the middle of the summer.

All they could do was look for ways not to make it worse. Nate started freezing quarts of fresh orange juice when supply outstripped demand, because he was not about to waste it. He had ten quarts stored in the freezer downstairs. If a couple of tables filled up, he grabbed one and ran it under hot water, fast, to defrost it.

He quietly cut back on the size of the wine orders without mentioning it to Stew, ordering three cases of wine rather than five even though each bottle ended up costing more because he missed out on the volume discount. In the short run, it looked better to spend $300 less on wine. It ran counter to what Nate knew to be true—you had to spend money to make money—but you had to have money to spend it.

He and Jonah began to hope that the *New York Times* would take the summer off along with everyone else. They used to think that the only thing worse than a bad review was no review at all. Now they added a third circle of hell: a great review in the middle of the slowest summer in recent memory.

David Waltuck looked at dozens of places before he found the one that most closely met his requirements, a space on a busy restaurant block across the street from the always-crowded Gramercy Tavern, surrounded by restaurants that would drive traffic but were different enough to make his new place, Élan, an alternative rather than a direct competitor. The space had been a restaurant, which meant savings of both time and money: He needed to change the look in the front, but he could use the existing kitchen, which meant that he could be ready to open, and so to recoup his costs, more quickly. A vanilla box held no appeal for him: Waltuck was happy to inherit a useable space, recast the front in his image, and get back to work.

The rent was $30,000 a month, but the first three months were free, a standard reprieve in a restaurant lease to give the owner time to remodel or rebuild as necessary. The previous owner insisted on an additional $400,000 in key money to cover HVAC improvements—heat, ventilation, and air-conditioning—which Waltuck was willing to pay, if grudgingly, because that was time saved as well, upgrade work he didn't have to do, permits he didn't have to chase. He could devote his energies to making the room beautiful and to devising a menu that offered Chanterelle favorites, like a signature seafood sausage, alongside newer dishes.

He installed a twelve-seat bar in the front and a banquette anchored by a big curved booth, along with freestanding tables, in the forty-eight-seat dining room. It was all done in quiet neutrals, cream, gray, brown, and black, with cylindrical light fixtures descending from the ceiling in both rooms and a set of Chuck Close self-portraits that had hung at Chanterelle installed across from the bar. Waltuck intended Élan to be more casual than Chanterelle had been, to take a few chances with the food that he might not have tried at a restaurant with four stars to sustain. Today's diner wasn't as interested in the kind of dining experience that had put thirteen-year-old Jonah and Nat in suits and ties, and he had to acknowledge that.

Élan opened in late June, and while an immediate rush would have been gratifying, Waltuck had a more tempered perspective. He had his regulars, and it was summer, and he didn't have anything resembling a social media presence to let the uninitiated know what was waiting for

them. Despite his skepticism about hiring someone to wrangle publicity, he and his partner had brought on a publicist, at least for the early
months, and he'd had some coverage on Eater and Grub Street, which
was nice but felt tangential. Waltuck wasn't convinced that it paved the
road to lasting success. He relied instead on Chanterelle's mailing list,
thousands of loyal customers, many of whom were eager to see what he
was up to this time. That would be his foundation until the fall, when
vacationers returned to town and the street would be full of people who
were used to coming to this neighborhood to eat.

One day, when the weather was particularly nice, he opened the
floor-to-ceiling front windows to let sunlight cascade over the bar—
and just like that, as though someone had cued the actors to walk on-
stage, people started to wander into the restaurant, attracted by the
notion of a meal in the sun-bathed room. The front filled up with animated, happy customers, and Waltuck had his first optimist's glimpse
of how the future might look.

Luke changed from a T-shirt and baggy shorts into a dress shirt and
slacks for the lineup meeting on July 23, as though he wanted to dignify
what he was about to say, to make it more of an announcement than a
concession. Jonah came in quietly and sat down, even though he usually skipped lineup. He needed to be there in case people got upset.

"How's everybody today?" asked Luke. No one spoke, the only sound
the *click-click-click* of Luke's ballpoint pen.

As soon as the last person sat down, Luke launched into his speech.
"I want to let everyone know that I've made a decision for myself, personally. I'm going to move on." Several sets of eyebrows rose in surprise.
"It's a decision I thought a lot about, and I have the full support of Jonah
and Nate."

Servers and runners came and went all the time, but Luke was a partner, and his departure fairly guaranteed further disruption down the line because he'd brought in some of the front-of-house staff, who might not be as eager—or as welcome—to work here without him. Shaky work schedules and empty seats were bad-enough signs on the barometer of restaurant health, but a departing partner was a big deal.

"I want to say how incredibly proud I am of what we've done," Luke went on. "We've opened a successful restaurant, so far, in what is probably the most difficult restaurant environment in the world. And this is a family affair—no big investors, no corporate backers, just friends and family. Hard work, a great concept, smart people, and a value system that others will model after."

The staff sat there, silent, for too long, so Nate broke in to ask Jonah to review the new menu items. There was a dish with what Jonah and Chris called burnt eggplant, but a server asked if they should call it charred eggplant instead, because a guest hadn't liked the idea that he was about to be served a burnt vegetable. Jonah settled happily into teacher mode, a nice refuge in the wake of Luke's speech.

"It's not okay to burn a steak, you want to char it," he said, "but with eggplant you actually burn the skin. Inside it's still creamy, and then you puree the whole thing to get a smoky, earthy quality. But if you keep getting weird reactions let us know. We can always say charred."

With that, everyone got up and went back to work. There was never any time to linger between lineup and the start of dinner service.

Jonah usually left the intelligence work to Nate while he focused on the food, but as the summer droned on he started to solicit opinions about how pervasive the slump was, in the hope that it would help him maintain the proper steady managerial air. Alex Stupak, the chef-owner of Empellón Cocina, said that they were slow, which made Jonah feel better. Peter Hoffman had advised Jonah to wait to launch brunch in the fall—and even though Jonah had ignored him, he took comfort now in the notion that brunch was a timing error and would pick up along with everything else at summer's end. He paid more attention to Nate's reports and concluded that this was a phase, and not one that was in any way specific to Huertas.

Jonah kept telling himself that a quiet summer had its advantages— they had the rest of July and all of August to get in shape for the fall, and by then all the big staff changes would be out of the way. Luke was leaving. Chad and Chris were leaving in early August. Jonah got Alyssa to come on full-time as the lead line cook, with the promise of a promotion to sous chef once they opened for lunch, and hired a line cook to work the fry station. He'd already seen how self-sufficient Alyssa was, how she managed outward calm no matter how crazy it got or how overwhelmed she might feel, and the new cook, twenty-four-year-old Max Loflin, had an impressive amount of experience. He'd worked at a pizza place during high school, found a mentor at a French bistro, and then bought a one-way ticket to Barcelona, where he worked at a hostel in exchange for food while he learned about the cuisine. He worked at one of John Besh's New Orleans restaurants on his return—and had built up a set of practical skills that were good enough to get him trails at Eleven Madison Park, The Modern, and Jean-Georges. Huertas was the oddity on that list, smaller, far less formal, but Huertas promised a tutorial in how to open a restaurant, and Max wanted to know that as much as anything. He wasn't quite as buttoned-down as Alyssa was, but he knew his stuff.

The real kitchen, the one Jonah would have moving forward, would be in place a couple of weeks before Labor Day. The outside help had stabilized the kitchen while they got under way, but now it was up to the full-time staff, plus the one additional cook Jonah would have hired already if every delayed extra shift weren't money saved.

He knew what customers were spending down to the dollar, and the $42 check average at the bar gave him reason for hope; it kept a bad summer in the back room from devolving into a catastrophe. He wanted to do two turns in the dining room every night—at their peak, in the early weeks, they beat two turns—but the room didn't even fill on week-nights and turned only a handful of tables on the weekend.

The dicier things got, the faster Nate fired ideas at him: They should do the family-style large-format dinners sooner, or try a five-course tasting menu with no choices instead of the current four-course with options for two of them. Smaller, nicer proteins. Jonah resisted it all, or at least thought about it more slowly than his partner might have liked.

The dining room was Jonah's pride, the place where he showed people what he could do as a chef, while the front room was not that much of a creative challenge. He considered half steps—they could use the back for private parties and push that aspect of the business. They could try to find new ways to lure customers who were, as he saw it, "really serious about the dining experience." He sensed some resistance to the set menu, but he wasn't prepared to consider a wholesale shift this soon. There was always the danger of changing too much too fast. Better to see if September lived up to their expectations, which he continued to assume it would.

He and Nate talked instead about ways to save money in August, which meant a judicious pruning of labor costs, a move he'd been unwilling to consider only weeks earlier—nothing that would unnerve staffers and encourage defections, but a reasonable trim that would only last until Labor Day. He knew who needed to work and who wouldn't mind having an extra day off, and they ought to be able to navigate for four or five weeks without creating a new crisis. He could improve his already economical food costs, and Nate had already found ways to minimize the outlay for liquor.

Jonah was not going to let himself panic, or even spend too much time worrying about the daily reports. Disappointment had only crept into his brain since Memorial Day, after all, and had little lasting chance against a dream that had seniority by more than a decade.

He preferred to think about his second restaurant, a useful, pleasant distraction that was always on his mind. Jonah used to say that it wasn't much harder to open seventy-five seats than forty, but now that he had to fill almost seventy seats, he wasn't so sure. Maybe the next place ought to be forty seats, a vermút and pintxo bar, or a bar that served tortillas and papas. He thought about Maialino and Marta, both of them bigger but both of them in hotels, and wondered if that was the smart move, if the pluses of shared risk compensated for added responsibilities like room service—not that any hotels had come calling, but a worthy debate in case they did down the line. He thought about taking a space in a food hall, should anybody ever offer him one, because it was another way to have someone else foot part of the bill.

Jonah saw a piece on Eater about the way in which David Waltuck prepared General Tso's sweetbreads, a version of a Chanterelle dish that Waltuck had retooled for Élan, and it made Jonah think about how risky that venture seemed. Thirty-five years after Waltuck opened Chanterelle, the new place was, as Jonah saw it, "still him and his food," and he wondered if that would be enough to survive in the current restaurant climate. More than one restaurant was an insurance policy. If Jonah were selling drinks and pintxos at some crowded little bar on a more densely trafficked street in the West Village, or in Williamsburg, it might take the edge off of Huertas's July.

Whatever the project, Jonah wanted to work with Chris, and thinking about that possibility helped to restore his equilibrium. They'd been talking about it since they cooked next to each other on the line at Maialino. They might be on different paths at the moment, Jonah striking out on his own, Chris working his way up inside a large company, but there was a reunion on the horizon; Jonah knew it. He figured he'd give Chris a year at Marta and then they'd talk seriously about what they might do next.

July 2015. By then, July 2014 was going to be the kind of wreck they joked about from a far better vantage point.

Jonah lifted his hand and traced an ascent in the air. "Labor Day should be like this, and then—" He raised his hand farther, let it float along at that new level, and smiled.

The one-story building that Gavin Kaysen found in Minneapolis started life as a stable, and then became a warren of small offices with a warehouse at the rear. He would have to gut the space and start over— first create a vanilla box and then start the build-out—but the location made the effort worthwhile. The building was in the city's North Loop, a warehouse district where old industrial buildings woke up one morning to find that they'd become stylish condominiums with faded photos of the original carriage works lining the walls, and a fledgling coffee bar took up residence diagonally across the street from a short row of gentlemen's clubs. Another nearby club was slated to be transformed into a boutique hotel—and The Bachelor Farmer restaurant, which opened in 2011 in an old warehouse a block in the opposite direction, had shown that the neighborhood could sustain an ambitious restaurant. The momentum was reassuring; this was not going to be the kind of byzantine challenge chefs could face in New York City. Minneapolis clearly welcomed the upgrade.

The prices, given what Kaysen had seen during his New York City search, were ridiculously low: Rent on the 6,400-square-foot space was under twenty dollars per square foot, including taxes—less than half of Jonah's rent for more than three times the space. That kind of rent changed everything; it enabled Kaysen to spend more on food and staff and decor without getting anywhere near the perilous edge. The warehouse space would turn into storage and prep facilities, and at the back of the dining room he would build a showcase display kitchen that ran the width of the room—with a counter providing front-row seats for a handful of diners who could watch his kitchen staff cook and plate every course. He would have a bar up front, booths along the opposite wall, and tables throughout the room, 120 seats with space left over for a 40-seat private dining room.

And he would have two things that were hard to come by for a first-time chef-owner in New York: enough space, and not too much noise. Rent would have precluded the former, and style dictated the latter, if he'd stayed put on the East Coast; a jammed, loud restaurant had been the epitome of New York dining fun for several years. Kaysen was going to have room between tables for people to walk by without turning sideways and apologizing, and just enough noise to make the place seem like everyone was having a good time, all because he was in a position to define his terms.

He signed a twenty-year lease, ten years at the current rent with two five-year renewal options that came with a comforting price cap. He would call the place Spoon and Stable—spoon, because he liked to collect them, including the ones his brother would turn into a wall hanging for the dining room, and stable, a nod to the past.

At thirty-five, Kaysen was months from opening his own place, eager to think about the menu and the ways in which he could utilize local products. It was more complex—and satisfying—than simply ordering from vendors. He wanted to talk about duck with the guy who owned the Wild Acres game farm, not only about acquiring some but about what they were fed and how they were stored once they were killed and cleaned. Plastic bags, came the answer. Kaysen thought that dry-aging them might work better, the owner was willing to give it a try, and from there, Kaysen had a supplier of exactly the kind of duck he wanted, and Wild Acres had a standing order for sixty to eighty ducks per week.

So much of the project was reassuring: the proportional costs, the matter-of-fact process, the kind of reasonable behavior that was not so common in New York. The flip side of that was that everything was so straightforward. The calm was unnerving. Kaysen had anxious moments when he missed the manic excitement of restaurant life in New York. This was light-years from what he remembered: dining out as a popular competitive sport, everyone in a rush to be able to say that they'd been to the next new place, so many times that they had little trouble landing a table.

It remained to be seen if Minneapolis locals would support what Kaysen intended to do, or if anyone might take a drive up from Chicago, say, to check him out—or if food just didn't generate that kind of excitement here. Kaysen's wife reminded him of what he'd said when he first took the leap and made his decision: If he concentrated on great food and great service, people would seek him out.

9

GHOST TOWN

Jonah and Nate stopped cashing their paychecks in August. They cut the checks so that no one would notice and inquire, and then they tucked them in their wallets rather than deposit them. For one month—it had better not be more than a month—they would have to live off of savings that had now become further personal investments in Huertas, and, in Jonah's case, off of his wife's paycheck as well, which he hadn't done since he'd been out looking at spaces, a rather substantial step in reverse. Nate monitored daily numbers to see if they'd need a bank loan to manage payroll, and a couple of concerned investors wondered if Jonah ought to turn the whole place into a bar that served pintxos and raciones, and abandon the menu del dia altogether.

It was a reasonable enough question from people who read their monthly statements, because the bar continued to be busier than the dining room, which wasn't saying much at this point. Jonah felt he owed them a response he did not quite have. He still wasn't ready to give up the dinner menu, but Nate summoned him to a meeting off-site, no distractions, to talk about what they could do to stop the free fall. It was too easy to get sidetracked at the restaurant, to get caught up in immediate tasks—and as the sole front-of-house partner, without pay at the moment, Nate felt compelled to take a more assertive role in Huertas's future. He urged Jonah at least to make the menu flashier, and fast, in case a critic was planning his fall calendar.

"Stop thinking about food costs," Nate told Jonah, "and let's get a kick-ass review."

Nate had a point: They weren't going to get a great review for being economical, and the current dining-room menu was hardly drawing crowds. Jonah agreed to come up with a five-course tasting menu, no choices, to replace the four-course version. He'd change the added course frequently to encourage customers to come back, he'd spend more on ingredients, and he'd stick with the $55 price, which ought to be an additional draw.

The investors' suggestions about a bar was the safer bet, but it felt too much like giving up, so Jonah and Nate agreed to go bigger instead, and hope that the results were impressive enough to draw a crowd after Labor Day. They added a happy hour, not because either of them cared about happy hour but because it made economic sense without turning Huertas into a full-time bar: The staff was there anyhow getting ready for dinner service, the lights were on, so they might as well serve drinks and a small menu to try to wring some profit out of the late afternoon. And they agreed to hold off on lunch service for now. It seemed like too much of an effort on a street that came to life at night.

Jonah wanted to launch the new menu right after Labor Day, but he was voted down by Nate and the publicist. Part of the point of a revamp was to draw media attention, and there was too much competition in September. August was dead for websites as well as for restaurants, and they, too, needed to draw traffic every day. If Huertas launched the new menu in late August, it would be that much easier to generate coverage.

People who were away but wanted to be up on the latest food news could read about it on their phones and tablets and laptops and make plans to check out the menu on their return.

Jonah agreed to start serving a new menu quietly, mid-month, with the official debut on August 28.

It was hot and muggy, brunch was dead again, and dinner didn't promise to be much better. Late in the afternoon, a host and a server sprawled facedown on the bench seats of the first booth, their heads against the wall, their feet wriggling in the aisle. A muffled moan rose up.

"It's soooooo slow," said the server. Between the weather and the scant reservation list, being snappy and attentive was going to be a struggle.

In the kitchen, Jenni picked individual leaves of purslane from their rubbery branches while Alyssa sliced eggplant in half lengthwise, and then sliced each piece into half-rounds. Nate was away for the weekend, and Jonah, at Jenni's urging, was at a family friend's annual party, both of them gone before anyone focused on the fact that this was Luke's final shift. It was an odd night before it ever got under way—Jenni running the kitchen alongside a manager who was most of the way out the door.

"I feel like I'm behind," said Jenni, even though she knew she wasn't, and that there wasn't much of a pending crowd to prep for. "I know I'm not—but you know how sometimes you get that feeling?"

Alyssa, preoccupied with the eggplant, muttered a supportive "uh-huh" and kept cutting. She knew that Jenni's nerves came in part from being in charge, so she joked about it being a women's kitchen for the first time and consulted the reservation list to make sure they knew what was coming. There was a party of eight in the dining room, always a challenge, because it meant eight sets of four courses that had to go out simultaneously, and who knew what kinds of curveballs they'd see

in response to the standard allergies-and-aversions inquiry. They tried
to comfort each other: No matter what, that table would be out before
the next back-room reservation even ordered.

The front-of-house staff was jittery as well—no Nate, no Jonah, and
no idea what to expect from Luke on his last night, since Jonah had
failed to inform his soon-to-be ex-partner that he'd be away and hadn't
said anything official about the departure to the staff. Luke and Stew
did an afternoon ice-cream run to keep spirits up, carrying back treats
that were puddles after only a block's walk. When it was time for lineup
everyone took their seats quietly and waited.

Luke rattled off who would be the dining-room captain, who was in
charge of running pintxos, who the new guy was who would arrive at
six thirty. If anyone got into trouble, he, Luke, was there to bail them out.

He reviewed the menu and the previous night's performance, nota-
ble for several dishes that had gone out late. "A cheese plate went out
twenty-five minutes late," he said. "It could be a fast item, but it hadn't
even been made. Twenty-five minutes late."

He looked around the room. "What's an internal clock?"

For a long moment no one spoke, until Stew said, "Be aware to make
sure dishes go out on time."

"One minute to us is three to a guest," said Luke, with a nod. "It's a
different perception. Not everyone complains. I don't, but if I'm pissed
I won't come back, and I'll tell people what happened."

The memory of the couple Luke had left sitting for forty-five minutes hovered in the air for a moment, until the kitchen staff appeared,
as a group, to say good-bye. Jenni stood behind Luke, her hands on his
shoulders, while the dining-room captain made a little speech about
how much everyone appreciated Luke's contribution. He had created
an organizational system for the front of house that was still in place,
and they were all grateful to him for that legacy.

He thanked them in turn for their hard work and reminded them that "the vast majority" of online comments were positive, which meant that people were still happy after they'd paid the bill, gone home, and had time to think about it.

"I want to thank everybody," he said, "who put ideas into action."

Stew presented him with a bottle of whiskey, and everyone applauded. Luke asked Jenni if she wanted to add anything, and she wrapped her arms around him and kissed the top of his head.

"I hope everybody has the chance to do this at least once," said Luke. "It takes so much energy, but you learn so much about other people and about yourself."

That was it. Everyone went back to work as though Luke weren't leaving permanently at the end of the night. Jenni tied her apron on and looked over at Alyssa.

"Al," she said, trying to sound authoritative. "How're you doing?"

Alyssa surveyed her station. "Good."

Jenni tried a small joke about Dad not being around tonight, and the first orders started to pop.

A new five-course, less frugal menu.

Food was where the fun started, after all, and for the first time in months Jonah found himself thinking about it before he was fully awake, in the moment before the alarm on his cell phone went off: Instead of duck with chard and carrots, he might serve duck with carrots, no chard, but three kinds of duck, the breast, a homemade sausage, and the heart. That was more impressive than duck breast with vegetables. With four courses he had to stick to a more traditional duck entrée, but five gave him a separate slot for vegetables. His brain was doing what it liked best, before he was conscious that it was. He woke up happy.

He'd already worked up a stuffed squid with pork sausage and pepper rice. They had two new pintxos, one with a duck mousse and one with bluefish inside a thin cucumber wrap. After much trial and error, they had an almond ice cream that they'd developed with Davey's, the ice-cream shop up the street. Jonah had made batches and batches of almond paste until he got one that was smooth enough to keep the ice cream from being granular, and then the owner of Davey's had turned the paste into ice cream using his homemade base. It was the dining room's new dessert, a Spanish riff on an Italian affogato, which was gelato with espresso poured over it, with Huertas's version using ice cream to replace gelato, a reduction of Pedro Ximénez sherry instead of espresso, a couple of Marcona almonds, and two small lengua de gato cookies.

When Jonah got to work he told Nate, with some surprise, of how pleasant the morning had been. It had been a while since Jonah woke up being the chef rather than the owner. He liked thinking about the duck as duck, rather than as a revenue source.

Nate pronounced it the best news he'd heard in a while. If Jonah would do what he did best—run the kitchen—and let Nate do what he did best—crunch the numbers and lob solutions—they might just head into the fall in good shape.

The mutual good mood didn't survive the day. Two of the servers who'd come in with Luke had left with him, but that was only the start. The real blow was defections from two people who'd been at Huertas since the start. Stew gave unexpected notice, as did the line cook who'd started at the same time—Stew, for a bartender's job that paid more than either Jonah or Nate made, and the line cook for a promotion to sous, a job "that she was smart enough to get but not smart enough to turn down," said Jonah, with uncharacteristic bitterness. Both departures felt to him like a personal betrayal, because he'd asked Stew if he was interested in a promotion to manager and he'd said no, only to take a better-paying job someplace else. Jonah thought he'd been clear with the line cook about opportunities to advance, but somehow she'd missed the message—and didn't seem to feel any obligation to a chef who had hired her when she lost her previous job on a day's notice. He felt anxious and hurt. At a restaurant as small as Huertas, it was impossible not to feel that they were leaving him, not the company.

Having Alyssa full-time was a big help, but now he had to hire and train another line cook rather than rely on a dependable cook who already knew the food. Nate was going to have to step in to bartend when he should have been focused on the community board, which had just put Huertas on the agenda for September 8. Everything was lined up—the new menu, the likelihood of a full liquor license—but people he relied on had abandoned him, and Jonah berated himself for not having been a good manager, a good coach, a supportive presence.

Starting immediately, he announced, Saturdays were pintxo audition day: Any cook was welcome to create one, and if the staff liked it, it would go on the menu. He vowed to give everyone more positive reinforcement.

"Not like they're fucking perfect," he told himself, "but they're good. I should have said more."

He had to hire a new line cook, fast, which became a convenient outlet for his frustration. Jonah was blunt, and hardly alone in his appraisal: There were no line cooks of acceptable caliber out there—or if they were capable, they were in too much of a rush. They wanted to trade a culinary school diploma for a job on the hot line, or to jump straight to sous chef after too little time on the hot line. True, Jonah had spent only a year on the line before he got his promotion, but he'd already spent eight years in professional kitchens. He had yet to see that on a résumé, whether it came from a culinary school graduate or someone who'd learned on the job.

Jonah had already run some ads, not anticipating the line cook's departure but hoping that he'd need another body in the fall, and the responses had by now reached joke level: Applicants with barely enough experience didn't show up for a trail, or showed up without their knives, or late, or sloppy, or with their knives and on time but with rudimentary skills. It took Jonah about ten minutes to figure out whether a candidate had potential—some of them doomed themselves halfway through a diced onion without even realizing that the trail was effectively over.

One promising candidate impressed Jonah, worked for ten days at the wood oven, said he had to miss his next shift because of an out-of-state court date, and never came back, even though he'd left his knives at the restaurant. Another applicant showed up armed with little beyond attitude—and an immigration issue Jonah could solve if he'd hire the guy, which Jonah would not, given the cook's inability to roll an acceptable tray of croquetas.

It got so bad that Jonah started scheduling two trails at once, on the assumption that one of the cooks wouldn't show. And then, suddenly, he had too much choice: a twenty-year-old kid who was a couple of classes shy of a degree from Monroe College's culinary program, and a cook who'd worked for eight months at chef Fabio Picchi's Il Cibrèo in Florence, Italy, which for three decades had served refined regional Tuscan cuisine. Jonah considered culinary school a "parochial" experience and was wary of graduates, although Jenni and Alyssa were exceptions to his rule. The Monroe student, Alberto Obando, might be, too. He had a work ethic: He was a scholarship student who had held down a part-time job and been a teaching assistant, so someone—multiple someones, clearly—thought he had potential. Monroe had overhauled its program a few years earlier when the new dean, Frank Costantino, rerouted the advertising budget into financial aid and embarked on a national recruitment program with a simple goal: to offer minority students a rigorous culinary education without the prohibitive costs of more high-profile schools. Costantino wanted to build a team for state-wide and national culinary competitions, to turn out graduates who could compete for top kitchen jobs. Alberto was one of his stars.

Alberto was impressive on his first trail, and Jonah was prepared to have him come in for a training shift, but he hesitated when he heard from the cook at Il Cibrèo, who clearly knew what he was doing. It wouldn't be fair to Alberto to offer him a training shift—essentially a job offer, unless it was a disaster—until he saw what the other cook could do.

If both of them were capable, it came down to a question of fit, of who provided the skills he needed the most. Alberto would cook what-ever Jonah asked him to cook, in whatever way Jonah asked him to do it, while the guy from Il Cibrèo would be more creative. Alberto was likely to stick around, while his competitor might be more ambitious, in more of a hurry, as the departing line cook had been. Jonah hadn't thought about this aspect of a candidate's profile before, but now he realized that it mattered at a small place like Huertas. Hiring Alberto would take more effort from Jonah because of the training required—but in the end, he'd have a custom-built line cook.

Jonah gave Alberto one more trail, brought in the other candidate, and managed to give both of them a job—Alberto as Huertas's new line cook, the more experienced applicant dispatched to Marta, where Chris was working in advance of a September opening.

He and Nate successfully doubled up on their effort to retain Stew with promises of more money—although they couldn't match what he said he would get at the new place—and more authority for that pend-ing cocktail program. The opportunity to create a cocktail menu once they had a full license was too tantalizing for Stew, who sometimes spent his break at the Indian store down the street, thinking about inventive combinations of herbs and spices. The promise of more places down the line didn't hurt, either. Like them, he believed in the promise of life after Labor Day.

The five-course menu launched on August 28, which happened to be the one-year anniversary of the first time Jonah set foot in the space. He showed up at the Wednesday lineup to talk about Thursday's launch and to give everyone a much-needed pep talk. He told them they were going to be fine. They'd weathered a slow summer and a lot of staff changes, but fall was going to be busy and fun. He knew it.

A server asked Jonah what he was going to do to celebrate the anniversary.

He shrugged. "I guess I'll spend the whole day in the space," he said.

And then nothing happened. The days after the menu launch were as dead as the days that preceded it, and Jonah found himself surrounded by staffers who were holding their breath—and worse, looking to him to keep their spirits up. He tried hard to act as though relief were mere days away, to sound eager for the fall rush and excited about the new food, but the extended effort finally took its toll. For the first time in his life, he lost out to dismay. Planning the restaurant was more fun than this. Opening the restaurant was more fun than this. Running the restaurant was turning out not to be much fun at all, at least not this summer, when he tried every smart move he could think of and none of them worked. The one fix that might work, the new menu, was eclipsed daily by disappointments that had nothing to do with food, and it was getting harder to tell when, or if, he was going to catch a break.

"This is the first time," he said, "that I haven't wanted to do this."

Although he wouldn't confess any of it to his coworkers, and told himself that this was a temporary dark mood, Jonah began to dream not of expansion but of rescue.

"If someone came in today and said he'd buy the place for two million dollars," he said, which was enough to pay off his investors and
suppliers and have something left over to underwrite a smarter second
chance, "I'd say okay. I'd probably do it again, but differently."

Restaurants fail all the time. The unluckiest ones disappear overnight,
missed only by the too-few customers who frequented them, the lease
sold to the next hopeful candidate or the landlord left without a tenant.
Eulogies for more illustrious restaurants like Waltuck's Chanterelle, ones
that at their peak had been booked weeks in advance, speak philosophi-
cally of their glorious heyday, their contribution to culinary history, and
their regrettable if unsurprising end. Restaurants age quickly, like the
chefs who run them, and twenty or thirty years is an enviable run. The
end is sad—they will be profoundly missed—but mortality is inevitable.

The few that last longer are historical landmarks as much as anything, frequented by regulars who enjoy the clubby attention and one-
timers who want to say they've been to The Four Seasons or Le Cirque.
Industry veterans summarize the process with a shrug and a range of
failure statistics, from one in five to 80 percent to the hyperbolic and
unverified nine out of ten. Feeding people for a living has always been
for the foolhardy and passionate—or, more and more, for someone with
an unassailable concept and multiple outlets, as stories of exponential
growth bully closure stories out of the way.

The *Zagat Guide* tracked openings and closures based on their sub-
scribers' reports, a consistent if flawed methodology, as it relied on anec-
dotal reports from the field and couldn't possibly catch everything. Still,
it provided a sense of the landscape, and the most recent numbers were
unnerving: While there were 160 openings in 2014, compared to 111 in
2013, 82 places were reported to have closed, which was a four-year

high. Tim Zagat told Eater that high rents were part of the problem, and in fact real estate prices were an equal-opportunity scourge: Danny Meyer had already announced that Union Square Café, the eldest sibling in the USHG empire, would relocate at the end of the year because of a rent increase. According to the *New York Times*, the initial rent on the space, in 1985, was about $48,000. It went on the market a week after Meyer's announcement at an annual rent of $650,000.

But that was a change of venue, not failure. If Meyer had the resources to relocate rather than close, newer restaurateurs had far less choice. Jonah's month started with a $14,000 rent bill, followed by food costs, payroll, utilities, and a publicist. If he didn't make enough money to cover costs, he had to find extra funds—and if he ran out of resources like uncashed paychecks, he was going to be out of luck.

In the midst of a decade's frenzy, though, the definition of bad luck changed, from an absolute state to a potentially temporary affliction. Restaurants were no longer a binary system, either open or closed; bad business, properly processed, could pave the way for bigger success.

It was even possible to succeed, fail because of it, and then succeed again.

Chef Stephanie Izard got famous fast as the winner of season four of *Top Chef*, which she parlayed into two Chicago restaurants—but only after an earlier, lesser-known phase of her career that involved a success unwieldy enough to land her in the hospital. The first time she passed out at work, she was at the host stand of Scylla, her first Chicago restaurant, midway through a call to confirm a reservation—which would have been someone else's responsibility if there had been a someone else. She woke up on the floor with the phone still in her hand, so she got up and called the person back.

"I'm so sorry," she said. "I was trying to confirm your reservation. I just happened to faint," at which point she passed out a second time.

When she came to she was on the floor again, which was how a staffer found her.

"Can you please call back that reservation so they're not freaked out?" asked Izard. After that she let the staffer take her to the emergency room, where the doctor pronounced her dehydrated and exhausted, a sobering if not quite surprising diagnosis. Izard, who by the time she was twenty-seven was the owner not only of a restaurant but of the building that housed it, had taken occasionally to crashing on a couch at the restaurant, still in her kitchen clothes, rather than waste time getting home and into bed. Wherever she slept, she was at work at seven a.m., six days a week, through the dinner shift and kitchen cleanup before she headed for a nearby bar to drink her adrenaline down to a manageable level. Dehydrated and exhausted made perfect sense.

Izard was done in, she came to believe, by a boom mentality in restaurants and real estate, the kind of giddy, anything-can-happen atmosphere that crushed common sense: The Eurocentric past was giving way to a populist food riot, and people with money wanted to be part of it, to invest in the next hot chef as a way to buy a little chunk of the excitement. Mortgage money was still hanging off of trees, just waiting for a young culinary school graduate who'd already worked her way up from a resort kitchen in Phoenix to a sous chef's job in Chicago. It didn't matter that she'd never run a business; no one seemed to care that she didn't have a business plan.

She got a loan to buy a $750,000 building, came up with a menu, hired a staff, and opened Scylla without so much as a general manager to make sure there was someone other than the chef to confirm reservations. She had an accountant to monitor income and costs—even if she had no idea that one thing an accountant might do was to call with a request for $20,000 to pay taxes, which was more than Stephanie's income in the first year. She had to be able to pay her employees before she could consider giving herself a raise.

Scylla was simply more popular than Izard could handle, on both a business and an emotional level. She had no life outside the restaurant—and not much of a life in it anymore, having collapsed under the weight of responsibility. She'd already called the realtor who'd found the building for her, a couple of times, to broach the subject of selling, only to pull back at the last minute in the hope that things would somehow get better. She was responsible for twenty employees who'd have to look for work if she closed—as would she. If she gave up, Stephanie would be a chef who went out of business, a failure, not exactly the profile she wanted to present if she ever tried to court investors again.

But there was no time to take a step back, create a functional business model, and hire the right people to bail her out. She called the realtor again and meant it this time: If he could find another restaurant to take over the space, she was ready to give up. The building went back on the market in May 2007, and the three-year-old Scylla closed that summer.

Two weeks before the new owner took over, Stephanie got a call from the producers of *Top Chef*, inviting her to audition for season four, which was going to be filmed in Chicago.

She was about to turn thirty and unemployed. She said yes.

"Everything happens for a reason," she thought. "Perfect timing."

Izard's win, that year, bought her another try. The people she hadn't known she needed at Scylla—business partners from the Boka Restaurant Group, who at that point had two chef-driven restaurants and were on their way to partnerships with six chefs in multiple locations—approached her on the strength of the win and offered her a second chance, done right this time. It was two years before Girl & the Goat opened in Chicago's gentrifying West Loop, by the time they found and outfitted a space, but her new partners were in no rush.

"People kept being, like, 'Where's your restaurant?'" said Izard. "I remember my partners said, 'Well, we don't want the headline in the paper to be 'Top Chef?'" as though the chef hadn't lived up to her title.

"I was, 'Yeah, I don't either,'" she said. "It puts more pressure on."

Girl & the Goat opened in 2010, and two years later Izard colonized the opposite side of West Randolph Street with Little Goat Diner, an 8,200-square-foot space with 120 seats that served everything from breakfast at seven a.m. to late-night weekend meals at midnight. She won a James Beard Award in 2013 for Best Chef, Great Lakes Region.

The days of passing out on the phone were over; she had partners to help shoulder the load, and she had overhauled her personal life. Izard got married in 2013, and her husband, a beer brewer, suggested that they could take on "three main things a year" as an overarching survival strategy, propped up by a new daily discipline. They woke up at five thirty in the morning on workdays and went to the gym together. She was at the restaurant before nine to make sure that prep got off to a good start and was out by nine at night. Twelve hours a day, six days a week, with quiet nights at home and early-morning exercise to take the place of late-night partying and recovery. Long-term, it was the only answer.

Now that she had the kind of success she could manage, she got to confront the question of what to do next. She thought about getting into the quality fast-food race with a chicken place and considered setting up her own processing plant, but decided in the end that it was too much of a stretch, probably $1 million to set it up right, and hard to control in terms of consistent quality. She fielded requests from hotels, in and outside of Chicago, and wondered if she ought to consider opening a place in New York City, to prove that she could.

The prospect felt a little bit like the chicken project, too difficult to monitor for a chef who tasted every dish every day with her team, even the dishes that were on the menu all the time, to make sure that the execution was up to her standards. She liked being part of the Chicago chef community—but the issue of expansion nagged at her because it was the expected next step. Chef Paul Kahan, a longtime friend, had figured out how to juggle seven restaurants and a bar, and she saw him as a mentor, "more of an overseer-restaurateur-chef," while she was still very much the "day-to-day chef." She talked to him about the options she considered and the offers she received, because she did not want to make another misstep.

She also hoped to start a family; that was one item on the three-item to-do list, and the existing businesses were the second. A cookbook could be considered part of the existing business, but the list was filling up, and a big out-of-town project felt like too much for the third slot. She decided to stick to the neighborhood for now, and embarked on plans for an Asian market-style restaurant a five-minute walk from her other places—a big open space full of stalls, with an early-morning noodle take-out window for employees at Google's new headquarters nearby. It wasn't the long-term answer to what she wanted to do but rather an interim step while she figured out where, exactly, she wanted to end up.

"It's a strange transition," she said, "that I'm still trying to figure out."

Rebound lore was like scary stories told around the campfire, a communal effort to keep fear at bay. Izard's story was hardly unusual. Some of the biggest successes in New York City, names on Jonah and Nate's short list of groups they wanted to emulate, had once been that close to disaster, more than once, only to rise from the ashes to survey the scene from an unassailable height. Their sagas made people brave; the next good idea could make the past evaporate.

David Chang opened Momofuku Noodle Bar on a shoestring in 2004, when he was twenty-seven. It didn't do much business, so he changed the menu, opened late night to get industry customers, and started to draw crowds: After a disappointing $500,000 in revenues the first year, the restaurant brought in $1 million in the second year and $2 million in the third. He opened Momofuku Ssäm Bar as an Asian burrito place in 2006, this time with $1 million in loans to repay, and faced possible bankruptcy before he salvaged the restaurant with a loan from his father, expanded hours, and another new menu.

"If you look at ten years of Momofuku," he told *ForbesLife,* "almost everything has come out of a mistake—a terrible fucking mistake." And yet he had prevailed: The *New York Times*'s Jeff Gordinier, who labeled 2004 a "game-changer" in the world of New York City restaurants, named Chang one of a handful of chefs who got the revolution going, "an empire-building star."

Gordinier included April Bloomfield as well, who failed out of the usual sequence and yet barely broke stride. After The Spotted Pig, she and partner Ken Friedman opened John Dory, a seafood restaurant that went into and out of business in less than a year—but months after that they opened The Breslin in a boutique hotel, and a year later opened what the *New York Times* called a "retooled" version of the closed restaurant, called The John Dory Oyster Bar, as though to blot out any memory of earlier failure.

Those kinds of stories made it possible to dismiss the threat of irreversible bad news. A truly talented chef could survive a misguided menu, staff defections, a miserably slow start, a bad location. There was no reason for Jonah to be discouraged; Chang and Bloomfield had been in far more dire straits, and now they were opening restaurants at an almost incomprehensible clip. Trouble could be a springboard for the next try, and worth the risk. Bad news might be more dramatic than in years past—the lows seemed to hit faster and harder—but recovery could be outsized as well, as long as he didn't give up.

In his 2006 book, *Setting the Table*, Danny Meyer summarized more than twenty years of experience and wrote, "The road to success is paved with mistakes well handled."

Almost a decade later, Chang told the *Forbes* reporter that he liked to recall what he considered his dad's best advice: Make mistakes. Just don't make the same mistakes twice.

10

THE CRITIC

Pete Wells was unhappy. The *New York Times* restaurant critic arrived at an East Village restaurant he planned to review, only to be told that there was a long wait for a table for four. Maybe two hours. They could take his name, which would not be his real name, and let him know. It wasn't as though another night would be any better, so the question for Wells, his wife, and two friends was how best to wile away the time. They were already hungry, because he hadn't factored in a two-hour delay. One of his companions had heard about Huertas, and it was nearby. They could bide their time over drinks and pintxos there, and that way he'd know whether it warranted another look.

Wells kept a long list of places that might merit a review, although inclusion on the list was no guarantee. He couldn't possibly get to every one that piqued his interest. It was a best-intention list, one that he pruned on a regular basis, deleting places that languished for too long. Restaurants could sit for more than a year, elbowed out of the way by a more compelling prospect, before they were excised. Huertas was a relatively new entry, and its USHG lineage made it a bit more intriguing than another small, independent restaurant might be, but he hadn't gotten to it yet. Might as well.

None of Jonah's strategies to attract a critic's attention had made a difference, not the five-course menu del dia or brunch, not the home-made vermút or the homemade almond ice cream or even the slow-poached egg in the rotos. What was about to get Pete Wells in the door was somebody else's no-reservations policy, which Jonah had rejected for the very reason he now stood to benefit from it—because it left peo-ple stranded with nothing to do for hours at a time.

Wells went to great lengths to remain anonymous, as had *Times* critics who preceded him, and restaurateurs worked just as hard to find out what he looked like. Nate had long since searched the Internet for an image of him and found one of a man of exasperatingly average appear-ance, although there was no way to tell if or how Wells had changed since it was taken. Nate asked around and came up with not very much: medium brown hair of unreliable but probably medium length, maybe a beard, maybe stubble, maybe clean-shaven. The most recent intelligence came from a friend at Eleven Madison Park who said he'd seen the critic on the Wednesday after Labor Day with a little bit of stubble, which could be predictive unless he had shaved since then. Nate understood how futile it was to speculate on someone's facial hair, and yet it made him feel better to be doing something, so he redrew the image he carried in his head, adding and subtracting hair but not too much. At least they knew he hadn't had time to grow a full beard.

As it turned out, the critic's wife was not quite as inaccessible. Her name popped up in Wells's biographical information, and there were plenty of photographs of her; better still, she didn't seem to change her look. Nate shared photos of her with everyone at Huertas and instructed them to be on the lookout. Wells might come in alone, or with a bunch of people other than his wife, but this greatly improved the odds of spotting him.

Which Nate did, on the Friday after Labor Day, when he came upstairs from the basement office and saw four people sitting in the first booth, one of whom looked like Wells's wife, one of whom had to be Wells. Nate considered the hair on the man's chin and decided that yes, this was how stubble plus two more days would look. He pulled the captain aside for a consultation and she agreed, so they let the staff know as quickly and quietly as they could: The restaurant critic from the *New York Times* was about to eat at Huertas.

They still assumed that *New York* magazine's Adam Platt had preceded him, way back in June, but by now that was beside the point because he hadn't written anything. They had Pete Wells, as sure as could be; that was definitely his wife, and the odds were slim that she'd be out with a man who closely resembled descriptions and old photos of her husband, and yet wasn't.

Anyone who could find an excuse to stand at the service station did so, to eavesdrop and ferry information to Jonah and Nate. The kitchen knew before the order came in that the party in the first booth was looking for a stopgap before dinner—which frustrated the cooks because it didn't give them much of a chance to show off. Lots of pintxos, but only one or two of each—except for three croquetas—the tinned mackerel, the small meat plate, an order of olives. Three different vermút—the house preparation, a spritz, two vermút de verano—and then a beer, a glass of Rosado, and a kalimotxo.

They ordered two raciones—the boquerones plate, which displayed only the kitchen's ability to turn out paper-thin potato chips and find an excellent supplier of Spanish white anchovies, and the huevos rotos. That was good, because anyone who had seen a plate of the real thing would appreciate Jonah's version. Word came back from a server that Wells wasn't eating much of the raciones, but his friends seemed to be enjoying them. Eventually they got the call from their intended dinner destination and headed out the door for the evening's real meal.

No one knew what to think. There were bad signs: Wells hadn't intended to eat at Huertas, he hadn't been seduced into abandoning his other dinner plans, and even if he was reviewing the other place and had to go there, he didn't get much of a sampling of what the kitchen could do. There were good signs: He must've heard something good about Huertas or he could have picked any of the other places in the neighborhood, he tried a lot of stuff, and the plates came back to the kitchen empty. And Nate had spotted him, so that everyone, from the server who explained the provenance of the cheese and jamón, to the cooks, to the bartender, was that much sharper than they might have been.

Nate lingered at the pass with Jonah, trying to make sense of what had just happened. "Maybe," said Nate, "he was checking us out."

Jonah searched for the right word.

"Auspicious," he said. "It could be an auspicious moment."

Community Board 3 had an unwritten rule about upgrades to full liquor licenses, and the Huertas lawyer had tried to get Jonah and Nate to listen: "If they give you beer and wine in a new place and you want a change—changing booze to full liquor, outdoor seating, whatever—they think that a year will give them a good indication of who you are and what you're doing," said Levey. If they could wait until next April, they'd probably get the upgrade without any opposition. Barely six months in, the board might be difficult.

After the summer they'd had, they hardly felt patient—and surely their past experience, and the critical reception Huertas had received so

far, would be enough to convince the committee that this was a substantial, quality operation. "They wanted to jump a little early," was how
Levey saw it, but he agreed to get them on the committee's September
agenda despite his misgivings. He'd be happy to be proven wrong.

Two nights after Pete Wells's visit, Jonah and Nate headed over to
the Community Board 3 licensing committee, happy but not too happy,
because Wells's appearance was a fluke and now he had to decide
whether to come back, and confident about the odds of a full liquor
license but not smug, because this was a notoriously tough board,
chaired by a lawyer and composed of local volunteers who saw themselves as the neighborhood's defense. Before they left Huertas, they told
the staff the odds were 90 percent in their favor.

Nate believed it, and had a cocktail menu ready to go once the State
Liquor Authority rubber-stamped tonight's approval, which could be as
soon as two weeks. Jonah tended to focus instead on the 10 percent and
to prepare accordingly, mindful of what Levey had told them. "Nate
doesn't realize it, but I think we're going to get pushback," he said. "Not
from neighbors, but from the board. They'll say, 'You've been open less
than six months. You've got balls coming back here.' They're going to
treat us like arrogant little kids, so we have to go in there with a lot of
humility. Definitely going to get pushback."

Wilson Tang had e-mailed him with advice: Don't sound desperate,
because you don't want the board to think you need the full license to
keep from going out of business. But don't sound too cocky, either.
Jonah walked into the meeting wishing he were more certain of the
right spot between those two extremes.

The meeting room was at the back end of a long hallway papered
with announcements, a square, low-ceilinged room with rows of folding
chairs facing the wide table where committee members sat in a row, the
chairperson at the center of the group. To the left, the board president

sat behind a big desk and kept an eye on everything—the applicants, the clock, the wandering child whose parents were there to complain about someone else's liquor license request.

The committee reserved its formidable ire for a liquor license upgrade applicant who'd opened on a residential side street ten months earlier, had been denied an upgrade at an August meeting, and was back without having addressed many of the committee's concerns. The place had all the trappings of a sports bar—five televisions, enough noise to draw complaints—though the owners swore it wasn't. A woman from the neighborhood block association stated the group's strong opposition to the full liquor license and, while she was at it, to the bar itself. The committee urged the owners to withdraw the application, regroup, and present a better plan. If they persisted, they faced one of two unpleasant outcomes—either an outright denial, or a set of restrictions designed to minimize the perceived impact on local residents.

Huertas was up next. The board chair gave a brief summary of the restaurant's history, including the fact that its beer and wine license had been approved eleven months earlier, in October 2013, with the stipulation that it be "a full-service restaurant," but that six months had passed before it opened for business.

She turned to Jonah, Nate, and their lawyer, who had come to the front of the room to stand alongside the committee's table.

"You had your door open on Friday, and it was horrifically loud," she said.

Did she stalk applicants on the assumption that they would try to deceive her?

"There was a party in the front room," said Jonah, quietly. "Unusual circumstances."

The lawyer pointed out that of the twenty-two letters of support, fourteen were from neighbors, and of the 242 petition signatures, about

140 were from the area. He rattled off the accolades that the restaurant and Jonah had received.

"It's a pure restaurant," he said, as opposed to a sports bar masquerading as something else. "But we're hearing people saying, 'Gee, I'd love a cocktail with that tasting menu.'"

"When we were before you last year," said Jonah, "we really would have loved a full license, but we didn't have a track record." He felt that he had one now.

A committee member asked Jonah about his work history and Nate about his position at Blue Smoke, to which they responded with some pride. Their résumés showed how serious they were.

The first committee member to voice an opinion was impressed. "At first, I was going to say no way," she said, "but they have background, and they're responsible, and it's a real restaurant." She was inclined to support the application for an upgrade.

Her comment hung in the air just long enough for Jonah and Nate to think that they were home free—and then, too fast to comprehend, the objections started to fly. The chair complained that five months after opening was too soon to ask for an upgrade. She complained further about "people who come into the neighborhood from outside" with expectations. The words "privilege" and "pedigree" sounded like pejoratives.

"I don't want to say you deserve this because you have better training than a guy from Queens who doesn't get a license," said another board member.

Jonah and Nate were speechless. Of all the objections they'd anticipated and planned to address, they'd never imagined getting turned down because they were from the Upper West Side and their families were well off, which was how they interpreted the comment. Jonah had worked since he was fourteen, Nate had worked in college, and besides, this wasn't supposed to be a competition against some nonexistent person from Queens. Each application was supposed to stand or fall on its own merit—and yet they couldn't object, couldn't show their feelings, because they might have to come back to these same people for a second round, relegated to the questionable appeals population that included owners of party hotels and sports bars.

Even the lawyer was blindsided, although he assumed that the comments referred not to the partners' family background but to the presumption that all the press coverage and their impressive résumés would make them exempt from the one-year rule, entitled to special treatment.

"It'd be a shame to put this off," he said, cautiously, "if you're going to grant it eventually."

The committee took a straw poll to see if there was commanding sentiment in one direction or the other, but it was as close as it could be: Three members were inclined to approve with stipulations, while four wanted to deny the application outright.

"We take a really hard line," said one of the four, by way of explanation, not apology.

Levey tried again—Jonah and Nate were not asking for any other considerations, not for later hours, not for outside seating, nothing but a liquor license.

"They're really good guys," he said.

At that, one of the committee members complained that he was getting tired and wanted to end the conversation unless one of the four who leaned toward rejecting the application had had a change of heart.

No one had.

The committee chair dismissed Jonah and Nate with a meager word of encouragement: Come back and try again when you've been open longer.

It was all they could do to get out the door without saying something they'd regret. Nate was in a rage over the rejection in general, and over the specific references to privilege and pedigree; what did their parents' tax bracket have to do with whether Huertas ought to have a liquor license? Jonah, whose cocktail-fueled holiday season had just evaporated, got very quiet.

They had two options left if they wanted to resolve this before April. The faster move was to appear in front of the entire community board, not the liquor license subcommittee, and hope that the full board would see fit to contradict its own members, which was unlikely. The other option was to go straight to the SLA, even though it was slower and more expensive. The SLA met only monthly at its Harlem office, its agenda was backed up with appeals of decisions made at the local level, and it cost more than $4,000 in filing fees, payable in advance, refunded if an application was denied, though that was cold comfort. If the full community board rejected the application, Jonah would have to explain two no votes to the SLA instead of one, so that made no sense. The lawyer figured that the SLA approval process would take six to eight weeks, so there was a slim chance that Jonah would have cocktails for the holidays, if not for people who were planning big holiday parties ahead of time.

Big, lucrative holiday parties, which had just become a far less likely source of revenue.

The best strategy was to wait out the subcommittee and come back next April, because a yes vote then meant an automatic approval from the SLA, but neither Jonah nor Nate felt that they had that kind of time.

It was hard for Jonah not to feel "a little spiteful," he said. It would be one thing if there were a crowd of noisy sloppy drunks outside Huertas every night at three a.m., but all he wanted to do was pour a drink, particularly a gin and tonic—Spain's unofficial national drink—if a customer wanted one.

. . .

Huertas lost $7,000 less in August than it had in July, but not because more people showed up and spent more money. Sales were flat. Jonah and Nate cut losses by cutting expenses, got to Labor Day on fumes, and waited for the uptick. Instead, the first three days after Labor Day were the worst in Huertas's short history, and the days leading up to Wells's visit and the community board meeting, little better.

Privately, Jonah considered a possibility he never would have imagined on opening night: If the big fall surge didn't hit soon, he might have to close the restaurant. Worse, he didn't think that he had made any fatal mistakes; he didn't see the glaring misstep. They had customers, but not enough, and the new dining-room menu had yet to attract bigger crowds. They had plenty of press coverage, none of which seemed to be having an impact. The liquor license would have improved sales figures, but there was no way to tell when they'd show up on the SLA agenda, except that it likely wouldn't be in time for the holidays. He looked at every angle and came to the same conclusion: They were doing everything they could and it wasn't enough.

The slim good news—a big article in the *Village Voice* and the Pete Wells drop-in, which didn't qualify as good news unless he came back— was not enough to keep him from some rather apocalyptic second-guessing.

"It's so fucking hard in New York City," he said. "The whole experience has really soured me—now I'm sympathetic to people who say the negatives outweigh the positives. I'm running the business really well, doing a great job on labor and food costs, everything that's in our control. But I can't control sales."

He kicked himself for not sticking with his original plan to open in Williamsburg, which was "expensive but packed," because the endless stream of tourists would have more than made up for higher rent. He fulminated on the lack of sidewalk seating, which wouldn't matter this winter—if they survived the winter—but could put a dent in sales again next summer. People strolled the blocks with sidewalk cafés without knowing where they were going and picked an appealing one. Huertas had to settle for people who'd made up their minds to eat there.

Jonah was grim about the obvious fix: "What makes money is a bar with five TV screens and sliders," remembering the community board applicant. He had not spent half his life dreaming about that.

He couldn't afford to provide health insurance stipends, which would have drawn a better level of employees. He hadn't raised enough money to insulate himself for five years, the way a big company could. And the money he had came from people he knew well, and liked, which had seemed like an advantage at the start but now grated on his nerves.

"I would caution people not to take money from family and friends," he said, in a reversal of his initial desire to work with empathic investors. "Not that I had other options—and I felt incredibly competent, but now I feel an incredible weight. It's people I know."

In August he'd imagined what he might do if a phantom buyer walked in with $2 million and offered to put Jonah out of his misery, to stake him to the kind of smarter second chance that had propelled Chang, Bloomfield, and Izard. By mid-September his imaginary price had come down to what it would take to pay back the investors, his own contribution a wash, though he had no idea if such a bailout were possible at this point.

"I'm not even sure that deal would come to me," he said.

He wondered if he had passed a fail-safe point without realizing it. "Failure has crept into my mind the way it never has before," he said. "I never thought I'd fail. But I'm a very rational person. It's within the realm of possibility. Having that even in my mind is a new thing for me."

. . .

Nate watched the reservation list for anything that might provide a clue to another Pete Wells visit, although some of what got his attention would have seemed unremarkable if he hadn't been on the lookout. A table of four was more interesting than a table of two, because the word was that Wells paid three visits to any place he was going to review, and he needed enough people to order a range of dishes. A very early or very late reservation piqued Nate's interest, because some people said that a critic might eat two dinners in one night. An odd e-mail—a broad category that at this point included anything other than the common first initial and last name—caught his eye.

The guy who'd supplied the stubble intelligence told Nate that recently Wells had opted for more dramatic disguises and a wider range of dining companions to try to stymie vigilant chefs and managers. The same friend said that when Wells's predecessor, Frank Bruni, was spotted at Eleven Madison Park in 2009, the kitchen sent six extra courses to everyone in the dining room, to impress Bruni without it looking as though he had received special treatment.

Six extra courses on the fly. Nate could barely imagine a kitchen that operated like that.

And then odd little things began to happen. Nate approached a woman at table one, at the window in front of the bar, because he thought she was a regular at Abraço, the coffee place around the corner, and he wanted to thank her for signing the liquor license petition. Halfway through the brief conversation, he realized he was wrong. He recognized her from somewhere else.

"You're in the industry," he said.

She was, in a way: She wrote about food for the *New York Times*, where there was great buzz, she said, about Huertas.

"Yes," said Nate, thinking like his speedy self and not like Jonah, whose internal brakes would have kept him from saying what Nate was about to say: "We may have had a special guest."

"I can't confirm or deny," said the writer, and Nate, who could not think of what to say next, found a quick excuse to go back to work.

The next night the man who'd eaten with Wells showed up at the bar, and Nate moved in for the strategic hover. It turned out to be Jeff Gordinier, the *Times*'s Food section writer who had suggested pintxos to Wells as a smart way to fill the time before dinner.

Nate retreated to the service station by the kitchen and watched as Gordinier sent out a raft of texts or photos, surely to Wells, or at least Nate wanted to believe that. When it felt right, not intrusive, not too blasé, he went back for another chat, hoping that the writer might convey a message to Wells: They ought to try the dining room, Nate said. The wine pairings were a great deal.

Pete decides on his own, came the reply.

The night after that, a restless Nate had drinks with a friend who worked at the NoMad, the second restaurant from the team who in 2011 had bought Eleven Madison Park from Danny Meyer. Chef Daniel Humm, who'd won his first Michelin star at twenty-four, and his business partner, Will Guidara, had opened the NoMad restaurant and bar in 2012, in the hotel of the same name, and in only two years had arrived at a point where they'd transcended mere mentions on Eater and Grub Street and were, as Nate saw it, "all about reviews and San Pellegrino ratings," the annual list of the top fifty restaurants in the world. It was a far different universe from the one where Huertas lived, in terms of food and ambiance and cost, but NoMad had survived Pete Wells's multiple visits, prevailed, in fact, and Nate wondered if his friend had any advice on how to prepare, short of six extra courses for the entire house.

Simple, his friend replied: They changed the entire menu the day after Wells's first visit, reinvented it overnight, so that there was no chance he would have to repeat a single dish.

Nate's head started to spin. He and Jonah wanted Wells to eat in the dining room, of course, to experience the new five-course menu del dia. That way, Jonah was in control of the menu. But what if Wells sat in the front again? They couldn't come up with a completely new set of pintxos and raciones every single night. Jonah decided to look at the itemized check from the first visit, which was tacked up on a bulletin board in, the basement office, to see what Wells and his friends had ordered. At least he could make sure that the server passed new pintxos first.

That night Nate dreamed that Wells came in and he seated Wells at table forty, the best table in the dining room, the one at the back of the room, alongside the glass doors. That was the dream: Wells came in, and Nate seated him. Clearly, table forty was going to be it, if they got their chance.

Jonah and Nate called a managers' meeting and issued a mandate that hearkened back to Luke's service mantra: For the next six weeks, starting today, they were to treat every one at every table as a potential critic, in case the cryptic enthusiasm of the two *Times* writers was a coded message. Jonah would make sure that servers got to taste everything during the day, not a few of the dishes in a hurry at lineup, so that they could better answer any questions. He and Nate intended to consider all the beverage pairings and make substitutions when it seemed right—though right, given their heated debate on whether cider worked with the huevos rotos, might prove to be a bit elusive. As an experiment, they would put two different bottles of cider on a table with the instruction, "Drink as much as you want," Nate said, and then they'd see if the sweeter or the funkier cider prevailed. At that point they could argue some more, since no one was about to let customers dictate what got poured the next time Wells came in.

In the meantime, they debated where to put the critic, since a dream about table forty didn't quite qualify as a strategy. They had no idea how many people would be in his party, or whether he would reserve for the back dining room or visit the front a second time, so they considered every variable. Table six, the two-top right in front of the service station, was the nicest front-room table, but whoever ate there could hear too much of what the servers might have to say about the customers—which would mean that Wells would hear too much about how they intended to care for him. The front tables by the windows were nice, but it could get crowded and noisy. Table forty in the dining room really was the best, but it was a four-top. What if he came in with only one other person? They couldn't seat him at a table for four, because it would look like special treatment, or maybe they could, if the rest of the room was full. They reconsidered the two tables by the front windows, but no, only the one on the south side of the restaurant. Under no circumstances was he to be seated on the north side, which was too close to the bar.

Nate got to work a little early on September 17 and announced, out of nowhere: If there's a dining-room reservation tonight it's Pete Wells. Nate had been checking the list for days—there weren't many dining-room reservations—and had already announced, more than once, "If it's Pete Wells it's this one," based on nothing more than hunches, or names that caught his eye, or a combination of those two things and an early booking. Everyone took him seriously, even though his pronouncement was little more than congealed nerves, because that was the newly announced policy, to treat every guest like a critic.

Wells walked in the door at six forty-five, alone, told the host he had a reservation for four people at seven o'clock, and went up to the bar. Stew was busy with other customers, so Nate, who had been near the door and saw Wells get out of a cab, handed the critic a menu, walked behind the bar, and pretended to be busy at the computer until Stew came over to input an order.

"Pete Wells is right over there," muttered Nate.

Without a word, Stew turned to wait on the critic as though he weren't the most important guest imaginable. Nate, who at that moment idolized his bartender, tried for an air of capable nonchalance as he walked back to the pass to give Jonah a fast heads-up.

"Well," said Jonah, who'd been reviewing their accounting on his laptop, which was what he did when the restaurant wasn't busy. "I guess I'll go to work."

He had fifteen minutes to prepare before the rest of Wells's party arrived at seven, and a few minutes more while they sat down and thought about whether to try the beverage pairings. The menu was the menu, no latitude there, but the execution, for this table on this night, was all Jonah.

The three men who were joining Wells arrived at seven, and as they walked past the kitchen on the way to the dining room Jonah recognized Ed Levine, founder of the website Seriouseats.com, whose son had played youth basketball with Jonah—and who was part of a table for five on the following night. The challenge increased exponentially: Jonah had to cook the best meal of his life, and when he was done he had to revamp the menu del dia to avoid any duplication for the ballplayer's dad, who undoubtedly would report back to Wells on his meal.

First out, the pintxos, which on any other night would barely have caught Jonah's eye: the gilda, which they always served; some charred Padrón peppers; garlic shrimp on toothpicks.

The egg course was a bit showier. A fried egg white sat under corn and tomatoes cooked with chunks of homemade, pimentón-cured bacon. A raw yolk perched on top of that. When the diner poked the yolk with a fork, it ran down into the warm corn and tomatoes and thickened the oil the vegetables had been cooked in, creating a sauce.

The fish course was skate served with turnips in a sauce of pureed turnip greens and fennel, a little flourish that made the point about Jonah's low-waste philosophy. He saw no sense in discarding the turnip tops if he could turn them into something delicious.

The meat course was Jonah's homemade chistorra sausage, this version made with lamb instead of the traditional pork or beef, flavored with garlic and pimentón and served with a slow-cooked bean stew.

For dessert, a goat-cheese cheesecake, a dense little puck topped with candied almonds and served with a nectarine sauce.

At each step, Jonah, Nate, Jenni, and the dining-room captain and servers huddled over the plate like surgeons and operating-room nurses considering the specifics of a patient's anatomy, Jonah bent almost double as he arranged even the smallest element on the plate. There was no time for discussion, and no one was about to contradict Jonah as he adjusted a sprig or a bean or wiped the already-clean rim of a plate, but hovering seemed the supportive thing to do.

As the egg course headed to the back, one of the servers reached over to nudge the corners of Nate's pursed mouth at least up to even, if not into a smile. "The boys are nervous," was the subterranean chatter, as staffers reassured them about how great the food looked and how happy the table seemed. Caleb, one of two servers attending to Wells, measured the collective angst of the knot of people at the pass and reassured them.

"This isn't my first rodeo with him," said Caleb, who had served Wells at an Italian restaurant on the Upper East Side. Wells never reviewed the place, for whatever reason, but Caleb saw no need to share that part of the story with his coworkers.

Faced with the need to appear very calm, staffers siphoned their nerves into their cell phones and texted friends to say that Pete Wells was back. Those friends tended to be in the business, given the no-weekends off, late-night schedule of most restaurant people—who else socialized at two a.m. on a weeknight?—which was why the front room suddenly got very crowded. Animated customers ate and drank and craned their necks toward the dining room, even as they tried very hard to look as though they weren't. Several restaurants operated without their general manager or bartender or sommelier that night, because they had no idea what Pete Wells looked like and intended to sit at their tables until they got a glimpse. They told the Huertas staffers that they were there to support the gang and fill the place up, and then they admitted their ulterior motive.

It was all peripheral noise. The only talk that mattered was what the host overheard as Wells and his friends headed out the door: Empellón Cocina served what they called a cheeseburger taco, he said. It was right next door. Was anybody game?

With that, the men headed next door for more food, leaving Jonah and Nate to read several courses' worth of empty plates as though they were tea leaves. It could be a very good sign, an indication that the group had liked every single thing they were served. Or it could mean that the portions were too small. The cheeseburger taco could be nothing more than curiosity mixed with convenience, or it could mean that Wells was still hungry—but not interested in more food from Huertas.

There was no way to tell and no time to dwell on it, because Jonah and Nate had to figure out a new menu and get the food orders in by eleven. Wells might as well be eating at Huertas two nights in a row, even though he wasn't, because of his friend, who was.

They slid into an empty booth to discuss their options, with no idea of what was available.

Jonah considered putting chistorra sausage in the egg course, but Nate vetoed that. Wells had tried the chistorra. It was too similar.

Nate suggested fish for a main course, maybe throw in a shared tortilla with pan tomate and serve chistorra migas without an egg. Jonah didn't think that was good enough, so Nate backtracked: What were the best dishes Jonah had done so far?

For a moment Jonah thought about inventing a new dish, but this was hardly the right time for an experiment. They agreed: Diners loved Jonah's duck, and the scallop crudo had gotten raves. One customer had said it was the best crudo ever, so it went on the list along with duck served with turnip and fennel migas.

Jonah had a goat's milk cheese from northwest Spain, the Leonora, which he could turn into a pintxo on top of bread. Nate gave him a thin smile.

"You're going to put cheese on toast," he said, imagining how that would sound in a text from Wells's friend, no matter how good the cheese turned out to be. They agreed on a smoked trout pintxo instead.

For dessert, the Spanish version of an affogato. Nobody else in town had that almond ice cream.

They agreed to add a shared tortilla to the list, placed the necessary orders, and headed home, confident that they'd come up with a great last-minute menu—the only items that would show up twice were the gildas and the complimentary plate of chocolate and almonds at the very end. But on his bike ride home Nate had another idea, so he pulled over to send Jonah a final text. They should stick with the egg dish Wells and his group had just eaten, the one with corn and tomatoes. That way they could make what seemed like a spontaneous offer when they saw their returning guest, as though they hadn't known in advance that he would show up. They'd make an order of huevos rotos for him, while everyone else at his table got the egg dish that was on the menu, which sent the right message: "'We can do something on the fly for you because you were just here,'" was the way Nate saw it. "It's incredibly hospitable. It's the Danny Meyer ethos: We want to cook for you."

11

ANXIETY

Olivia, who had been a host at Huertas for a week, was making calls to confirm reservations for the last Friday in September. About halfway through the list, she got to a table of two.

A man picked up the phone.

"I'm confirming Friday at seven for two," she said.

He asked her to remind him of the name the reservation was under.

Bianco, she said.

He mentioned that his dining companion had a shellfish allergy, and Olivia reassured him that the chef would create an alternate dish for the scallop course.

Olivia might be new, but she had quickly become as alert for possible clues as everyone else. Had Mr. Bianco asked what name the reservation was under because she had interrupted him in the middle of something important—or because for a moment he'd forgotten which fake name he used when he booked the table?

As soon as she hung up she looked at the e-mail address he provided when he made the reservation, a weird and seemingly random assortment of letters. Huertas's reservation software allowed her to search contact information to see if a customer had been there before. She stared at the screen. Mr. Bianco had in fact been there before. He was the party of four in the dining room, seven days earlier. He was Pete Wells, and he had just confirmed that he would be back tomorrow. And she, with her brand-new review antenna, had picked up on it from a moment's hesitation on his part, just long enough for her to wonder, Doesn't this guy know his own name?

She ran back to the kitchen to tell Jonah and Nate.

That night Jonah and Nate sat down again to plan Wells's next—and almost surely final—meal. Everyone said he showed up a maximum of three times, and even though the first time had been a fluke, this had to be it. Jonah strove for the right balance, down to the smallest detail: The smoked octopus pintxo was a hit, but he'd recently served it balanced on a tiny spoon, which might scream "look at me" and might be more self-conscious than he wanted it to be. He'd perch it on a chip with aioli instead. Still great, but not so precious.

Ideas tumbled out as he imagined the meal, each choice narrowing the options for the course that followed it. He'd revamp a classic Basque stew of tuna, peppers, tomatoes, and onions; make it lighter; substitute scallops; and turn the rest into a jammy sauce. Migas with a slow-poached egg, charred broccoli, and anchovies. Duck, but a different preparation than the one he'd served to Ed Levine. This time he'd do duck with turnips, carrots, and a carrot and duck jus.

But it wasn't a Spanish preparation, and he didn't want to get too far offtrack. "Maybe turnips are a talking point," he said, as much to himself as to Nate. "Maybe like grelos, a Basque green, usually served with smoked pork, so that's like turnips with duck. We'll make that point." He resolved to tutor the servers before service, so that they could explain the connection.

He didn't have a dessert, but one would come to him.

The only logistical issue was the octopus. If Wells started at the bar as he had on his first visit, he might order something, and it might be the charred octopus and potatoes that was always on the front-room menu, which would require two last-minute adjustments. First, Jonah would have to substitute a different pintxo on the menu del dia, to avoid serving him octopus a second time. Second, and probably more important, he had to figure out how to step over to the wood-burning oven, in full view of his most important customer, to prepare his single order of charred octopus. That was not a good move; Wells could reasonably wonder if the dish would be different, possibly not as good, when made by the cook who normally worked the wood oven. If Wells went to the bar and ordered octopus, Jonah would have to find an excuse to hang out at the oven after he made that single order, to look as though he often spent time there, and nothing unusual was going on.

He and Nate tried to imagine every conceivable aspect of the meal, despite the late hour and the fact that Jonah had to be up early to do a cooking segment on the *Today* show, which until the Wells confirmation had been the biggest media event on the horizon. Now the proportions of the day had changed. After a little bit of sleep he'd make an egg dish on TV, hit the farmers market on his way to Huertas, and hope to find a dessert idea somewhere along the way.

Before Jonah and Nate closed up, they allowed themselves to address a question they would share only with each other: Did a second visit to the dining room mean they were in the running for three stars? It was too much to hope for, for a casual place like Huertas, but they allowed themselves to fantasize, just for a moment. One star would be a disappointment, although they would never say that to the staff, and no stars would be a disaster, but Wells wouldn't be coming back if his experience so far had been that bad. They tried to convince themselves that they were in very good shape for two, and hoped they wouldn't be punished for the fleeting hubris that led them the consider the possibility of three.

Two stars would make a big difference. Jonah had seen it at Maialino. "There's a moment in the meal when the guest realizes, these are professionals, all the little things are being taken care of. That's the moment when they let their guard down, relax, and have a good time." Two stars from the *Times* would convey that more clearly than all the coverage they'd had so far.

Whatever they got, it would be nice simply to have the process end. The restaurant vibrated with nerves these days, hours after everyone else had gone home.

Jonah had a childhood memory of walking with his dad up the long block from the grocery store to his family's apartment, laden with bags, and it came back to him as he walked along the western leg of the Union Square farmers market on the morning of Wells's visit. He usually shopped at a smaller market a couple of blocks from Huertas rather than drag a lot of bags three times as far or have to spring for a cab, but he wanted plenty of options, because he was shopping for inspiration. He liked to stroll the length of the market before he made a purchase—particularly today. He was still shy a dessert, beyond a simple flan, and the pressure to come up with the right one didn't make being creative any easier.

The weeks between summer and fall were full of jewel-toned fruits, as bright peaches and nectarines yielded to more somber Italian prune plums and Concord grapes, and the scent of the grapes wafted through the market. Jonah walked past one stall, then another, looking for a way to make the flan more exciting, wondering what he could do to make a grape memorable.

Then it came to him. Grapes were small and round and had thin skins. Cherry tomatoes were small and round and had thin skins. At Maialino, they put Sungold cherry tomatoes into the deep fryer just until their skins burst, and Jonah had always thought that the same technique might work with grapes. The skins would crisp up and slip right off; they'd be a little bitter, and crunchy, which meant that he could use them instead of pine nuts, a more traditional Spanish presentation.

He bought grapes, hustled back to Huertas, and spent a half hour frying sample batches until he got it right: A thirty-second dip in the fryer and the skin gave way with a gentle squeeze, leaving the inside of the grape intact.

Jonah had his menu. A friend at a bigger restaurant called to see if he should dispatch people to make Huertas look busier, and Jonah turned him down. The dining room wouldn't be busy when Wells arrived at six forty-five, but by the time he left it would be pretty full, which was preferable to an onslaught.

Tonight might almost be fun. Wells could have bailed after the first or second visit, but he hadn't, so Jonah had one more opportunity to stick to what had worked so far, to cook for himself, to offer Wells a meal that Jonah loved. Holding to that standard made all the rest tolerable. If Jonah was happy with a dish, if he was proud of it, he could withstand the occasional request for sauce on the side, a less runny egg, the deletion of what seemed to him an essential ingredient, lamb sent back to be cooked for too long; possibly even bureaucrats and licensing delays and staff betrayals.

By the time the restaurant opened that night, the staff was reduced to magical thinking and superstition.

The dining-room captain and one of the servers wished that there were a way to time-travel to midnight to know that they'd survived.

Olivia tried not to have second thoughts. "God, I hope I'm right," she said. "I'll feel so guilty if I put everyone through this for nothing."

Jonah cut the citrus wedges for the bar himself rather than have one of the bartenders do it, as though uniform segments were the ticket to success.

And Nate smiled when Wells walked in the door holding a bicycle helmet, grateful for good karma wherever he found it.

Jonah monitored every plate that went to Wells's table—table forty, even though it was a party of two—and every plate that came back. He was happy that Wells ordered the cheese course, which might mean that he wanted to experience the full menu. He saw it as a good sign that Wells and his guest lingered even after he paid the bill—they must have been there for almost three hours—which they wouldn't have done if Wells was disappointed.

He distracted himself by wondering about the timeline. If September 26 was the final visit, would someone call about taking photos the week of the twenty-ninth? If they took photos the week of the twenty-ninth, would it run in time to help with the holidays?

He got his answer quickly—the *Times* dispatched a photographer and informed Jonah that the review was scheduled for October 7; he should expect a call to fact-check the details. There was nothing left to do but wait until the afternoon of October 6, since reviews went up online the day before they appeared in the paper.

And then Ryan Sutton, the lead critic at Eater, showed up twice in a matter of days for the menu del dia, first on a late-night visit by himself, identified by another diner who recognized him and quickly sent a heads-up text to Nate, "Just FYI, Ryan Sutton at bar," and again in a party of three. His colleague, Robert Sietsema, had already reviewed Huertas, so no one had bothered to research his appearance—but here he was, acting as though he was going to write something. There was no time for hard-earned relief at having finished up with the *Times* critic: It seemed likely that Huertas was going to have its fate sealed, one way or another, twice in one week.

Alyssa had started to get overdraft notices back in August, which had to be a mistake. It wasn't as though she had suddenly started spending money on clothes or home decor. Her life was circumscribed by work: She took the subway in from Astoria, cooked, took the subway back, slept, did laundry, and paid the same monthly bills she always paid. And yet she seemed to have less money than she thought she should, through August and into September.

When she finally had a chance to look at her account, she saw the problem immediately: Her loan repayments for four years at CIA's main campus, in Hyde Park, New York, had increased automatically when a temporary reduction expired, and she'd forgotten that it was going to happen. Alyssa owed close to $80,000, as she'd paid for all of her CIA bachelor's degree with student loans. At the time, she thought that the degree was essential because she hadn't gone to college, so she powered through the program in three years, no summers off, even as she worked at a nearby restaurant. If she'd come to regret that decision, to think she could have gotten where she was on experience alone, she could hardly ask to have the loans forgiven on the basis of her bad judgment.

Alyssa had spent her externship at Gramercy Tavern, graduated in December 2010, and went back to Southern California to spend the holidays with her family. She started on the line at Maialino the following

March, followed by a stint as a private chef—only to get to here, worse than broke. Paying off her loans was like having three rents, she thought, on a paycheck that barely covered the first one.

"Forget keeping my head above water," she said. "I'd just hoped for my nose."

She was well-paid for a line cook, at $13 an hour—most New York City line cooks earned an hourly rate of between $8 and $12—but Los Angeles restaurants tended to pay more, so she decided to go home. The math was inescapable: Alyssa couldn't afford to work as a line cook in New York City and pay off a four-year culinary education. Jonah had said that he might still promote her to sous, even though lunch service was on hold for now, a casualty of a slow September and the new menu— but he hadn't brought it up recently, and she didn't see how he could give her a raise when things were so slow and there were no added shifts for her to supervise. In truth, she wasn't sure it would make enough of a difference.

Alyssa had been cooking professionally since she was seventeen, nine years of working the line for too little money, even while she was at school. She'd been cooking for a paycheck longer than Jonah or Jenni had, and all she had to show for it, she felt, was a mountain of debt and not enough of a prospect, here, to make staying a rational choice.

She didn't have the kind of food dream that propelled Jonah and Nate. Alyssa's idea of success was closer to the ground: She wanted to open what she called a "threefold" business with her brother, who didn't want to spend his life helping their mother with her tax prep and immigration business—a sandwich shop; an adjacent store that sold the breads they used in the shop as well as meats, cheeses, and pastas; and a small restaurant with a bar. "A delicious bar room," was how she described it, "with a dining room that chefs could rent for pop-ups or I could use as I please. Maybe a tasting menu this Saturday? Get out the word: 'Chef's trying something new.'"

First she had to retire the debt, though, and the only way to do that was to cut her limited expenses ever further. She would go back to Southern California, move back with her mom in the house where she grew up, and find a job so that she could start to dig herself out.

Alyssa made up her mind in September but didn't tell Jonah because she didn't want to undercut morale with the *Times* review at stake. When she did quit, after the review came out, she would reassure him that this wasn't the standard two weeks' notice. She wanted service to be steady. She'd stick around until mid-January.

It was the right thing to do, she knew it, and yet it was hard to see past the debt, hard to stay positive about having a little place of her own.

"I'm not even sure I'll continue cooking," she said, the exhaustion talking. "But then, I don't know anything else."

12

THE VERDICT

Huertas Gets Tapas Right and Set Menus Wrong."
Eater's two-star review went up at twelve thirty on Tuesday afternoon—or rather, the headline went up, linked initially, incorrectly, to the earlier review by Robert Sietsema that had enabled Jonah to put the word "superb" up on the Huertas website. The word "Wrong" in the headline implied that Ryan Sutton had found fault with something, but probably nothing of consequence, not with two stars attached. They were halfway to Nate's stated goal for the day, two stars from Eater and two from the *Times*. While they waited for the right review to appear, and wondered what cranky comments Ryan Sutton might make about the back-room menu, Nate focused on the stars and walked over to shake Jonah's hand. Stars lasted, while details faded away.

"Great job," he said.

Then the new review appeared.

"My companion sighed when I announced we were ordering the five-course menu at Huertas, an ambitious young Basque spot in Manhattan's East Village. 'You mean we all have to get the same thing?' Indeed, the same thing. There are no real choices, not in the back room of this pintxos bar. And therein lies the problem." Sutton mentioned in passing the "stunning array of affordable hors d'oeuvres and preserved fish" in the front room before returning to his central complaint, "an expensive incongruity" of lamb sausage with lamb leg on the fixed menu.

"Sometimes, lack of choice ends up working against the consumer," Sutton wrote. "This is one of those times."

The upshot, for Eater readers: Visit the front room, a "smoky, sexy wood-fired affair," and avoid the dining room.

Anger was pointless, even though it was Jonah's instinctive response, heartily seconded by Nate. Why review the menu del dia if you reject the concept? What's the point of complaining about the framework when you should be talking about the food? Readers didn't care if the people who accompanied Sutton chafed at the menu format. He should have spent more time on the food and less on the template, and let readers decide for themselves if they wanted to give it a try. The review surely would have been more positive if he had.

The staff went through the motions of afternoon prep like zombies, slowly, because they all had their cell phones out and had to stop every two minutes to hit "refresh," which made it difficult to walk quickly, carry anything, or work near flames. No one knew exactly when the *Times* review would post. In the meantime, they worked hard to construct a comforting rationale that would enable them to dismiss the Eater review as an aberration. The *Times* was going to be the definitive judgment. It had history, decades of being the make-or-break opinion, and it had a week's run. Eater coverage would be obliterated by new coverage before the weekend. The *Times* review was the product of three visits over a month's time, not thrown together in a week.

Having been spurned by Eater, the Huertas staff had no choice but to find fault with it—either that or consider the grim possibility that Sutton's was the first vote in a unanimous day.

People at the *Times* already knew the verdict—random copy editors, fact-checkers, digital staff, none of them with any vested interest in the outcome, while at Huertas, the clock seemed to be slogging through mud.

The cooks cut vegetables in a syncopated rhythm interrupted by phone checks, assembled their mise en place, pretended to care about family meal, and didn't talk much. The front-of-house staff readied the tables and checked the glassware and flatware for spots, and refreshed, and waited, and refreshed again. Jonah and Nate repeated their public position, glad that they'd kept their stated expectations lower than their private hopes: No stars was almost surely not a possibility. They'd be proud of one star, or at least they said so, and thrilled by two. Jonah reminded himself of what Danny Meyer had told the Maialino staff when that restaurant got two stars: A casual place ought to be thrilled with two. Three was often a curse, because people regarded three-star restaurants as having somehow fallen short of four.

Jonah had another set of numbers in his head, which he tried to ignore: forty covers in the dining room a week earlier, but only six on Tuesday and ten on Saturday. They were nowhere near stable. Whatever number of stars they got, it needed to be enough to make a difference.

Nate figured that he must have refreshed his phone three hundred times, and by late afternoon he found it hard to cope. He went outside to call his younger brother and confessed that he was so nervous he was having trouble breathing—as people inside suddenly started to shriek. He refreshed his phone again.

Two stars. A *Times* Critic's Pick. "A Serendipitous Trip to Spain." He darted inside.

It was not a solid two-star but a great two-star. People blurted out phrases as they got to them, too excited to calm down and read the review start to finish, as though no one else had a phone or knew how to read. The narrative, which started with Wells's frustration at the long wait at his intended destination, built in a crescendo of happiness:

"This kitchen knows where to get the good stuff," he declared, after a serving of Iberico ham.

"From the front door to the table, our service had been proactively friendly and enthusiastic," this, after Nate had warned the front-of-house staff that Wells rarely singled out service.

He ordered huevos rotos. "It was gone in 30 seconds."

And, "The way this night went was that by the time the other restaurant called, we didn't want to leave."

He was kindly disposed by the time he tried the tasting menu, so much so that he cut Jonah some slack for the garlic shrimp, not as sweet or firm as they should be, but, he was sure, "an anomaly; in general, the cooking at Huertas stands out for its pure, fresh flavors."

He pronounced dessert "a dream, a round and closely packed little goat-cheese cheesecake with a topping of candied almonds instead of a bottom crust. More tangy than sugary, the cake took beautifully to a sauce made from ripe nectarines." If he didn't get around to Jonah's crispy Concord grapes, it hardly mattered. Nothing mattered except the pendulum swing from a cranky Eater review to what felt like a rave from the *Times*.

The summary toward the end of the article made everyone dizzy with joy: "This night and a later one made it clear that dinner in Huertas's back room ranks among the best deals in town, up there with the how-do-they-do-it bargains at Contra and Delaware & Hudson. Mr. Miller shapes his menus so skillfully that it's hard to imagine wanting more."

It could not have been any better; that was the quick consensus as the phones began to ring and people shouted out more lines from the review and texted it to everyone they knew. They scoffed at the Eater review, buried now under an avalanche of intelligent praise, as they repeated "among the best deals in town" and "it's hard to imagine wanting more."

Jonah clung to the routine of getting ready for service as though it were an anchor, as one by one people came over to congratulate him, clap him on the back, try for an awkward hug. He'd been holding it together for weeks, for months, and he had to measure out his relief carefully so that it didn't swamp him. Happiness seeped in, in increments. His mouth relaxed into an almost goofy smile, and his shoulders no longer sat quite so tight, as though protecting him from the possibility of bad news. His usual slump was powered now by delight. He could relax, a little bit.

Nate was less moderate about celebrating. He put Queen's "We Are the Champions" on the sound system and cranked the volume way up, as everyone reeled around the room like pinballs, bouncing from one squealing embrace to the next, unable to hold still. They sat down, they stood up, they checked their phones for more congratulations, and then they read the review over again. It was impossible to read it too often.

Jonah and Nate agreed: It would have been a three-star review if they had linen tablecloths and a slightly more polished air, which made it the best possible review. It read better than any two-star they could recall, and it avoided the raised expectations, and almost certain letdown, of a three-star.

And then it was almost five thirty. They had to peel themselves off the ceiling and get to work.

Nate grabbed the short wine tumblers and poured an inch of cava, a sparkling Spanish wine, for everyone at the lineup meeting—which today included not only the front-of-house staff but the cooks and the prep cook and Juan, who rarely got to leave the basement prep kitchen these days, between butchering and prep and maintenance work. It was Jenni's day off, but Alyssa called and put her on speaker so that she could share in the good news.

By now Wells had tweeted the review to his seventy-four thousand followers, and Nate gleefully recited the message: "How I fell into @huertasnyc and why I didn't want to leave," with a link to the story.

"I couldn't be happier with you guys right now," said Jonah. "It's a victory for everyone. He didn't just love the food but the experience. And special thanks to Jenni and Nate."

Alyssa held her cell phone up.

"She can hear you," she said.

"Hi, Chef," Jenni yelled, ignoring his rule about calling him Jonah.

"Now I'm self-conscious," he said. He raised his glass. "I'm sure this will taste better with two stars."

With that, everyone went back to work.

One of the hosts consulted the reservation list and smiled.

"The two parties that canceled tonight are going to regret it," she said.

The party started before the party started. Nat, the long-ago bar mitzvah boy who had taken Jonah to Chanterelle and worked alongside him there and at Gramercy Tavern, showed up early with a friend who was a wine purveyor. Jonah's parents arrived—and because it was a quiet Tuesday in the dining room, Jonah and his dad had time to stand at the pass and pick apart the San Francisco Giants baseball game. Nate circulated with an empty wine bottle, had every staffer sign the label, and wrote the date and drew two stars on it as well. The publicist came by with an instant revisionist analysis, all the better for making sense: She was glad the Sutton review had run today, because the *Times* had over-shadowed it.

"Three weeks from now it would have been of concern," she said. "Today it evaporates."

Stew dismissed the review altogether because Sutton had referred to an almond cake, when in fact it was an apple cake.

"Sloppy," he said.

There were already five cases of beer downstairs, stocked in advance in optimistic anticipation of a celebration party that would begin as soon as they could close up the kitchen, and a growing number of champagne bottles from friends. For once, they wished for an early, sparse crowd in the dining room so that they could get around to having a good time, fast. They had that luxury, now that they knew the slow times were about to end.

Nate surveyed the busy bar, which was always good on Tuesdays because of the $1 pintxos. Life, he figured, was about to be better than this all the time.

"I am ready for the burn every single day," he said. "Enough of this boredom." He glanced at Jonah, who was concentrating on the plates in front of him, and leaned over the pass.

"I'm waiting for you to smile, man—jump over the pass," said Nate, bouncing up and down on his toes. Jonah kept plating the five dishes in front of him. The review was a thrill, but he had his eye on the opportunity it presented, which was to convince a raft of new diners to put Huertas on their short list. Pete Wells had done what he and Nate could not, though not for want of trying: He'd filled up the back room, at least for the foreseeable future: They started the day with only eight reservations for Wednesday night, but by the time they finished with Tuesday's dinner service they were up to twenty-seven.

Jenni blew in just before nine thirty, happy to sacrifice her night off for a party, carrying a rectangular two-layer Duncan Hines chocolate cake with Duncan Hines chocolate frosting and crumbled Oreos between the layers and homemade cream cheese frosting on the outside. She threw an apron on over her dress, filled a large pastry bag with more chocolate frosting, and made space for herself at the pass, opposite Jonah.

She held the bag poised over the cake.

"I'm going to write 'Thank You to the Staff,'" she told him. "Anything else?"

He smiled. "'Four stars in one day?'"

Jenni piped a star and realized that it was too big to fit four in a row, so she grabbed a spatula to lift it off just as a server bumped into her, damaging the top of the cake. She slathered on more frosting to cover the mess and started over.

"It has to be perfect," she said.

She tried again and got closer, but the final star slid over the edge of the cake like a Dalí clock, so she swiped all of them off again and refrosted the top. On the third try she got it: four stars in a row with "#AllDay" under them.

Luke arrived carrying a bottle of champagne and wearing a suit, his new uniform as an assistant general manager at Quality Meats, a midtown steakhouse owned by the restaurateur who had created the original TGI Fridays and his son—just as Jonah and Nate decided that nine forty-five was late enough to stay open and closed the front door. Jonah walked up to the bar to pour himself a glass of vermút while everyone else broke down the kitchen in triple time. He looked at his cell phone for the first time in three hours. Twenty-five e-mails and four text messages; not that many, he thought, but then, everyone he cared about was at Huertas.

The servers set up the dining room for drink service, as Jonah dispatched his final responsibility of the evening, the only unpleasant consequence of the *Times* review, given his feelings about public speaking. He stood on a chair in the front room as everyone clapped and yelled, and announced, "I'm going to regurgitate my speech from opening night," which he did. He had wondered who would be there when he opened. He had allowed himself to wonder, too, who would be there when he got this first great review.

"I'm so glad it's you," he said, in a hurry to get down from the chair.

The cases of beer went, the champagne went, and the party moved next door to Empellón Cocina. Serious drinking—what one server referred to as "frat party drinking"—was one aspect of the previous generation's kitchen culture that had endured, in great part because bars were the only places that were still open after a long dinner shift. It was difficult to go straight home and to sleep after all those hours of split-second effort, and yet it was important to go to sleep fairly soon because morning was going to arrive too quickly. A drink with other staffers was an efficient way to downshift, even if it got harder to remember to leave after every subsequent drink, and restaurants often adopted a nearby bar as their after-work hangout.

On a night like this, it could easily get out of hand. There was so much pent-up energy, almost six months of it, enough to blur the usual indicators that it might be time to stop, or at least to slow down.

Empellón kicked the Huertas crowd out just after one, and they stood on the sidewalk, some of them already well past reason in terms of alcohol consumption, and debated whether to look for a late-night bar where they could continue the festivities. The consensus was that it was time to go home, because they had to be back at work in the morning and had no idea what kind of mob scene they might face. They drifted toward the subway or split a cab, hoping for a couple of hours' sleep before they faced twenty-seven dinner reservations and who knew how many *Times*-reading walk-ins.

Jonah might have lingered. There would be other restaurants and other reviews, but never again a great first review in the *Times*. Several of his friends from Maialino and its three-week-old sister restaurant, Marta, had shown up to help him celebrate, and the consensus was that the best way to acknowledge a *Times* review of this caliber was to continue the party. They were right, on some level, and he hesitated, but common sense prevailed, and he and Marina headed home. He had managed only recently to scale his schedule back by two hours, coming in at ten thirty instead of nine thirty and leaving closer to eleven, sometimes even ten thirty, than midnight. That was over, starting today. He was back to nine thirty to midnight five days a week, maybe six, until he saw what the crowds were like.

Jenni was a little apprehensive when she saw the reservation list for Wednesday, the night after the review posted online, the day it appeared in the paper itself. They'd survived sixteen-hour shifts back when Huertas opened, but they were out of practice after a slow summer, and that first run had been a sprint. The coming onslaught was supposed to last, supposed to be normal from here on out. "The prospect of those days again, without stopping, there's a little fear. But we'll be fine," she said, as much to convince herself as anything else. "We're putting out a lot of food."

No one was prepared for how much food, or how fast. The kitchen usually marked time by the appearance of Antonio, the late-night dishwasher, who arrived at nine thirty, a couple of hours after the front room started to fill up. When he didn't show up on time on Wednesday night, Jenni's anxiety spiked. It was nine thirty, the back room was packed, and the front room was a zoo. Why wasn't he there yet?

Because it was only seven thirty, she realized; it only felt later. Jenni had already put up so much food that she'd assumed she'd been at it for hours longer than she had. The kitchen had to duplicate the madness of the last two hours for two more hours before Antonio showed up, and then for another two hours of service after that.

Jonah tried to keep track of the parade of people to the dining room, to see if he could distinguish between the potential keepers and the people who ran from review to review. The first rush was older than he'd anticipated, "and not sort of old, but really old. Eighties. Canes." Later on the crowd got a little younger, if still older than the people in the bar—but the point was, they kept coming. Every table in the back was full for four hours straight, until he left Jenni in charge of closing up the kitchen at ten thirty. People who made reservations for two showed up with three; parties of four became parties of six, and couldn't Huertas squeeze them in? The path out the front door narrowed, as clots of people lined the bar and the standing counter across from it, and anyone hoping to get in or out had to angle their shoulders to pass.

Before the review, he'd had Juan prepare 75 gildas for dinner service. Today he had asked for 110 or 115—and as he surveyed the scene, he realized that he would probably need more than that on the weekend.

"My biggest priority," he said, with an enormous grin, finally, now that he saw the crowds, "which I haven't even done, is to put out an ad for a cook."

Huertas had fifty reservations for its first Saturday brunch after the review, but that was only part of the new order. Jonah received his first unsolicited résumés, which with luck would make his search for another line cook easier. And the purveyors regarded him with a new respect: One of his standard orders arrived on Friday accompanied by free product samples—cornmeal and spices—and a seafood information sheet, in case Jonah wanted to spend more of the money he surely was about to make.

Wells's tweet had spawned a set of tweets and retweets, including one from Serious Eats's Ed Levine. "Pete Wells is right: Huertas is a terrific restaurant. The $55 prix fixe menu is a worthy successor to the original Torrisi concept. Go now," he tweeted to his 134,000 followers, invoking the name of Major Food Group's hole-in-the-wall first restaurant, Torrisi Italian Specialties. It was a magical association. MFG's two chef partners, Rich Torrisi and Mario Carbone, had been teen cooks like Jonah, but they attended CIA and landed at a run of famous kitchens owned by role models who included Marcus Samuelsson, Mario Batali, Daniel Boulud, and Wiley Dufresne. They opened Torrisi in 2009 and a year later joined Jeff Zalaznick—whose background was in investment banking and food website development—to launch Major Food Group. Its expansion model was based, it seemed, on equal parts skill, fearlessness, and speed—they now had four restaurants and profitable offshoots that included a bar and Yankee Stadium outpost—and not a small amount of audacity, including the decision to close Torrisi after five years and replace it with a new concept.

The company website referred to MFG as "a new breed of restaurant group with the aim to conceptualize and operate restaurants that are respectful of the past, exciting for the present, and sustainable for the future; restaurants that uphold the highest level of food quality and fine dining service in a fun and inviting atmosphere for the guest." All that Jonah and Nate knew was that they seemed to do everything faster and better than anyone else—that they had, at least for now, laid claim to high-energy fun. To be mentioned in the same breath with them was a compliment and a challenge, because MFG's restaurants had managed to become that most elusive, enviable, and profitable thing—they were irresistible. Nate marveled at the fact that even the partners' last names sounded cool.

The *Times* review seemed to blanket the known universe with goodwill. Peter Hoffman stopped by to congratulate Jonah. David Waltuck called with congratulations as well, and to let Jonah know that the *Times* review of Élan would run the following week. He only hoped, he said, that his review was as positive as the one Jonah had received.

Jonah was touched by the call. Waltuck had been more than generous to a couple of kids, a great teacher and mentor. The business about the pending review was sobering, though. For everything Waltuck had accomplished, he was waiting, just as Jonah had. His remarkable past would have no influence on whatever was coming.

Alyssa was on her third coffee before Saturday dinner service even began, with a Gatorade chaser after the second one to make sure she stayed hydrated. To help her get through the night, she had set aside a second Gatorade, some Starburst candies, and leftover family meal cookies from Blue Smoke, the USHG barbecue place whose new chef had worked alongside Jonah at Maialino and had brought over food to congratulate the Huertas staff on the review. She raised her arms heavenward, part stretch, part supplication—she hoped she had stashed away enough caffeine and sugar to keep her going—as Jonah called out the first order of the night.

An hour later she was red-faced and sweating. Jenni was sweating. Jonah had rolled his pants up to his calves in a failed attempt to cool off, exposing a pair of dark, striped, rumpled socks that lacked the resilience to do anything but puddle at his ankles. The stack of completed order tickets ran halfway up the spindle where Jonah speared them and it wasn't eight o'clock yet; as they piled up, conversation evaporated into a call-and-response, Jonah chanting nonstop, "Fire six skate, two menu, two menu, four menu, two menu," and getting confirmation from his harried cooks. Jenni had started the evening using two spoons to make whipped cream quenelles to accompany the apple cake dessert, perfect little footballs of cream that she placed just so. By eight she had abandoned perfection for speed: She turned a single spoon against the side of the plastic container of whipped cream. It wasn't quite as elegant, but it was pretty enough, and faster.

Jonah kept an eye on Alyssa, not that he was worried about her but because the volume at her station could trip up even the most experienced cook—and once behind, it was hard to catch up. The roast and sauté station always bore the brunt when a crowd showed up. Forty people in the dining room times five courses, three of which were her responsibility, meant 120 plates of food, plus however many front-room orders came in for the four raciones she had to make. She could end up sending out 150 plates a night, easy, and they had to be on time and in sync with the rest of a table, allowing for special orders or slow eaters. The volume might be predictable, but the rhythm rarely was.

On the first Saturday night after the review there was a ninety-minute wait at the bar, for the first time since the opening. Instead of having six parties in the back, they turned most of the tables three times, booking even the fringe times of five forty-five and ten thirty. Sometimes Jonah ran out of room to lay out new order tickets on the pass.

Huertas made more money in one night than it had for the entire first week of September.

. . .

David Waltuck did not quite get his wish for a review that was as positive as Jonah's. The *New York Times* review made a respectful nod to his four-star history at Chanterelle, and gave Élan the same two stars and Critic's Pick designation that Huertas had received, but not the equivalent level of praise. Jonah had gotten off light, with a ding for the shrimp and a wistful yearning for one more croqueta—hardly a complaint, to want more of something. The gist of the review was, Go to Huertas and eat, right now.

For all the compliments that Wells laced into his review of Élan, the summary judgment was not the kind that would necessarily spur the new generation of diners to rush right over: "Standing out in the open," it read, "Mr. Waltuck's cooking is revealed to be as variable, as prone to peaks and valleys, as anyone else's." The critic felt that the move from a four-star temple to a new, more casual place had "liberated" Waltuck, inspiring him to create successful new dishes like pot stickers filled with mashed potatoes and served with shavings of summer truffles, or sea urchin mixed into guacamole. But the results were inconsistent.

"Occasionally, what seems like a fun idea will land like a bag of wet laundry," wrote Wells, referring to foie gras lollipops that he found a "grim treat." General Tso's sweetbreads were "another game gone wrong," although he admitted that he didn't like the dish when he found it at Chinese restaurants, either. He loved the signature seafood sausage with sauerkraut beurre blanc that Waltuck had brought forward from Chanterelle, which he judged one of the best items on the menu, despite the fact that it came out "looking hopelessly behind the times."

It seemed that a sixty-year-old chef, even a legendary and beloved four-star chef, could have a little trouble finding his feet in a world populated by chefs who were less than half his age and had new notions about what and how to feed people.

"At times," wrote Wells, "Élan seems a little unfocused, as if Mr. Waltuck is hedging his bets by combining a grown-up bistro with a gastro pub in the crazed-carnivore style of the past decade."

By Waltuck's estimation, "there was not much of a blip" in the weeks that followed the review, but he had his eye on a bigger prize. Late November and December were the important months, more for lucrative private holiday parties than for a general increase in the number of reservations: lots of people, lots of alcohol, guaranteed numbers in advance. Waltuck opened with a full liquor license, a nod to his distinguished history, and that would help to make the holidays an insurance policy against January and February, which were quiet no matter how popular a restaurant was.

In the midst of all the post-review excitement, Jonah had to take a day to tape his *Knife Fight* episode at a studio in Brooklyn, competing in the first round against Einat Admony, an Israeli chef and cookbook author who owned three restaurants with her husband, a food-show veteran who had already won *Chopped* twice.

Jonah was uncomfortable from the moment he arrived. There had to be four dozen crewmembers and onlookers milling around, which wasn't conducive to concentration, and they wanted to record a lot of voice-over dialogue that they would cut and insert later on. They told him they wanted "brash and cocky," which was not his style. "I won't talk shit about someone else," he said, so he watched himself, hoping to avoid saying anything that could be edited into more attitude than he felt.

The format was similar to *Chopped*, with a bit more leeway—rather than a new basket of secret ingredients for each course, the contestants got one basket, a half hour to figure out what to do with it before they started to cook, and one hour to transform as many ingredients as they wanted to use into as many courses as made sense to them. They could bring a couple of items with them, so Jonah came armed with the dry pasta they served at Maialino, figuring that he could turn almost anything into a pasta dish.

His first-round box contained salsify, maple syrup, and brisket, the meat impossible to cook in so short a time without a pressure cooker. There was nothing to do but get started. Jonah turned out pintxos for the first course, a shishito pepper wrapped in salsify, grilled, and dressed with lemon, sea salt, and maple syrup, and crostini with raw salsify, anchovy, and capers. Next, he made chitarra carbonara with salsify, pasta with a sauce bound together by a salsify puree that had a touch of maple syrup added to it. The only thing he forgot was to adjust for salt, which he forgot at home, too: He was used to making pasta at Maialino, where he had worked with a tank of water, so he added too much salt without realizing it until he tasted the results. He tried to compensate for the mistake by adding less cheese at the end, but he had to admit that the dish was on the salty side, and the judges agreed.

They said that Jonah's brisket was the best dish of the day—except that it was tough.

For dessert, he turned out a salsify flan with sea salt and maple syrup standing in for the caramel.

The two chefs had a moment together while the judges conferred, and Admony told Jonah that she thought he had won, because the judges pronounced one of her dishes the worst of the round. Jonah thought that she had won because his pasta was too salty and his delicious brisket, too tough.

She was also far better known than he was, and one of only two women in the sixteen-round competition, which might mean something, he thought.

"I really hate losing," said Jonah. "I just hope they don't cut it in a way that makes me look like an ass."

He did lose, whatever the reasons, and would have to wait until the show aired to find out how he came off in the process. He rushed to work after a seven-hour shoot consoled by one thing—at least he didn't have to go back for another round.

When he finally got to Huertas, at six, the tickets were rolling and the restaurant was already half full. It felt weird—as though he were a chef who owned several restaurants and had trusted, talented employees who ran the kitchens for him. It felt the way he wanted the future to feel.

Alyssa saw her station like a chess game—there was what she was doing right now and what she knew she would be doing for each of the eight steps that followed. She saw the sequence of an order in her head, start to finish, and had been known to slap away a line cook's hand if he got too close to one of her plates, even though all he wanted was to be of help.

"Don't touch my stuff" was her work philosophy. She would find a way to get things done, no matter how busy the restaurant was, if people left her alone.

The last Friday of October was a test, though: There were seventy-six covers, a record for Huertas so far, and she simply ran out of room. She turned the two burners up high in the hope that the flames would extend to heat the four pans she'd crowded onto them, filled the flat-top with more, and perched two waiting pans on the piano, the steel rim that ran in front of the burners, which was hot enough to burn her if she didn't watch out but not quite hot enough to cook the contents of those pans. They sat there until a space opened up, so that she didn't have to waste seconds stepping away to get them: She lifted a finished pan off the heat with her left hand, shoved its replacement into position with her right, and kept moving in a counterclockwise half turn, to plate the contents of the first pan and send the dish on its way.

The shared rice dish for the dining room should have made the kitchen's life a little easier, because more family-style dishes meant less plating, and two of the mini-paella pans would feed four to six people. They were supposed to sit on the flat-top for a half hour, filled to the brim with liquid at the start, ending up with a nice crust at the bottom. It worked as long as nobody touched the pans—but the slightest jostle early in the process sent liquid sloshing onto the flat-top, where it turned into a crusty little moat that got in the way of the sauté pans that were waiting their turn. At the evening's peak Alyssa had fifteen little paella pans burbling away.

Antonio would have cleaned the flat-top when he arrived, but Alyssa was so frustrated by the end of the night that she started scrubbing, just to have someplace productive to put her energy. It didn't help that she'd given notice as soon as the review came out; she was killing herself on her way out the door.

She was back at nine the next morning to work a double shift, brunch through dinner.

"How many tonight?" she asked Jenni.

"Seventy-five," said Jenni, proudly.

Alyssa felt her eyes well up. She prided herself on her work ethic, but she didn't know where she was going to find the strength to get through another shift like the previous night's.

"I can't do this," she said, just as Nate walked up.

"What's the problem?" he said.

Alyssa screamed, "We can't do this!" and walked over to her station to start doing prep. She sang Christmas songs to herself to try to calm down.

. . .

The story served up with the late November opening of Gavin Kaysen's Spoon and Stable was irresistible, in a city that had never been on the national short-list of essential dining locations: Local boy makes good, works abroad, wins awards and honors, turns his back on New York City, whose residents consigned the state of Minnesota to the category of flyover, and comes home to cook and raise his family. He had given up the life that many cooks dreamed of, and expected his old neighbors to embrace food the way they did in important food cities, which was a nice compliment. He had rejuvenated an office building built out of a stable, a fast walk from a dying sex strip, to become part of the city's next phase.

A potent mix of Minneapolis pride and plain curiosity got people talking before the opening, and the opening itself clinched things. His guests included Daniel Boulud and Thomas Keller, one legendary chef from each coast making the trip to Minneapolis to celebrate their spiritual heir and Bocuse d'Or teammate. With Kaysen as team coach, they were training for the competition that would take place in January in Lyon, France—the culmination of seven years' effort to put the United States in serious contention for the first time. That was the level of excellence Kaysen had brought home, and the city was eager to express its gratitude.

It was easy enough to find him, to walk over before or after a meal for a fast hello: Kaysen, a small, trim man in impeccable whites, stood at one end of the open kitchen and expedited, calmly but quickly, to a random chorus of "Oui, Chef" as one cook after another fielded an order. Behind the display kitchen, hidden like the wizard behind the curtain in Oz but far more productive, the prep kitchen staff readied the ingredients that enabled Kaysen and the visible cooks to turn dinner into performance art.

The duck, fed and dry-aged according to Kaysen's specification, appeared as a laser-edged rectangle, its paper-thin, translucent skin as brittle as torched sugar on a crème brûlée, and in duck meat loaf sliders. There was spinach with cheese curds, a regional treat as channeled by the classically trained chef, and a version of his grandmother's pot roast that involved chanterelle mushrooms and broth poured tableside; he wanted to incorporate home on the menu, but on his culinary terms.

No longer did a food-obsessed local have to find an excuse to drive to Chicago to eat. Soon enough, traffic would run in the opposite direction, and any hope of a reservation would be two months out. People stood in the snow in the hope of snagging a first-come, first-served seat at the bar.

13

SUCCESS

Success seemed definitive, back when it was out of reach: Huertas wasn't yet doing enough business, but as soon as it was, as soon as it reached a tenable plateau, Jonah could do two things that he couldn't do when the restaurant was empty. He could attract more talented cooks, which would ease the time commitment for the existing staff and stave off burnout, and he could think more seriously about what came next.

It was more complicated close up. First off, there was no depot; it wasn't as though Huertas arrived and that was that. The October numbers were great, close to double the bottom of the summer: Revenues were $176,000 in October compared to about $88,000 in both August and September, compared, for that matter, to $120,000 for opening month. The average check was up to $50 from an initial $42.

The sheer volume was startling. "We're selling so many cans of seafood, we just bought every one that our supplier had," said Jonah. "We sold them out of scallops, clams, mussels. They get a big shipment from Spain and it's a month until they get another, so we said we'll take everything because we're going to blow through them."

Even a random dip on a midweek night seemed an aberration, corrected before anyone could get too worried about it. Jonah and Nate felt confident enough to cash their paychecks—they were holding on to a half dozen at this point—but they stopped short of cocky.

"If we could flatline here," said Jonah, "I'd be happy." He was too competitive for that to be quite true, but the staff understood what he meant. If life would just hold steady, he'd feel secure enough to make plans.

They wouldn't know if they were safe for weeks yet. The consensus among more seasoned restaurateurs was that a *Times* review guaranteed a six-week window of opportunity: six weeks to turn the curious into return customers, that was it, before the easily distracted public moved on and Jonah got a better sense of exactly how successful he was likely to be long-term. The *Times* review had hauled Huertas back from the brink and given it the healthiest possible shove in the right direction. Now all that mattered was what they did with the fresh start.

With Alyssa leaving, Jonah wanted both a sous chef and a line cook, and the first batch of résumés after the review made him hope that the drought might be over. It didn't take long for him to realize that the new applicants were as "underwhelming" as their predecessors; the only difference was that now there were more of them. He got a sous chef applicant who'd only worked in corporate kitchens and big food service operations, never in an actual restaurant. He got a line-cook hopeful who wasn't a cook but a paramedic who wanted to change careers. Jonah was willing to give him a trail because a paramedic ought to be responsible and hardworking, and he could teach the guy what to do as long as he knew the basics. He didn't.

Jonah knew people who could handle either job, but they worked at restaurants where he'd worked, and there was a firm no-poaching rule. If Jonah wanted to hire someone who worked for a chef he'd worked for in the past, he'd have to ask permission, and he preferred to find a cook who didn't require that kind of favor. He didn't want someone else to swipe one of his cooks someday.

The logical in-house solution was to move Alberto up from the wood oven to the fry station, full-time, and move Max, the fry cook, up to Alyssa's station, because it was easier to find a beginner to work the oven than to find a cook with experience. It wasn't the perfect answer, though, and Jonah was reluctant to make those two promotions if he had doubts going in. Max didn't work clean enough to satisfy Jonah or Jenni, even though he had an honorable explanation—if he faced the choice on a jammed night between getting food on a plate and wiping down the piano that ran along the front of the range, it was food on the plate every time, and Jonah couldn't quite argue with that, even though he thought there was a way to do both.

Alberto made Jonah nervous only because he was a kid three months into his first full-time job, and yet everything he did suggested that he could handle a step up. He watched what Jonah did carefully and had no interest in kitchen drama; he didn't raise his voice or get emotional or give anyone a hard time. Everything about him was precise, from his short dark hair to his disciplined posture to his kitchen uniform, which somehow always looked crisp. He was like Jonah in that way—he kept his head down and got the work done.

If minorities had more of a numerical presence in restaurant kitchens than women did, over time, it was in part because historically immigrants had filled the lowest-paying entry-level jobs—a downstairs community, literally, in New York's upstairs-downstairs vertical universe, which of necessity separated a kitchen's upper echelons from the prep cooks who supported them. When Jonah made braised tripe, he did so in the main-floor kitchen, because hot dishes had to walk fast from the pass to the dining room; when he spent summers on prep, it was in a windowless basement, the ingredients to be carried upstairs when he was done. Women might land in the basement, if they worked on the pastry side, but that, too, was a practical decision, if an ironic one; while the job of pastry chef was an upstairs position in terms of the hierarchy, most desserts were made in advance, so pastry could live downstairs and settle for a dedicated assembly space in a corner of the main kitchen.

A young, ambitious cook like Alberto faced a pervasive assumption about his destiny, a ceiling based on generations who lacked the skills— or access to the skills—to run a kitchen. He'd grown up cooking, like Jonah and Jenni, but his single mother couldn't simply decide to send him to culinary school. It was too expensive; it wasn't an option. If not for Richard Grausman, an author and educator who had devoted himself for thirty years to students like Alberto, he would not have become Jonah's presumptive fry cook—or if he had, it would have been years from now, his progress dependent on employers willing to give an eager but untrained kid a chance.

In 1990 Grausman piloted a cooking program in New York City public high schools that led to the formation of C-CAP, the Careers Through Culinary Arts Program, designed to provide culinary training to underserved high school students, and college scholarships for those who distinguished themselves in an escalating set of cooking competitions. As a high school senior, Alberto's future hung on a two-course dinner he had two hours to prepare from classic French recipes he'd had to memorize: Sûpreme poulet chasseur avec pommes château, or hunter's chicken with turned, sautéed potatoes, and crêpes sucrées with crème pâtissière and sauce au chocolat, crepes with pastry cream and chocolate sauce. He won a $7,000 scholarship; recipes from the past would help to pay for opportunities he otherwise might have missed.

In addition to his classwork at Monroe, Alberto became a teaching assistant. He helped the culinary dean open the program's dining lab, a small restaurant that was open to the public and staffed by culinary students, and ran the lab even as he kept going to class. He completed the requirements for a two-year associate degree while he held down a part-time job, including two classes he finished online, and then he saw the ad for a position at Huertas.

Alberto was only three classes shy of his bachelor's degree, but there were days when he didn't see the point, as it made little sense to think about homework when he might profitably invest that energy in his career. His girlfriend and the dean tag-teamed him—he was too close to the end to blow a degree now—and he promised them that he'd get it done, even though he wasn't sure when, or how.

He was more focused on his future. Alberto believed in the one-year-and-out rule, a common philosophy among young cooks: If there wasn't progress or the firm promise of it after a year on a job, it was time to move on. If he ever felt stuck at Huertas—spent too much time at the wood oven or the fry station, or even at Alyssa's roast and sauté station down the line—he'd have to leave. A great job, by definition, had forward motion, because he saw himself doing exactly what Jonah was doing, someday. He wanted his own place, too, but he wanted to learn about other cuisines, particularly Asian food, and he wasn't going to get that here.

Patience and impatience; it was hard to find the balance. Alberto had a lot to learn, so he had to be careful not to get ahead of himself, even as he kept his eye on his long-range goal. Huertas was part of his continuing education. The Monroe classroom kitchens were old-school, and he had been screamed at by his share of instructors. He was intrigued by somebody who seemed able to manage without too much drama, and he tried to emulate his boss's approach on everything from his mise en place to his calm demeanor in the kitchen.

"Jonah's so attentive to detail," he said, "and it's not, 'You have to do it this way,' but, 'It's better if you do it this way.'"

Alberto already worked the fry station on Max's days off, and he knew that even a seemingly simple task like making potato chips was trickier than it looked. "The hardest part of the fry station is balance," he said. "Pintxos, and orders with things I have to fry—balancing space and time. I'm going to be as efficient as possible." If he got the chance to be in the main kitchen all the time, not up at the oven, he would have more opportunity to watch Jonah, to learn how to handle himself once he had his own kitchen to run—and to prove his merit, which with luck would mean another promotion before he hit the next one-year mark.

Once the post-review euphoria subsided, Jenni found herself in an unexpected and equally outsized funk, at an uncomfortable emotional distance from the rest of the staff. The review, the crowds, and the accompanying crazy hours reminded her that she was, after all, a salaried employee—still a sous chef, not yet the executive sous, and too often the one who stayed late to close the restaurant. She'd been there since the beginning. No one could say that she'd devoted any less energy than the partners had to making Huertas a success—but she didn't have her own money to invest, as they did, so she didn't have the status. It was time for Jonah to more fully express his appreciation to her, and she let both Jonah and Nate know how she felt: She was not being compensated sufficiently, financially or emotionally.

"Everyone says I should be a partner," she told them, because in fact that was what some of the staffers said when she complained to them. At the same time, she didn't want to push too hard and precipitate an unnecessary crisis if they weren't ready to promote her or give her equity. "I just deserve to be compensated," she said, and left it to them to figure out how. They could make her a partner, give her a deserved promotion, or give her a raise with a specific timetable for promotion and equity down the line. They should figure it out and come back to her. Jenni didn't have a plan if they balked, because she wasn't going to quit in a huff and look for another job. She assumed they'd do the right thing.

The easiest answer, to Nate, was to find the second sous chef who had so far eluded all of their efforts, which would enable both Jonah and Jenni to cut their workweek by ten hours. Jonah was more willing to discuss a partnership, because he wanted Jenni to be happy. She'd taken a big gamble on him—and now that it was starting to pay off, he wanted to find an appropriate way to thank her. A partnership meant that she stood in line for payouts with the other partners and the investors, so it wasn't money out of pocket today. Once they were in a position to write disbursement checks, they could include Jenni—and they could use the partnership offer to insist on a five-year commitment. That had advantages when they opened a second place and needed a reliable person to run the Huertas kitchen.

Nate was blunt: He reminded Jonah that Jenni was a sous chef who had never managed a kitchen before, and restaurants weren't in the business of giving equity to sous chefs. If Jonah really wanted to, they could slice off a percentage or two of equity shares, which could mean a few thousand dollars for Jenni after the investors were paid off, but that wasn't a real partnership, and it might not mollify her. Better to give her a big raise immediately, he told Jonah, $5,000 or $6,000 a year and a monthly stipend so that she could go out to eat. She'd feel better, and they'd buy some time to see how she handled added managerial responsibilities.

Or they could tell her that she would get equity at Huertas's one-year anniversary, which would provide them with the same window of time to reflect on the decision. They could hold off on a promotion until they hired an additional sous chef, because at that point it made sense: They couldn't expect her to have the same title as someone new who reported to her. There were all sorts of appropriate ways to do this, and no reason to rush ahead with wrong moves just because Jonah felt an emotional debt to her.

They settled on a $4,000 raise, to $42,000, and a stipend to communicate how important she was. She needed to spend more time checking out other restaurants so that she could contribute more to the ongoing development of this menu and of whatever menus they developed for future locations.

Jonah had always been proud of his work ethic, as a teenage kitchen volunteer and as a line cook. If Maialino needed him to oversee the sous vide chicken, he would bag up 120 pounds of chicken, get them into and out of the circulator, and have them ready to be finished on the flat-top. When the circulator balked, he loaded the bags onto a wheeled cart and pushed it a couple of crosstown blocks to Gramercy Tavern to use their machine, and accommodated the Tavern's cooks if their machine broke down, without ever letting himself fall behind. On a day when the cart's wheel caught the curb and dozens of bags of chicken splattered on the ground, he cursed privately at the guy at the nearby halal food cart who didn't step over to lend a hand—weren't they in the same business, after all?—but all that a passerby saw was a tall, skinny kid righting the cart and reloading the bags. A small tantrum might have been an appropriate response, but Jonah preferred outward calm.

When he got promoted to sous chef at Maialino, he figured that the proper style boiled down to expecting the same kind of commitment from anyone who was still a line cook, even though the executive sous was technically in charge of managing the crew. The notion of leeway didn't figure into the equation. If he could survive a trolley's worth of spilled chicken parts without a whimper, everyone else could handle an equivalent challenge at their stations.

Jonah was unyielding—not noisy, not theatrical, just insistent about results and uninterested in excuses. "There, if somebody wouldn't stand up to tough love, I didn't care," he said of Maialino. "Get me someone else. I don't care about your personal life or about what happened on the way here."

But that kitchen had a big staff that put out about five times the food Huertas did, breakfast through late night. He didn't spend every shift with the same handful of people, as he would at his own place. He believed that a small kitchen required a different approach, and defining—and refining—it turned out to be an ongoing struggle. "Managing people's happiness is the hardest part of my job, and my biggest concern," he said. "I didn't used to care if people liked me. Now I do. Now they're going to do better if they like me. I have to think about that," he said. "What can I do to get the best out of them? Riding them really hard may be the best way to get the best work out of them tonight, but long-term I have to be more nurturing. I don't want to be an asshole."

He evaluated his managerial style, halfway to Huerta's first-year anniversary, as "much nicer and easier going" than he had been at Maialino, but it came at a cost. He kept up an ongoing dialogue with himself about everyone in the kitchen: Would Jenni be sufficiently pleased with a raise; would Max step up and prove himself worthy of the roast and sauté station; could he find a better candidate, and how would that affect Max's morale; would Alberto prove to be the smart move at the fry station, and if so, what expectations would he have about the next step? He had to keep his eye on all of them, to evaluate not only how they were doing but how they seemed to feel about it—and at the same time watch the prep cook and the dishwasher for any early signs of dissatisfaction. He always had an eye on Juan, who essentially ran the prep operation downstairs, to make sure that he was content.

Occasionally Jonah got around to thinking about himself. He had retired the summer's sad notion of a deep-pocket stranger who bailed him out, but he still thought, sometimes, about how vulnerable he was. There were clear benefits to working for someone else. Now that Chris had started at Marta, he could build his résumé without having to hang on to uncashed paychecks, and he still had time to open his own place down the line. Jonah could probably sell Huertas from a less needy position at this point and retreat into a more insulated job as a managing partner with equity, but he tried not to think about that. He was supposed to be on his way, not looking for a safe haven. Still, it was useful to think about options, even if he didn't intend to pursue them. Possibility took some of the edge off of the day-to-day pressure.

Not quite enough, in the estimation of his wife and his mother, who wondered if his hair was starting to thin slightly at the crown. It would hardly be a surprise, given that his father was almost completely bald and had started to lose his hair in his late twenties, but if they were right—he didn't think so, but if they were—stress had to play an equal part. If that was true, he could slow down the process, however inevitable genetics might be, if he could just find a sous chef and a line cook, improve the brunch numbers, keep the business at its current level, decide what to do next and when to do it, make the investors happy, stop beating himself up for not paying them back yet, and be a decent guy but not a pushover through it all.

. . .

Jonah might not be ready to think about a second place, but one of Huertas's brunch regulars was developing an upscale food court in the West Village, and he wondered if Jonah and Nate wanted to take a look. Gansvoort Market was going to open a couple of blocks away from Chelsea Market, which in 1997 had turned the ground floor of an old Nabisco factory into a square-block temple to food that now housed everything from a butcher shop and a bakery to a fish and seafood supplier and a Cambodian sandwich shop. Gansvoort was going to involve a smaller, more eclectic mix of food tenants just down the street from the new Whitney Museum, scheduled to open in the spring of 2015 at the southern end of the elevated High Line Park, already a magnet for tourists who descended its stairs hungry and thirsty.

After six months of being the needy ones—can we please get a liquor license, more customers who spend more money, return guests, a brunch crowd, a decent line cook?—Jonah and Nate were dizzy at their new role as the object of someone's desire, as speculative as it was. The location was so tempting. This was a "premiere spot," said Nate, and Jonah agreed; he would have looked at the West Village in the first place if he could have afforded the rents, which were even higher than they were in the East Village. Names got made in the West Village, where people seemed to go out to dinner every night, and not merely to grab a burger—unless it was a Michelin-starred version, of which there were two, the $26 Black Label burger at Minetta Tavern, opened in 2008 as part of chef Keith McNally's downtown restaurant group, and the $25 burger with Roquefort cheese on April Bloomfield's menu at The Spotted Pig.

They decided to take a look. Donostia, the Spanish restaurant that shared the first Eater review with Huertas, had already signed on at

Gansvoort, so Jonah and Nate couldn't do tapas or pintxos, but the developer wondered if the partners had another idea they'd like to present. The stall he had in mind was only 200 square feet and lacked a gas hookup, so they'd have to come up with a concept that didn't require cooking. They had three months to put together a proposal, which he hoped they'd do.

Jonah and Nate had an idea before they got back to Huertas, or rather, they could see how to adapt an idea they'd had for a while, to make it work in such a limited space: They could do a vermút bar and serve meats and cheeses, sandwiches and prepared salads that they made at Huertas and cabbed across town, to the rhythm of repeated credit-card swipes from a new customer base. They'd never considered this kind of operation when they talked about a second place. They'd always imagined a full-on restaurant and not necessarily a Spanish one, although Nate was more wedded to Basque food as a brand than Jonah was. But the location was compelling.

"It's worth it from a branding perspective," Nate told Jonah, "to have a foothold in the West Village near the High Line and the Whitney and the Meatpacking," which was what the meatpacking district had been newly christened by the people who were developing it. It was worth taking the time to see if the numbers made sense.

The numbers that refused to budge, even with the first-week boost from the *Times* review, were brunch revenues, which had settled back down into disappointing if not crisis range. Jonah said what both he and Nate were trying not to think: They ought to cancel brunch and concentrate instead on being open seven nights a week, which they planned for some time after the first of the year, even though they both knew that dropping brunch was not an option, not now. They'd been singled out by the *Times*. The last thing they needed was a set of stories informing readers that Huertas had failed to make a go of brunch.

. . .

First Avenue liked to sleep in after a late night. At midnight it looked like rush hour, the sidewalk clogged with pedestrians, plenty of cabs ready to lurch to the curb to take them home, but it was slow to come back to life in the morning. McDonald's opened at six, Cosmo's Launderama and the 7th Street Village Farm market at seven, and Subway at nine. Other than that, the street was lined with heavy metal pull gates held in place by big padlocks, with flattened boxes and garbage bags bundled up at the curb.

At nine thirty on the Tuesday before Thanksgiving, Jonah was by himself at the pass, no music, no distractions. He consulted the previous shift's to-do list, adding unfinished tasks to an updated list for the coming night's service:

Freeze squid

Squeeze OJ

Soak 2 qt chickpeas

Pickle carrots

Put stuffing bread in oven

Sear chicken legs and wings (salt and pepper)

Bread crumbs

Cook breasts

Roast bones/make stock

Cook eggs

Scallions

Arugula

Mixed greens

Almond cake

Duck rillettes

The stuffing bread wasn't for service but for a staff Thanksgiving project Jonah had come up with, a nice way, he thought, to show his appreciation for everyone's hard work. Huertas would be open on Wednesday, which would be slow, and Friday, which would be full of people who didn't want to cook, but Jonah was taking Wednesday off because an owner could decide to give himself a break. It wouldn't hurt to help everyone else have a decent Thanksgiving meal.

He'd put up a Thanksgiving sign-up sheet where people could buy whole turkeys at the restaurant's cost or order portions of prepared meals—slices of sous-vide turkey breast, braised leg meat off the bone, stuffing that only needed to be baked, all of it for $12 per portion to cover costs. Front-of-house people helped to chop vegetables for the stock and stuffing, Jonah turned out a stock that combined turkey and pork and mushroom stocks, and he planned a stuffing that included homemade sausage, bacon, fennel, "and then the usual suspects."

Every morning, he roasted whatever bones he had on hand to turn them into stock. Chicken bones went into a pot with vegetables and water and were ready in a couple of hours, but pork or lamb bones went on last thing at night and simmered on a low heat until the first person arrived eight or nine hours later to open the restaurant. This time Jonah was the first one in, because it was his project, his staff meal, and he wasn't going to ask people for help beyond the slightly comic efforts of servers showing off their marginal knife skills.

The State Liquor Authority, Zone 1, met on December 10 in a small office building just off the corner of Malcolm X Boulevard and 125th Street in Harlem, across the street from Red Rooster, opened in 2010 by chef Marcus Samuelsson and named for a long-ago Harlem speakeasy. Red Rooster, all primary colors and bold style, was intended as a place to celebrate the neighborhood's history and invigorate its food scene—while directly across the street the three members of the SLA determined a restaurant's fate in a room that was equally committed to bureaucratic anonymity.

The hearing room was not a hopeful space by any means, its low-slung ceiling lending an oppressive air before a word was spoken, the day's decisions made by political appointees whose tenure often ended with the election of a new governor, short-termers compared to the members of the community board subcommittee. Rows of folding chairs filled most of the room, and an aisle up the middle ended at a microphone that faced a wide wooden desk where the commissioners sat. Today there was only one, alongside an administrator who tallied votes. A second commissioner was absent. The third, the SLA's director, was in Albany, and his face appeared on a monitor to the applicants' right. A restaurant owner could make eye contact with the commissioner at the front of the room or with the image on the screen, but not with both, at least not simultaneously.

Jonah and Nate were the only men who weren't wearing suits, and they and their lawyer took seats toward the back, rows behind the other applicants and their lawyers, all of whom had the comfortable air of people who'd been here and prevailed before. One woman sat in the back across the aisle from them, clasping a stack of papers, but she was not there to ask for a license. She represented a group of small business owners who opposed one for Starbucks, which wanted to sell beer and wine as well as coffee at a new outlet near a wine bar and café that she owned.

The Starbucks representatives reassured the board that underage customers would not be able to purchase wine and beer, that they would watch out for older customers buying alcohol for younger ones, and that the combination of an early end to alcohol service and the chain's sit-and-sip environment would discourage the dedicated drinking one might find in a bar. They dismissed the woman's concern about what this would do to local bars and restaurants that already existed on slim profit margins and might not survive having customers siphoned off by an outlet of a deep-pocket chain. Instead, they said, bringing alcohol to Starbucks would improve business for everyone by drawing more people to the area.

The director and the commissioner voted, and Starbucks got its license.

When it was Huertas's turn, Jonah, Nate, and their lawyer stood at an accommodating forty-five-degree angle to the desk, trying not to ignore either the board member or the director. They minimized the significance of the community board's no vote. Perhaps they had shown up a bit too early the last time, but three months had passed since then, and in that time they'd received a glowing review from the *New York Times*, with the attendant increase in business. Jonah was a responsible restaurateur and his customers were diners, not bar-hoppers, as the *Times* review attested. He'd like to be able to serve them a cocktail.

The woman in the room was sympathetic to his arguments. The director was not. Huertas had been open just over eight months, which still felt too early. He didn't want to set a precedent that encouraged other applicants to show up before their one-year anniversary. That was a "slippery slope," he said, and he did not intend to venture out onto it.

If the third board member had attended the hearing, each vote would have carried equal weight. With only two board members, the director's long-distance vote broke the tie. Since there were no objections beyond the timing, he said, Jonah and Nate should simply come back in April. With that, the Huertas team was dismissed, and the board called the next applicant.

Nate jumped on the lawyer as soon as the hearing-room doors closed behind them: Hadn't he said it was pretty much a sure thing? Wasn't there something he could have said or done to sway them? He peppered Levey with questions even as he wondered whether to replace him— while Jonah stood there, silent, sunk into himself, as disappointed as he had been thrilled when the *Times* review hit. A holiday season with drinks, gone. Big holiday parties, gone, at least some of them, because they'd decamp to a restaurant where they could drink. The added profits from cocktails that ran from $12 to $14, gone. The big, significant reason? It wasn't time yet, and it would set a bad example, which had nothing to do with the merits of their application.

Levey was philosophical. This was a disappointment but not a surprise, and perhaps the partners ought to accept, finally, that waiting until April was the realistic option. The director had said that the calendar was the only obstacle, as had the community board. It was time to take that seriously and to stop asking for what both sets of officials perceived as special treatment.

The three of them shared an elevator, silent, the lawyer went wherever he was going next, and Jonah and Nate headed for the subway station at the end of the block. They rode from 125th Street downtown to the 14th Street station without saying a word, Nate too agitated to sit down, Jonah slumped on an empty row of seats, his head in his hands, his watch cap pulled down low, earbuds in to fend off conversation. They transferred to the shuttle to the east side in silence, as Jonah thought about how to tell a hopeful staff that they'd been stymied again. Basically, a guy on a TV set had just punctured everyone's holiday dreams of bigger checks, a bigger tip pool, a bigger crowd at the door, the promise of stability even after the *Times* review wore off.

He texted the news to Jenni and Stew so that some of the initial disappointment would wear off by the time he and Nate got back, and he did his best to put on his so-what face before he walked in the door.

The rest of the staff would take their cue from Jonah and Nate, so they tried to seem more frustrated than angry, more irked by predictable, shortsighted bureaucracy—always a popular position to take—than anxious about the bottom line. They'd go back in April, at Huertas's one-year anniversary, and until then they'd settle for being a popular restaurant in the happy wake of a great *Times* review.

The bad news wasn't over. The wood oven had been cranky for the last few days, sending the occasional smoke hiccup into the room, but two days later it backed up completely. Smoke billowed through the restaurant, not enough to send everyone home but enough to force a decision. Jonah shut down the oven and shifted everything that usually came out of it to the kitchen, where he hustled to come up with a new way to char the octopus, as well as the mushrooms for the rice and mushrooms, two of the front room's most popular dishes. The already crowded flat-top was about to be working overtime.

The initial $40,000 savings on the ventilation system had bought them an alternative that didn't work, at least not at the moment. Until they figured out a solution that wasn't going to cost that much, the hulking domed oven was reduced to being a piece of the decor, no more useful than the wainscoting.

Six days after they shut it down, a neighbor called to complain about the smoke that couldn't have been bothering her because it no longer existed. Jonah forced himself not to point that out, because she was polite about it and had never called to complain before. There was nothing to be gained by antagonizing a neighbor. Maybe the smoke had bothered her when the ventilation system first acted up, and she had just gotten around to calling. He promised to take care of it immediately.

. . .

Starting a restaurant requires a plan, a willingness to sacrifice to implement it, and optimism based in part on the anticipated behavior of strangers. Maintaining a restaurant in the face of setbacks requires an almost foolhardy resilience and a certainty that there is a way out of whatever is happening at the moment, that this isn't the dead end. Definitive notions of victory and defeat are for businesses that revolve around something more concrete than making people happy at mealtime.

Three days after the SLA meeting, Nate and Stew stood over a little saucepan of sugar, water, and juniper berries, which Nate referred to as "my alchemy." They might not be allowed to serve gin, but no one could stop them from infusing a syrup with juniper berries, which give gin its flavor and aroma, to use in what Nate was determined to call "almost gin." It would be the base for an "almost Negroni," which in turn would be part of a new menu of cocktail imitators, classic cocktails made with wine and sherry instead of hard liquor. They'd market the lower alcohol content as a plus: People could drink more of these almost-drinks than they could the hard stuff.

Jonah sampled the contents of the saucepan. "Use the regular name of the cocktail, but put quotes around everything," he said. The SLA and the community board would have run out of excuses by the time Huertas reapplied for a full license in April. He was not about to give them any cause for complaint between now and then, and he didn't want to mislead guests about what was in that Negroni.

The new drinks boosted morale. They were a cautious battle cry, proof that Huertas was not about to be done in, not by bureaucrats, not by the ventilation system, not even by the pending gloom of January and February. An us-versus-them mentality was a good thing as the holidays approached, since nobody got to go home for them, not when the restaurant was open on Christmas Eve and, of course, on New Year's Eve, when there would be two seatings and a special menu. The restaurant family was as close to family as many of Jonah's employees got— and the more they felt like a tribe, the less they'd feel left out of the kinds of festivities most people, including their customers, enjoyed.

Jonah wasn't about to spend $50 on a wreath, but he okayed the purchase of some poinsettia plants and lights and encouraged the staff to be ingenious about the rest.

They strung wine corks into Christmas wreaths, built a menorah out of cider bottles, and one of the servers transformed empty rice bags into Christmas stockings that she labeled, one for each employee, and strung the length of the kitchen. Everyone got assigned a secret Santa with a $20 spending limit for a present, and there would be a party after the restaurant closed on New Year's Eve for anyone who wanted to hang around.

Alyssa bought a one-way plane ticket back to California for January 15 and tried not to dwell on how drastically things were about to change. Her first food job, at eighteen, had been at a restaurant on the Disneyland property in Anaheim, California, in a mixed-use outdoor mall called Downtown Disney. The park itself had three fine-dining restaurants run by the Patina Restaurant Group, and the more Alyssa thought about her options, the better Disneyland sounded. Her mom lived ten minutes from there, which meant that Alyssa wouldn't have to spend much money on gasoline. Her mom was going to buy a new car and bequeath her 2006 Lexus to her daughter, so no expenses there, either. No rent, no food costs—with the right job, Alyssa figured that she could make a sizeable dent in the debt in two or three years.

The Disneyland restaurants paid well and offered solid benefits, but the prospect of going from a small independent restaurant to a massive corporation with a capital-C culture was a little weird, she had to admit. Disneyland restaurants were a long way from beer pong and too many plates on too few burners, and it was not where she'd imagined herself ending up at this point. Huertas was the first small restaurant Alyssa had ever worked at, and she liked the autonomy, which felt like a compliment: Once Jonah saw what she could do, she was pretty much on her own. But it was over, at least for the foreseeable future.

"I'm having my quarter-life crisis," she said. "I need to get my shit together and stop playing New York City."

She spent more than double her secret Santa budget on a Unicorn Magnum Plus peppermill for Joc, the young extern who'd become an increasingly valuable member of the kitchen team, because it was the sort of thing an aspiring chef ought to have. For the New Year's Eve late-night staff party, she drafted Max to help her make big sandwiches on baguettes, full of leftover steak portions, cheese, mushrooms, and sauce, to go with the cava and beer, the tequila and Jell-O shots.

By the end of the year, Jonah was halfway to solving his staffing problems. He hired Lina, a line cook who had been an executive chef at a place he'd never heard of, unhappy enough to quit before she found another job—and while it was a big step down to accept a job as a line cook, they both knew that she had little choice. "Whether it's fair or not," said Jonah, "people in New York City want you to have experience at a good place in New York City." He didn't say that to her flat out, but he did say that Huertas was a good first step into a larger and more impressive network. She could look around for a sous chef position if she wanted to, but she'd end up at another anonymous place, which didn't really constitute progress. He had no trouble convincing her.

The elusive sous chef candidate, the one he really wanted, was Jeff, who was clearly overqualified and at his last job had earned more than Jonah did. He'd started cooking late, after a couple of years in finance, but had more than made up for the lost time—he worked at Eleven Madison Park after a culinary school externship there, and had landed most recently at Blanca, where he'd been a sous chef until he decided to quit and look for a less grueling job. With its two Michelin stars, Blanca was a famous anomaly—a tasting menu of over two dozen courses served at a counter at Roberta's, a Bushwick outpost of pizza and trendiness. For eighteen months he worked eighty hours a week on the tasting menu, spending two or three days a week just testing dishes. Sixty hours would seem like a relative holiday to him, and he'd be an exciting guy to have around.

"I bet I could learn some things," Jonah said. "I hadn't thought of that, to have somebody here who could be creative and bring ideas. That's the kind of person I'd love to hire."

Other chefs around town, some of them with more elastic budgets, were just as eager to hire Jeff, who said that he already had an offer of a sous job at Betony, a high-end midtown restaurant run by an Eleven Madison Park graduate. Jonah could talk about the potential for growth and advancement and hope that he fell in love with Huertas enough to bridge the wage gap, but it was a long shot. Still, he looked for ways to meet the guy halfway, and talked about opportunities down the line when they opened more restaurants.

The money was an ongoing dance. Jonah could offer Max $36,000 to $38,000 if he stepped up into the sous job, because that was a good raise in terms of what he already got—but an outside candidate would probably require something in the low forties, and someone like Jeff, even more. Jenni got $42,000, so Jonah couldn't go higher than that without creating a new problem. Kitchen staff didn't usually gossip about who made what, but she was involved in the hiring interviews; she was management, so she'd know, and be understandably resentful about being outearned by a sous who reported to her. Or he could offer enough to get Jeff to say yes, upset Jenni, and deal with the fallout. He figured that $50,000 would make this work, but that was what Jonah paid himself.

If he already had another place it might make sense because the candidate was so strong, but right now Jonah couldn't rationalize $50,000. They had decided to postpone opening on Sunday and Monday nights until they had a full kitchen staff, so they didn't have that extra revenue. They didn't have cocktail profits. It was not the time to spend too much money on a sous chef, much as Jonah was dying to hire him. Maybe Jeff would get nervous after too many weeks without a job and compromise on less.

14

DETOURS

Huertas rode into 2015 on a wave of year-end best lists, just the sort of lift it needed to survive the post-holiday slump in January and February. They still didn't know if the man they had identified six months earlier as Adam Platt had in fact been Adam Platt, but *New York* magazine's restaurant critic had been in at some point, because Huertas was the first place mentioned in the Bar-Food Revolution section of the magazine's annual Where to Eat issue. *Travel & Leisure* magazine anointed a dozen places in its Best New Restaurant: 2015 Edition, and Huertas was one of only four in New York City, alongside Marta.

"One of four," was the subterranean mutter around Huertas, whenever anyone needed a quick spiritual boost. "One of *four*."

Grub Street put migas at number eighteen on a list of its twenty best dishes for 2014. *Forbes* included Jonah in its 30 Under 30 list of restaurant industry newcomers to watch.

But in the midst of all the holiday list-making, a sobering rumor unexpectedly hit the online press: Peter Hoffman, who'd given Jonah his first full-time kitchen job at Savoy, might be closing his second restaurant, Back Forty, which he had opened in 2007.

When Hoffman opened Savoy in Soho in 1990, he was ahead of his time in terms of both location and menu. The *New York Times* dubbed him "a locavore before the word existed," and Jonah believed that his onetime boss would have been New York's answer to Berkeley's Alice Waters if he'd ever cared about promoting himself, which he adamantly did not.

By 2011, Savoy was surrounded by competitors and facing a pricey new lease, which left Hoffman with a dilemma. He could make the restaurant more expensive, more exclusive—or he could head in the opposite direction and make it cheaper and more casual like its younger East Village sibling, Back Forty, the kind of place a customer might visit more frequently. The latter option seemed the practical one. He told the staff on a Wednesday that Savoy was closing, to be reincarnated months down the line as Back Forty West. Four nights later, after a twenty-one-year run, Savoy was gone.

Now Back Forty was closing as well. The final night of service was even more abrupt—the rumor came a day after what turned out to be the restaurant's last night, confirmed by Hoffman in a written statement a day after that. He cited a "difficult landscape and lease uncertainty" as the reasons for his decision, and expressed the hope that customers would continue to visit Back Forty West.

The space was on the market two weeks later. The key money, the amount a prospective tenant was expected to pay up front to secure a location, was $250,000.

New York magazine laid the single-restaurant model to rest in a multipart story called "How the Restaurant Game Is Played," part of the same

Where to Eat issue that mentioned Huertas. Item 3-d on a list of survival rules was, "The More Restaurants You Own, the Easier It Gets," and writer Alan Sytsma told the story of chef Andrew Carmellini, one of the chefs for whom Jenni had worked, who surveyed the scene from atop a network that included seven restaurants, the food concession at The Public Theater, and brand licensing agreements at area airports and Madison Square Garden. Carmellini was a long way from his early days, when he had to sell $75,000's worth of musical instruments and recording equipment to finance the home stretch on his second restaurant, and he had a simple lesson to impart from his new, improved vantage point: More is better. The old model—a Chanterelle, a Savoy, which had endured for seventeen years without a sibling—was no match for higher rents and more competition. In his experience, not even a second restaurant was enough. Things started to get better once there were at least four. A singleton was as unstable as a unicycle.

Jonah understood the advantages of a larger staff from his time at Maialino—one USHG restaurant could draft help from another in a crisis, one accountant or human resources person could handle more than one place—but it was more than that. Four established restaurants gave a chef the credibility to raise speculative money before he had a space or even a firm concept, because people with discretionary cash wanted a piece of whatever he was about to do. That was real progress: eager investors who would offer him the money to find a space and then let him tailor a new restaurant to live in it; no more trying to find a space that fit an idea.

As for the right concept, the current buzzword for outsized success was "fast casual," even though that was difficult to pin down, like any nascent trend: It could be a locally sourced burger made from cattle raised on non-GMO feed and topped with small-farmer tomatoes and lettuce, or it could be a place with a menu but no tablecloths, or a place with small plates, or one with family-style meals. There weren't always servers; fast casual often meant lines and trays and either pick-up windows or runners to drop orders at a table. What mattered was quality and easy access, and the role model for that, sitting at the top of a heap of contenders, was the little hot dog cart that grew, past understanding: Danny Meyer had just filed documents with the Securities and Exchange Commission for an initial public offering for Shake Shack, which had started out in 2001 as a cart that sold hot dogs, hamburgers, crinkle-cut french fries, and frozen custard in Manhattan's Madison Square Park, a side project for the high-end employees of Eleven Madison Park. They weren't just any burgers but a custom formula developed with Pat LaFrieda Meat Purveyors; not any buns but Martin's potato rolls, all of it now served with wine or beer for a meal that sat squarely on a new frontier between takeout and sit-down. Shake Shack had grown to 63 outlets worldwide, with plans to expand, eventually, to 450. The IPO was designed to raise $100 million, and the company's valuation was predicted to be about $1 billion.

Something of that magnitude was almost surely a onetime phenomenon, which discouraged no one from imagining that it could happen twice. Even a sliver of that kind of success could protect a restaurateur from ever having to worry about rent spikes or difficult landlords or a delayed liquor license. The distilled lesson of Carmellini and Meyer and Waltuck and Hoffman was clear, without having to line up any more examples of single restaurants that teetered and fell: A successful neighborhood restaurant was not a survival strategy.

But when Nate asked around, it seemed that a single restaurant and a tiny offshoot were not the answer, either. As much as he and Jonah wanted to figure out their next move, it would not be the stall at Gansvoort Market. One of Nate's advisers cautioned him not to jump at the first offer, however flattering it was to be asked. The smart next move was not to be a tenant in someone else's business dream but to come up with a concept that he and Jonah could control, another place of their own. Jonah agreed. It made sense, even though he had to admit that somebody else paying the utilities, and being responsible for opening and closing, had its appeal.

Nate met Luke for drinks at Henry Public in Brooklyn Heights, closer to Luke's apartment than to Nate's—an appropriate accommodation, as Nate was the one trying to put together an agenda for another meeting with Jonah. Luke had been right about his role at Huertas: Nate was in what he called "constant conversation" with Luke, usually at Nate's instigation, because his departed partner provided a useful corrective to his admitted impatience and was more forthcoming than Jonah, who tended to do most of his debating inside his head.

And in the end, it was Jonah's restaurant, which made Nate feel the need to be even better prepared than he would have been if they were equal partners. He'd insisted on a second off-site meeting because he'd reached his limit again; he saw a crossroads where Jonah saw process, and he needed Luke to help him build a coherent case for change. In doing so, he also hoped to alter the dynamic of his partnership with Jonah, to start having the kind of input a co-owner had, regardless of the single-digit size of his equity stake. His day-to-day concerns—and proposed solutions—were part of a strategy to help Jonah define the company's future.

Nate and Luke worked until two in the morning, ordering boulevardiers until Nate swapped to hard cider to keep his head clear, talking about appropriate next steps as he scrawled notes on a lined yellow pad. He was jittery from a mix of exhaustion and excitement by the time he met Jonah for lunch in Williamsburg—at Reynard, a role-model restaurant owned by Brooklyn restaurateur Andrew Tarlow, who since 1998 had expanded from one place into a network of restaurants as well as a market, a clothing line, and the hotel that housed Reynard. Nate laid out three pages of notes and a graph that tracked weekly gross and net sales, and launched into his presentation.

The first page had two columns of handwritten entries under the headings "Nabe," and "Go for it!," which he saw as Huertas's only options, a nice neighborhood place or the first of many, the former obviously unacceptable. Nate had also generated a decision tree under the heading "We achieved a lot . . . we can't stop," and at the side of the page had scrawled "Do you want to be in this?" for both of them to answer. The second page was the "Go for it" plan, with the word "Energize" set in a circle marked with big X's for emphasis. The third page was a list of a dozen businesses worth studying—including Momofuku and Major Food Group—either because they had a huge first success that put them in a better position to move forward than Huertas was, or because they'd already become the kind of company that he and Jonah wanted to have.

Nate also had drawn up what he called "my thesis," a summary of three kinds of contemporary success stories that he wanted to present to Jonah. If a restaurant didn't fit into one of the categories—and at the moment, Huertas didn't—it was never going to spawn offshoots, never going to be the cornerstone of even a small restaurant group.

The first kind of success was what Major Food Group had pulled off with Torrisi, which sold "exclusivity and cachet."

"You had to come here twice to eat here once," he said, referring to the small space and long waits, which seemed only to increase people's desire to snare a table. "Twenty-five seats, a midrange tasting menu, and each of their subsequent restaurants is so well thought out. What brings New York foodies? A flamboyant menu and design, down to what the servers wear." And the partners weren't afraid of change, willing to revamp the format, or even shut down the space and start over with a new project, eager to try out a new cuisine. At Huertas, daring existed on a much smaller scale, and Nate chafed at it.

The second kind of success relied on celebrity to draw a crowd, whether it was Danny Meyer's name attached to a restaurant or a chef like David Chang or Mario Batali, but that was more a Catch-22 than an option. Jonah couldn't be more successful until he was more famous, which he couldn't be until he was more successful.

The third model relied on having a popular brand. Chang's small chain of Momofuku restaurants shared the same brand name and little peach logo—Momofuku meant "lucky peach" in Japanese—from the high-end Momofuku Ko to Momofuku Noodle Bar. They served Asian-influenced food up and down the price ladder, even if random dishes from somewhere else appeared on the menu. The people who lined up outside the noodle bar up the street had an expectation based on that brand—but Chang was a half-generation ahead of Jonah and Nate, who couldn't simply decide to be a big brand any more than they could decide to be famous. There was only one path left for them, which Nate had listed as a subhead under "exclusivity and cachet": They had to be "coolest mother—," and hope that fame and branding options followed.

The year-end lists—not the ones they made but the ones they missed—made a strategy more urgent. Nate's big disappointment, the thing that motivated him to call this meeting as much as anything else, was that Pete Wells and Adam Platt had left Huertas off their best-restaurant lists. For weeks before the lists came out he had reread the year's reviews from both critics, adjusted Huertas's odds as he read, and provided Jonah with a running commentary on his research. When he counted up the number of stars and considered the level and amount of praise, he figured they were in the running.

When the lists came out without Huertas, he reread the reviews of the chosen few. Some of them were not as glowing as Huertas's review, which was the point he wanted to make today. Those places had an indefinable something that Huertas didn't have. He and Jonah needed to address that, or face the possibility that they presided over nothing more than a comfortable local spot.

Jonah, who'd remained silent throughout Nate's initial presentation, looked at the "Nabe" column on Nate's yellow pad and shrugged. "Not much use for this side," he said. "You pay back investors after eight years and have a safe place? No."

That was all Nate needed to hear. Encouraged, he rattled off what he considered to be the right moves, all of which should be embraced as quickly as possible:

They had to stop vacillating and hire a sous chef, even if it meant paying the guy from Blanca $50,000 a year. The new line cook would take some pressure off, but a highly qualified sous was a long-term investment because he could replace Alyssa and assume the kinds of responsibilities that would free up Jonah to think about the next place. They could promote Jenni to executive sous chef, which would make her happy and cement the kitchen hierarchy. If they limited themselves to the applicant pool that was willing to work for under $40,000 for a chef who wasn't yet famous, they were always going to come up short.

They had to spend even more on food to achieve what Nate called "the wow factor," whatever Jonah decided that ought to be—more creative pintxos with more expensive ingredients, press pots of broth poured at the table, anything he wanted to do. Frugality was false economy, because nobody went home talking about a memorable piece of cod. They could raise their food costs a still-reasonable percentage point or two. They'd make more money if they did.

And they had to generate buzz, which meant opening on Sunday and Monday nights as soon as possible, preferably by the end of January.

Those were the nights that chefs usually had off, which for many of them meant eating at someone else's restaurant and posting photos of the food on Instagram. Huertas needed to be part of that.

Jonah hadn't stopped him yet, so Nate pushed ahead with the one idea he assumed Jonah would resist: Maybe they ought to get rid of the tasting menu altogether, even though it was essential to Jonah's original notion of what Huertas was going to be, even though Pete Wells had made a point of saying what a great deal it was. As far as Nate was concerned, the tasting menu was part of the fundamental problem— the front room and the back room were so different that people didn't know what to expect, or whether to make a reservation, or why they couldn't sit in back and still have some of the cool food that had flown by on trays as they walked to their table. He referred to a list he'd drawn up of successful, enviable restaurants and made his point: None of them had what he considered to be Huertas's competing formats.

Jonah looked at the list. He didn't want to argue; he was prepared to listen to Nate, but they had to consider the benefits of the menu, too. A set menu meant less craziness in the kitchen, which saved money because they could get by with a smaller staff. It meant less waste because they used the same list of ingredients for a week at a time. It was easier for the servers because the story stayed the same night after night. It was part of Jonah's original concept, the place where he got to show people what he could do—and the *Times* loved it. That ought to count for something. What was the hurry?

Nate had a single answer to everything Jonah said: They needed to make their message simpler, to build a brand that would multiply. Going for it, in his mind, meant a more varied menu, more choices no matter where a guest sat, not two separate concepts. The more he talked, the quieter Jonah got, the more Nate talked to fill the silence. Luke had mentioned a steakhouse whose food costs were an unimaginable 40 percent, but they made $2 million the previous year, which to Nate was proof that they needed to spend money to make money.

Jonah sighed. Steakhouses were different. They charged a lot more.

"Then what do you think?" asked Nate.

"It's not hard to expand the food," said Jonah, as though he were figuring it out as he spoke. "It does take more energy and more bodies in the kitchen to do more intricate things."

Nate took that as encouragement and circled back to the hiring issue. "You need to come in later than ten and not worry so much about maintenance," said Nate. "You need to trust other people in the kitchen, but I know that's not your MO."

"Maybe I need to change," said Jonah, "but that's how I lead. I work harder than anyone. I lead by example."

Nate persisted: Jonah should think more about the menu and less about daily kitchen tasks. He should change the pintxos more often and make them more interesting, and they could keep the tasting menu for now as long as it was "a really bombing menu." If Jonah needed more time to come up with new dishes, they could change the menu less often. Whatever they did, they ought to pay the publicist for more time and have some serious conversations about how to define and promote the Huertas brand.

Jonah took it all in, but he didn't jump to any conclusions, not yet. He'd delayed thinking about a lot of this, he knew it, but the longer he and Nate worked together, the more he thought it was important not to rush into things. They were a good balance: Jonah worked hard to compartmentalize his life, to spend time with Marina and his friends on his two days off, and not think too much about work, while Nate couldn't stop the conversation inside his head, which meant that it was Nate's job to push and Jonah's to resist until he was sure. Jonah was the principal owner. He had to distinguish between what was broken and what had to evolve, to fix the former and let the rest work itself out.

Jonah agreed with Nate about opening seven nights a week, though he saw no difference between the last week in January and the first week in February, and refused to consider an earlier opening unless he got the kitchen straightened out. He was happy to stretch the menu a little bit, but not to dismantle it, not yet. As for becoming the next Major Food Group—if it were possible simply to devise a plan to accomplish that goal, more people would be doing it. They would do their best, they would try to innovate, but being big was a cumulative process that seemed to involve timing and luck as well as a bombing menu.

A few nights later, Jonah sold what he described, with a touch of incredulity, as a ton of fried yellow saffron rice served with scrambled eggs and aioli, shrimp and peas and bacon—paella meets fried rice, was the way he saw it. He watched in bewilderment as serving after serving flew out of the kitchen, at $14 for ingredients that had cost about ninety cents. If Nate thought that worrying less about authenticity was a good idea, Jonah was prepared to try it, but he hadn't anticipated the crazy response to what he considered a "little bit silly dish." Yes, it was delicious, but it belonged on the menu at Mission Chinese Food, one of the restaurants on Nate's aspirational list, not here. The allure of Mission Chinese depended in great part on its disregard for geography or culinary legacy; the original San Francisco location offered kung pao pastrami and salt cod fried rice, and in New York, brisket qualified as what chef-owner Danny Bowien called "American Oriental food." People seemed to love his willingness to mix things up—Mission Chinese, a different kind of stutter-step success, had survived a Department of Health shutdown with its popularity intact, and had reopened in a new space on New York's Lower East Side, soon to be joined by the nearby Mission Cantina, which took on Mexican food with a similar irreverence.

If Jonah had a fledgling brand, it definitely wasn't fusion; Wells had acknowledged that he merged Spanish food with "the seasonal Green-market aesthetic," but it was still Spanish. Jonah had eaten at too many places that he considered "vaguely Spanish," back when he was doing research for the Huertas menu, and he'd always thought that it was a shame to mess around with the food. Better to do it the way it was sup-posed to be done. Huevos rotos felt authentic to him because it was still a plate of egg, potato, and chorizo, even though he transformed the basic ingredients into something he never would have found in Madrid. Fried rice? Friends of his had hung out at a Chinese place in an under-ground parking garage in Madrid, and Jonah joined them a couple of times, but it seemed a waste of time. He had one semester in Spain, so he ought to be eating Spanish food. He felt the same way about the Huertas menu—he much preferred a smart interpretation of an authen-tic dish to what he considered to be a culinary mash-up.

"My sensibilities are to stay away from novelty," he said, even as he absorbed the obvious lesson of the fried rice, which he refused to call paella on the menu, because it wasn't. He had to get out of his head and factor in his customers' reactions to the food, because the consensus was clear: They liked to be knocked out a little bit, and they clearly didn't mind a tasty surprise. They were a little numb from all the choice, these days—within two blocks of Huertas a hungry customer could choose Mexican, Spanish, Filipino, Japanese, Italian, vegan, Greek, or Polish food, as well as a place that specialized in schnitzel. Novelty clearly helped to get their attention, as ambivalent as Jonah might be about it.

"People would rather eat exciting than delicious at this point," he said. "Not to say it can't be both, but you have to think about what will be exciting, and putting that first is what you have to do." So he piped trout mousse into little puff pastries and topped it with trout roe, another pintxo he wouldn't have found in Spain. He wrapped leftover New Year's Eve filet mignon around pickled vegetables. He created a lamb dish that felt more French than Spanish to him. He put fried, battered calamari on the dinner menu and tried to drag it toward Spain, for the sake of his own self-respect, with a piquillo pepper vinaigrette and fried olives.

Someone else could have concocted an entertaining narrative about the fried rice, a story that started in a windowless Chinese restaurant in Madrid, crossed the Atlantic Ocean in the memory bank of a young food-obsessed New Yorker, and landed on a plate at his first restaurant in the East Village, and the publicist probably could have placed it on one of the food websites. It wasn't as though anyone was going to contact the Chinese place and have them scroll through their credit-card records to see what Jonah Miller had eaten on his single-digit visits during his semester abroad.

He would never do such a thing. Jonah had boundaries, like his food, like David Waltuck and Peter Hoffman. He'd always thought that was an asset; he had a clear sense of what he would and wouldn't do, and his skill and ambition existed inside that frame. His mentors had made their names on the food, not the personality behind it, and Jonah aspired to do the same—a sensible position, he figured, as he was by his own measure too low-key to sell wacky, more interested in creativity on the plate than in promoting an attention-grabbing persona. "Look at me physically, and my background," he said. "I'm not half-Asian, I don't come from a mixed family. Even the Carbone guys have that Italian American thing going, their names scream it," referring to two of the three partners in Major Food Group and Carbone, their latest restaurant. "My name, not so memorable. The Bloomberg website even had me as Jonah Hill for a few moments," mistaking a tall, half-Jewish kid from Manhattan's Upper West Side for a short, rotund character actor.

"I'm not eccentric enough, and I have a little too much self-respect to pretend," he said. The publicist always told him to be bubblier on television. Jonah considered himself to be bubbly enough—or as bubbly as he could manage and still feel like himself.

He was clear on what his brand would never be: huge, unpredictable, driven by personality or surprise. To improve his mood—it was a bit demoralizing to see how much people liked something he wasn't sure he wanted to cook—he took refuge where he always did, and thought about the next dish he wanted to develop. He would keep the fried rice on the menu, but he wanted to add a version of cocido madrileño as winter dragged on, a Spanish stew of chickpeas, carrots, chicken, blood sausage, and braising cuts like pork shoulder. The traditional way to serve it was with the broth as a first course, followed by the vegetables and then the meat. Jonah considered serving the vegetables and meat together, but he didn't want to tinker much beyond that. The chickpeas produced the most beautiful liquid. It would be a very nice broth.

In the meantime, an emboldened Nate kept lobbing ideas: guest chefs who invented pintxos in whatever style of cuisine they cooked, house-label vermút bottled by a woman in Brooklyn, an off-the-menu chistorra sausage served like a hot dog to make the customer feel like a cool insider, a whole rabbit, a customized button-down shirt for the pintxo runner. Hearth, a ten-year-old restaurant a couple of blocks up the street, had a thriving daytime business selling take-out cups of homemade bone broth from a kitchen window that opened onto the street, in the hours when the space wasn't in use. Nate eyed the front windows of Huertas and wondered how to monetize them. He urged

Jonah to consider what seemed to be the defining question, because quality clearly wasn't enough to make the difference: "What is the cachet piece of the puzzle?"

Part of it involved getting people to talk about Huertas, and not just the off-work chefs who might show up on Sunday and Monday. Jonah was in Williamsburg having brunch with Marina when he got a text from Jenni: Chef Bobby Flay, one of the first wave of chefs to become television celebrities, had just walked into Huertas. Jonah paid his check, dashed to the L train shuttle from Brooklyn to Manhattan, and got there in time to saunter over and greet his guest.

Alberto had to take a half step back when the new line cook started, and he tried to be philosophical about it. Lina had far more experience than he did. She ought to work the fry station and be the one who filled in at roast and sauté, and he would show his willingness to do whatever he was asked to do, on any shift they asked him to work.

His considered calm lasted about a week, until Jonah inadvertently left him off the schedule on a day when he was supposed to work, which sent him to Jenni, his direct boss, to find out if he'd done something wrong. She reassured him that it was a mistake. There was going to be plenty for him to do, even with the new line cook and the sous they hadn't yet found, because Huertas was going to open seven nights a week on February 8. He'd be bouncing around for now, filling in on other cooks' days off, but Jenni wanted him to understand the hidden advantage to having the new line cook: It would be easier to find space on the roster for more training shifts for Alberto. He'd already worked the roast station for the occasional brunch. The next step, once everyone was settled in, was to train him there for dinner, when the menu was far more extensive. That way, he'd be ready to step in for a dinner shift on a quiet night.

A sous chef continued to elude Jonah. The candidate from Blanca lost interest in the wage debate. One of Peter Hoffman's sous came over for a trail that Jonah pronounced "perfect," so he offered her a job and told himself that Peter might be relieved to let her go now that he had two sets of cooks and only one restaurant. He never had to have that delicate conversation, because she took a sous chef job at Roberta's. Jonah refused to get too nervous about it, though, despite Nate's urgency about the need to make big changes, because when he caught his breath and thought about more than this week or this month, when he took a longer view, Huertas seemed to be in pretty good shape. They were on track to make even more money in January than they had in December, which might be an indication that they'd survived the worst.

"I'm very nervous about saying such things, but it does seem we've turned a corner here. Maybe we've finally gotten to a place where there are enough people who want to be here night in and night out." He knocked on the nearest wooden table. If luck was part of success—and as the beneficiary of Pete Wells's two-hour wait at another place, Jonah had to admit that it was—then so was its darker side, superstition. He kept his optimism to himself rather than jinx everything, even as he resisted pressure from Nate to promote Max to sous chef and Jenni to executive sous just to be done with it. He had a couple of weeks, and he had a new line cook. He had a little more time.

And then, without warning, he had no time at all: Lina e-mailed her resignation to Jonah at the end of January, after less than a month on the job, without the nicety of two weeks' notice. She would pick up her stuff the next day. Jonah figured she had forgotten what it was like to work the line after three years as an executive chef—the sore feet, sore shoulders, another forearm burn, too many guests or too few, and the unyielding, split-second schedule, all of it on top of her family responsibilities. Nate wasn't interested in why she did it. Clearly she had "a shit attitude" and they'd be better off without her.

Jonah e-mailed her back. It would be wise of you to give us two weeks' notice, he wrote, because if you did you could list us as a place you worked. Without that, I can never help you out. Do not put us on your résumé.

Lina seemed not to care. She came in the next day, collected her tools, and disappeared, leaving Jonah exactly where he'd been almost four months earlier.

He had no choice but to do what he'd been avoiding for months—promote Max and hope for the best, and do it in a way that didn't rattle anyone else. They were adding the large-format dinners in a week, and he had to have everyone in place. He told Jenni first, because he also had to tell her that he wasn't quite ready to promote her to executive sous chef. If he'd hired someone from outside it would have been a necessity, to reassure her that she was in charge and to establish that she could tell the new sous what to do. With Max, what Jonah called "the leadership pyramid" was clear. Max had reported to Jenni when he was the senior line cook, and he would continue to do so as a sous chef.

She was a sous with no previous experience, nine months into her job, and she still had work to do on management skills. She knew it, particularly when it came to mistakes; Jenni tended to look for someone to blame for a problem rather than find a way to encourage a cook to do better so that it didn't happen again. She was on track and she was improving, so there was no need to worry, but Jonah didn't hand out promotions to make people happy. He'd promote her or give her equity when he decided it was time.

He sat down with Max next, to try to put his own philosophy to good use—not to bust him for bad habits but to inspire him to be a better role model, to help him find ways to build loyalty. Most sous chefs were promoted from within, which was good because the line cooks were familiar with their new boss, but bad if their shared history had any potholes. Max was obviously talented and had impressive skills, yet Jonah had written him up just a week earlier for not properly labeling food containers at the end of a shift, with both the contents and the date. It was hardly the first time he'd talked to Max about the need to work clean. Now Max would have to hold the other cooks accountable, which would cause resentment if he didn't lead by example.

Attitude mattered, too, as Jonah had learned after too many complaints about too little praise from the boss. Max sometimes adopted a pretty superior manner, and while he might be far more experienced than Alberto or Joe, the extern, he had to try not to flaunt it. "Your two favorite words should be 'please' and 'thank you,' and now I've added 'sorry,'" said Jonah. "I should say these more than I can count. If people are doing their best, you should thank them."

He reassured Alberto and Joe that he was aware of some friction between them and Max, he'd talked to Max about it, and he expected that Max was going to step up to the challenge of being a sous chef. If they thought otherwise, they had to come to Jonah with even the smallest problem. The last thing he wanted right now was to lose Alberto in the shuffle, so he gave him a bit of long-term good news—he could start training Joe to replace him at the fry station right away, so that he could finish his own training on roast and sauté.

Jonah wanted to be clear about the plan. Max was going to be Alyssa, with the title she hadn't had, and in a month or so Alberto would be ready to be Max, which meant working roast and sauté when Max was off, or when Max was expediting because Jonah and Jenni were off. By

March, Alberto would be working what he privately called the "make it or break it station."

Alberto had come as close as he ever had to a setback when Lina got hired and bumped him down, his progress toward dinner shifts suddenly blocked by a newcomer, the sort of chess move that made cooks look sideways for a more promising ascent. Now the same person who'd obstructed his rise had provided an opportunity he hadn't seen coming. He hadn't spent as much time on the fry station, all told, as he had at his entry-level job working the wood oven, and Jonah had just promised him dinner shifts if he didn't screw up.

And what came after slow dinner shifts? Fast ones. Alberto was in line to run the roast and sauté station on a Saturday night, and his first thought was that his girlfriend could not come in for that first weekend shift, no matter how much she wanted to be there. It was too much stress.

But he was getting ahead of himself. He needed to focus on right now, which was as exciting as it was unnerving. Thanks to a bunch of strangers—an unreliable line cook and a parade of flaky or unattainable sous applicants—Alberto was headed for the senior line-cook station for dinner service. Before his twenty-first birthday; before he had any right to expect it.

"That was fast," he thought.

With the new team in place for barely a week, Jenni asked for another meeting with Jonah, to make sure, she said, that they were still on the same page. She was worried about Max's attitude, worried about Alberto's inexperience, and worried that any of it would reflect poorly on her leadership while she was still a promotion and equity away from her goal.

Her future, as she saw it, included the promotion to executive sous and eventually to chef de cuisine, which would enable her to move out of the kitchen and into consulting just in time to have a personal life and a family. After that, she might have a food truck or open her own place, possibly as part of Jonah's company, which would make the start-up process much easier. She might even return to California for that step, although the possibility faded with every passing day. Wherever she ended up, the narrative she had in mind was one she'd been refining since the day she took the job at Maialino.

That was how Jenni saw her life—or at least how she presented it to Jonah. Privately she fretted over the consequences of getting what she wanted, because it would narrow her options. Jonah always said that she'd have to commit to five years before he'd consider making her a partner, which was where she got stuck, no matter how much she told herself that it was an essential part of her personal plan.

In five years Jenni would be thirty-one, which was fine if by then they had two or three restaurants and she was working anything close to normal hours. But what if they moved forward more slowly and she was tied to a business that ate up her time the way it did now? Thirty-one felt a little late to decide that she had to strike out on her own because things hadn't worked out as she'd hoped. It had taken Jonah two years to open Huertas, and he had the advantage of knowing people who were ready to loan him money. It would have taken longer if he'd had to go to strangers, which was what Jenni would have to do.

And thirty-one was too old to take a job at another restaurant because it could mean taking a step down to sous, or even to executive sous, by then, and having to work her way back up to chef de cuisine or executive chef, assuming that there was an opening. Something as simple as a boss who loved his job could keep her from moving forward, and she'd be stuck in a hierarchy that wouldn't budge, a salaried employee someplace else, her personal life still on hold. That was no progress at all.

It was so complicated. Jenni was in a hurry for proof—in part, she admitted, because she needed it too much. She assessed her self-esteem at "very low," which made reassurance more important than it might otherwise have been, and Jonah was slow with a compliment. Everyone in the kitchen knew: If he didn't say you were doing a bad job, you were doing a good job. That was as close as he usually got to praise, which was tough for Jenni to take.

"It's a weird coincidence," she said. "I have such a good job with a boss who doesn't compliment, when I'm a person who really needs a compliment." A partner's stake would be a big compliment, if the accompanying restrictions didn't bother her so much.

She knew what she wanted, wasn't sure if she liked the terms, and figured she had to keep pushing for the next step in case it turned out to be the right move. She couldn't idle in place; that was the one thing she knew for sure. But at the moment, she wasn't quite convinced that Huertas was going to get her where she wanted to go.

"There's such a back and forth in my head," she said.

The fraternity of professional chefs did not hang up a sign to welcome women and minorities to their ranks when Nancy Silverton and her contemporaries started out; kitchen equality was not high on the social-change agenda in the 1960s and 1970s except in places like Berkeley, where everything was up for grabs. Aspiring chefs were, by their nature, in it for themselves, looking for a way to express an individual creative vision on a plate. If a kitchen outsider prevailed, it had more to do with personality than with policy.

Silverton gave birth to her first child in 1982, on her day off, as though she could have willed away any conflict between work and home—and was back at Wolfgang Puck's Spago four days later, "obviously not full-time," she said, "but I was so driven that I wanted to see what everybody else was doing. And we know now, as experienced mothers, that really what happens the first six months is, they sleep. All you've got to do is feed them and change them, and they're sleeping." She had sacrificed "showers and sleep" when being the pastry assistant at Michael's meant getting to work at four in the morning, and she was prepared to continue to do so, and more if need be.

"Nothing is perfect," was how she saw it. There was no point in complaining, or, for that matter, in thinking about how gender might affect her professional future.

She liked to tell the story of her decision to become a chef, which involved a crush on a cook in a dormitory at Sonoma State—she told him that she loved to cook, wanted to work in the kitchen, and was a vegetarian, none of it true—because to her it illustrated her disregard for limitations. Silverton proudly ticked off the list of family members who inspired her: Great-aunt Mary, a suffragette who chained herself to the White House and landed in jail; Mary's sister, Evelyn, an International Ladies' Garment Workers' Union lobbyist; her mother, Doris, a longtime television writer, "political and very strong," as were her friends.

"It never occurred to me that I was a minority," she said. "It never occurred to me that women could be mistreated or misunderstood or left out, because I just wasn't brought up that way. I could do whatever I wanted."

Silverton attended Le Cordon Bleu in London and returned to Southern California after a stint at a Northern California restaurant, because it was the practical choice—a bigger restaurant scene meant more job opportunities. If the only available job at Michael's was working the computerized point-of-sale system at lunch, "a kitchen cashier," as she described it, Silverton would take it. Michael's was Santa Monica's answer to Chez Panisse, opened eight years later by twenty-five-year-old Michael McCarty, and Silverton wanted to work in his kitchen.

"I was old school," she said, "in the sense that all you had to do was get your foot in the door, prove yourself, and you'll move on."

The next opening was for an assistant pastry chef, which she took even though she had no desire to be a pastry chef. "Accepting that position was sort of similar to accepting the cashier's position," she said, "meaning that I had no interest in the sweet side of the kitchen." But Silverton worked with a chef who showed her how to maneuver in the "strict" world of desserts, to learn the science and then improvise without breaking the rules—which led to the job of pastry chef at Spago, and then to breads as well as pastries at her own La Brea Bakery. Eventually, she engineered a transition to the savory side.

She had come to think that having a balance of men and women in the kitchen "makes for a much more solid sort of cohesive, positive line," but she didn't set out to create that environment. If she employed enough women to occasionally staff an all-women line, it was a scheduling coincidence, not policy. Discussions of gender as a political issue seemed peripheral to Silverton because it had not been a factor in her own life. She had been raised not to think about it, so she didn't.

"I'm more of the camp, Shut up and let me work," she said.

As more women infiltrated the restaurant kitchen—once it became not a single chef and her forceful personality but a group of aspirants who wanted in—they bumped into backlash from men who had thought that the line was their exclusive province: Women often felt pressure to work harder than their male counterparts, to complete chores on their own when a man might reasonably have asked another man for help— only to be dismissed, if that work was acknowledged, by male colleagues who complained that women got special treatment.

Stephanie Izard blamed her chronic bad back on her I-can-do-it mentality, which too often involved lifting a full stockpot onto a burner to prove that she didn't need help doing so. Not that it improved her status with her peers: When she worked for chef Jean-Georges Vongerichten at Vong, he chose her to accompany him to a food event as a reward for all of her hard work. She still remembers coworkers muttering about her being singled out because she was a girl.

It wasn't possible to have a logical conversation with someone who felt that way, so Izard worked even harder, as though she could put more mileage between herself and the accusation. Jenni had been comparatively lucky in her career choices so far—the kitchens she'd worked in were far less contentious—but it wasn't possible to legislate equality in a restaurant kitchen. There was no way to ensure that the next job, if it ever came to that, would be in as supportive an atmosphere as the one Jonah provided.

The conversation about women chefs had gotten louder over the past few years, punctuated by things like *Time* magazine's 2013 cover story, "The Gods of Food," with three male chefs on the cover and not a single female chef on the list. Some women felt that stressing gender, accepting the label of woman chef, was a good way to highlight how few women ran kitchens, how far from parity the industry still was—even if they considered themselves chefs, not women chefs. Others felt as though women chefs, along with chefs identified by any race other than Caucasian, occupied a new half step on the American kitchen ladder, somewhere above chef de cuisine but definitely below chef. They heard an implied slight in their hyphenate status as a woman chef or an African American chef; they weren't full-fledged.

They agreed on one thing: It was harder to get ahead and, for those who did, to figure out how to handle success. The idea of a work-life balance hadn't existed when Silverton was coming up, not for anyone, men or women, though for women it was perceived as more of a problem. Izard had only recently arrived at the belief that she could in fact manage work and family, but it required preplanning, the imposed discipline of an annual three-task list, and strenuous effort; her instincts still told her to be at her restaurants all day, every day, a vestige of her earlier determination to prove herself in a room full of men.

Jonah and Marina could decide to start a family tomorrow and it would have no bearing on him physically—and as the owner, he could craft an accommodating schedule without worrying that an unenlightened boss might regard him as less of a contender for a promotion. For that matter, he didn't have to wonder if an imaginary narrow-minded boss already had him on a secondary list based on gender. It wasn't the sort of thing a job applicant could inquire about in an interview.

Huertas was safe for Jenni because Jonah clearly didn't care about anything but ability; he'd had a diverse kitchen from the day the restaurant opened. Huertas was risky because it might not grow fast enough to allow her to have a life outside of the kitchen—and yet safer than the unknown. Jenni vacillated about the commitment a partnership required because she had not one but two timelines to consider—the chronology of a chef's life, a narrow, short path that was hard to maneuver no matter who you were, and the women's version, which could be narrower and shorter still, depending on where she worked.

15

THE RISING STAR

Friends congratulated Jonah on all the attention Huertas got—and it did, by any comparative standard, between the stories, reviews, and year-end lists. He knew that, and yet he felt as though he were still asking for attention rather than dictating, nowhere near having to fend off media inquiries like some of the marquee names who could generate a headline, it seemed, merely by getting dressed and walking out the door. Danny Meyer joked that all he had to do to start a website rumor about a new venture was to peer in the window of a vacant space within range of someone with a cell phone. Social media and dedicated food sites were the hungriest customers around, which in turn made traditional media scramble to be faster on the uptake: Anything that well-known chefs and restaurateurs did was worth mentioning simply because they did it, or mentioned that at some point in the future they might consider doing it, or announced that it was out of the question. They were news incarnate.

Newer, less famous chefs and restaurateurs hustled to find a headline-worthy tidbit to offer. Jonah's Valentine's Day menu had to be set a month early not because he naturally worked that way but because the publicist needed it to show to website staffers. By February he had begun to wonder what story he could tell to avoid a repetition of the previous summer's soul-crunching quiet—but in the meantime, while he tried to come up with a worthy idea for a big story, he issued endless Instagram posts and tweets, as much a part of prep as roasting bones for stock or setting up a mise en place. Jonah, Jenni, and Nate perfected the cell phone hover and swoop, often in the middle of service, and posted photos of anything that looked like fun—finished dishes, happy staffers, sumptuous produce, the bustling front room—even though they had fewer than 3,000 Instagram followers and 2,000 on Twitter, in a world where David Chang had over 350,000 and 150,000, respectively.

The pintxo takeover—guest chefs doing their versions of pintxos, first Monday of the month starting in March—merited a brief announcement on Eater on February 18, which Jonah and Nate hoped would start a profitable cross-pollination with the visiting chefs' social media followers. They dreamed about having Mario Batali or David Chang accept an invitation someday, but for now they turned to friends who stood to gain as much as they contributed, in terms of exposure: Wilson Tang, the owner of Nom Wah Tea Parlor, who'd advised Jonah about the community board; Jean-Paul Bourgeois, Jonah's friend who was now the executive chef at Blue Smoke; Waltuck and Hoffman and a onetime Savoy chef de cuisine who'd opened and closed his own place and was between jobs.

That same day, Jonah got the kind of news he couldn't engineer: The James Beard Foundation included him on its list of two dozen semifinalists for the Rising Star Award, given annually to a chef under thirty who shows great promise. He scanned the list and figured he had no chance of making the finalist list, issues of talent aside; there were only three nominees from New York City, one a woman chef in Brooklyn and one a much-lauded African American chef in Harlem. The rest of the list reflected the kind of New York City backlash that had led Gavin Kaysen—himself the Rising Star winner in 2008—to decamp for Minneapolis. One way or another, whether because of a demographic or geographic imperative, this year's winner was probably not going to be a white male chef from New York City, and Jonah couldn't quite argue with that, as nice as it would be to win.

Jonah's off-menu chistorra hot dog had become so popular that he and Nate set up a meeting with their contractor, Nick Thatos, to talk about installing a new facade, replacing the horizontal windows with vertical ones that opened farther so that they could sell hot dogs all summer. Shake Shack had just ended its first day of trading on the New York Stock Exchange at a valuation of $1.6 billion, higher than expected, with a share priced at over $45, up from $21 the day before the launch. Jonah and Nate had no illusions about a Shake Shack–sized response, but they did have a hot dog, sales might translate into more people visiting the restaurant, and they had an opportunity to grab people's attention: Florence Fabricant, a veteran *New York Times* food writer, had asked if someone from the restaurant could drop off samples for her.

Three hot dogs, from the East Village to the *Times* on Eighth Avenue and West Forty-First Street, still warm, the Martin's potato rolls not soggy, the greens not wilted from sitting between the warm roll and the hot dog, the aioli and mustard not puddled together. Nate wasn't taking any chances sending a staffer, nor would he waste precious time walking blocks to the subway stop and standing on the platform. Jonah could wrap each element individually and pack everything up. Nate would take a cab straight to the *Times* and assemble the hot dogs at the last minute, in the lobby. He would hand them to Fabricant himself.

The only variables he didn't consider were street traffic, which made the subway alternative seem like a breeze, and the open design of the building's lobby, which wasn't conducive to prep work. A frazzled Nate announced himself at the *Times* security desk and convinced one of the guards to let him use the desk as a temporary workstation, to put the samples together before the columnist got downstairs. He worried that they hadn't traveled well—these were designed to be eaten immediately, not taken for a sluggish drive across town—but the buns weren't too wrinkled, the hot dogs weren't too cold, and it was all better than premade sandwiches would have been.

Fabricant's assistant appeared, whisked away the hot dogs, and left Nate in the lobby, hopeful, yet frustrated that he hadn't met the columnist herself and in need of feedback. He got an e-mail from one staffer who said only that the hot dogs had disappeared immediately, which sounded like good news even if it was secondhand.

"Add chistorra to your hot dog lexicon," began the short item in Fabricant's March 9 column, which dubbed the hot dog the "Basque dog" and went on to describe the pork chistorra and list the accompaniments. The only way to get the hot dog was to ask for it, because it wasn't on the Huertas menu. It was an insider special, set up that way to give it a bit of cachet, even if insider now meant the almost 2.2 million people who read the weekday *Times* in print and online.

Five days later food websites blared breaking news from the South by Southwest festival in Austin, Texas: David Chang had introduced the prototype for his new fast-food crispy chicken sandwich, to be sold at Fuku, whose first outpost would soon appear in the First Avenue space previously occupied by his high-end tasting menu restaurant, Momofuku Ko, just three blocks from Huertas. He cited the Chick-fil-A and In-N-Out Burger fast-food chains as the inspiration for the concept and an accompanying app—and blithely addressed the question of how well it would do, from the fairly unassailable perch of a chef with a strong brand that already offered diners a range of experiences.

"If the fried chicken sandwich is fantastic, and if the app is fantastic, great," he said. "But if it bombs completely, great. Out of those ashes something amazing will happen."

The agenda for the partners' third off-site meeting was short, and Nate wanted Jonah to understand the stakes: They had to give up the menu del dia. If they did, they'd be okay. If they didn't, "Summer's going to be like the last two weeks," he said, referring to a frightening dip, 125 fewer covers than they'd projected. "Times ten."

There wasn't time to try to figure out the sudden dive, which failed to meet even their most conservative projections of a single turn on weekday evenings and a turn and a half on weekends. And the liquor license wasn't going to come fast enough to save them: The lawyer was trying to get them back on the SLA agenda, but the board was getting a new director, which meant scheduling delays, so Levey had started to talk about a possible return to the community board. Wherever they landed, they would not be serving cocktails for their first-year anniversary on April 22.

They could no longer afford to discuss whether to make the change. The question now was how to do it, and how fast. Jonah needed to expand the front room à la carte menu and serve it throughout the restaurant— and they needed to make this look like preference, not necessity.

They had no choice, even though Jonah wasn't sure that the à la carte numbers would work any better. "My fears aren't conceptual," he told Nate. "It's more the bottom line. We're making a commitment and a bet—that simplifying the menu will bring in more people." He worried about how they'd compensate for losing the higher prices on the dining-room menu. They'd have to increase volume substantially to improve the numbers.

Nate had anticipated Jonah's concern and done some projections. If they eliminated the menu del dia they would have to raise the average check by $10, to $53, minimum, to make the same amount of money they were making now. And that wasn't really enough, as they both knew—they wouldn't be having this conversation if revenues were healthy. A jump of $12, to $55 for an average check, would be safer.

"Not insignificant," said Jonah.

"Not insignificant," allowed Nate.

"But possible," said Jonah.

"Or we can raise it only to $50, not $55," said Nate, "and then we have to add nine covers per service. Significant. Or raise to $52. That's six more covers a day." He had run every conceivable permutation; they were not leaving the little East Village restaurant they'd chosen for their conversation until this was resolved.

"Possible," said Jonah. He considered the obstacles: He'd have to figure out portion size for chicken breasts, for shared plates versus individual servings, and he might have to change the price on the duck. He worried about raising prices too high, and about how many dishes felt like enough of a choice, and about the impact on labor costs. People who liked to share small plates would be fine, but what about people who liked to have their own dinner? He wanted them to feel that they got enough food.

He tried to stick to the practicalities, but the timing was bad, and he wanted Nate to understand that. Jonah had just returned from a short belated honeymoon in Mexico that included dinner at Hartwood, a restaurant on the Caribbean coast of the Yucatán Peninsula run by two New York exiles who had turned a strip of land between the beach and the jungle into a destination for diners who would go anywhere for a remarkable meal. They relied on a wood-burning oven and a grill, ran the place on solar power, and cooked what they wanted to serve, no social media chatter, no make-or-break reviews, no new competitors every ten minutes.

Jonah came back inspired and frustrated. If it were up to him, in a vacuum, he'd do even more ambitious food in the dining room, head in the opposite direction from where this conversation was taking them. He'd come away from Hartwood and a handful of Mexico City restaurants thinking, "I can fucking cook better than this." But that was going to have to wait for a couple of years, if he got the chance at all.

Pete Wells may have extolled Jonah's ability to tell a story with the dining-room menu, to put together a meal that made sense from start to finish rather than indulge in showpiece dishes, but great food seemed to be bad for business, at least in this configuration, and they had to give it up.

Jonah was silent for a moment more. In truth, the menu del dia kept Jonah tied to the kitchen doing the kinds of things a chef ought to delegate to his cooks. It made no sense to teach Max or Alberto how to execute a dish if it was going to disappear when the menu changed a week later—it was faster simply to do it himself than to demonstrate, supervise, and intervene if it didn't go the way he wanted it to. That was a fundamental problem he hadn't seen coming: The dining-room menu fairly guaranteed that he couldn't back off to three days a week, which in turn meant that he'd never have the time to develop the next project.

"First-year anniversary?" he asked.

"Later in the spring," said Nate, with relief. "And we make it a media event. Blow-out tasting menus, get it while it lasts, blow people's minds for two months, and launch this after Memorial Day. You win the James Beard, and then . . ."

"Don't count on that," Jonah said.

Nate ignored him. Now that Jonah was onboard, they could get the publicist involved. There ought to be a long feature that cast all of this in a positive light.

The decision wore both of them out, and they lingered over their coffee, knowing that in a few minutes they'd have to head over to Huertas to get to work. Jonah wanted to talk instead about a new large-format menu he had in mind, an homage to something Peter Hoffman used to do on grills he set up on the street behind Back Forty—and to the tradition that inspired it. A Spanish calçotada celebrated the seasonal arrival of the Spanish calçot, a larger, milder cousin of the scallion that was charred and served with grilled lamb, along with wine poured directly into the diner's mouth from a porrón, a large pitcher with a long, tapered spout. Jonah didn't have a grill, and he still didn't have a working wood oven, but he could slow-roast the lamb and finish it on the flat-top, and use the salamander to get a good char on spring leeks, which would serve as a stand-in for the calçot. It was authentic Spanish food that required finesse to get it right, a nice thing to contemplate as he prepared to abandon the idea that had propelled him since he'd carried it around in his backpack to show to potential investors.

Nate was more interested in a couple of other new ideas, including take-out lunch service later in the spring, or a cart outside the new Whitney Museum during the block party to celebrate its May opening. It was too late to be a vendor at the party, but they could set up at the periphery.

"Maybe," said Jonah, who seemed done with decisions for the day. "Sounds like a headache."

. . .

Jenni's one-year anniversary with Huertas was at the end of March, and when she pointed it out to Jonah he said it was time to make some moves, sat her down in the dining room, and, without preamble, handed over a box of new business cards for Jenni Cianci, executive sous chef. He announced the promotion at the afternoon lineup, and the response was unanimous: Everyone already thought that Jenni was the executive sous, but sure, congratulations, now that reality had caught up with consensus.

She was gratified, if not quite as happy as she'd anticipated. The fact that he'd had to order the business cards in advance—that he'd already made up his mind—slipped past her, because she was focused on the fact that she'd mentioned her anniversary before he gave her the box. It felt as though she'd had to ask.

The next day Jonah's forecast came true, and then some: None of the three New York semifinalists made the list of finalists for the 2015 James Beard Rising Star Award. The foundation saw the future in Chicago, Philadelphia, Washington, D.C.; in Brunswick, Maine, and Los Angeles and Los Gatos, California.

Alberto could feel a busy night coming. The noise in the restaurant seemed to drop away, and all he could hear was "Fire, fire, fire," fast, one order after another.

It's coming, he told himself. Go in, do it, don't talk. Jonah was off, which meant that Jenni was expediting, Max was plating and overseeing the line cooks, and Alberto was on roast and sauté. Alberto had made himself even more nervous, the first few weeks on roast and sauté, by thinking about just how busy it was going to get and how many hours it would last—which bothered Max, who'd see the tight expression on Alberto's face, and tell him to relax, in front of everyone, which didn't make it any easier. Still, Max was right. Nerves were contagious. If Jonah thought that Alberto was competent to work the station, Alberto needed to act as though it were true.

It was hard at first, because it had happened so fast, and because he worked for three bosses with different management styles: Jonah, who got quieter when he was concerned; Jenni, who talked her way through a tense service, and Max, whose style Alberto thought of as "just get out of my way." When Alberto felt Jonah looking at him, he sped up and waited to see if a correction was coming, and took a breath only when Jonah looked away. When Jenni talked at him, he tried to respond without losing his rhythm. When Max bulldozed past, he tried not to take it personally. He expended a lot of energy on accommodation, even as he tried to keep up with the pace. He was determined not to be the one who landed the kitchen in trouble.

On a rough night he did a lot of short sprints from the burners to the shelves to the cooling drawers or the counter, not yet having achieved Alyssa's economy of motion, his heart racing as he tried to go as fast as he could without making a mistake. By the end of March he slid into a regular schedule, working the station Thursday through Monday from two in the afternoon to close, with his weekend on Tuesday and Wednesday. Not that his heart stopped pounding; it didn't. But the frantic rhythm at least become somewhat familiar, and the fear of the unexpected yielded to a more manageable fear of falling behind, which was something a cook had to learn to live with—to turn into a positive force—forever.

Saturday nights were the worst, most of the time, but the last Sunday in March promised to be a logistical nightmare: There was a buyout in the back room, thirty-six people arriving at six p.m. for a birthday celebration, and seven tables for the large-format dinner, and Jonah was off. Alberto could sense Jenni's apprehension, which seemed to him the only reasonable response to this kind of schedule.

Big parties were always a challenge—all that food at once—but the night started off with too many special requests, the sort of adjustments that could rattle a kitchen even when there wasn't a party of thirty-six. Jenni was calling volume orders—thirty-one duck croquetas—as the custom orders started to come in from individual diners scattered throughout the restaurant:

No fish for one of the women in the back.

No gildas at a table in the front.

No mackerel.

"Fine. Four croquetas and a morcilla tortilla," said Jenni, refusing to be derailed so close to opening. "Allergies all over the place," she muttered.

She stopped Max from using the wrong sauce to anchor an order of croquetas to the plate, encouraged the new fry cook to set out his empty plates in advance before the next batch came out of the deep fryer, and spun around to help Max with plating, even as she kept an eye on the ticket printer and wondered why two croquetas were still sitting at the pass, waiting either for a server to notice them or a cook to finish an order. Just as she was about to inquire, ten more appeared, and a server whisked them away.

Nate leaned over the pass to ask why two women at a front table said that they'd been sitting there for a half hour waiting for their food.

"Seriously, what did they order?" said Jenni, instantly on edge. She looked for the ticket in the row in front of her. "A tortilla and what, fifty dollars of food? Give them the food unless you think it's bad for business."

Nate spun and headed over to the table, came back to the pass, studied the ticket again, and returned to the table, muttering to himself. It was barely six thirty, the rush hadn't even hit yet, and the kitchen had taken too long on an order. One of the experienced servers, aware of how easy it was for a kitchen to fall apart on a night like this, gave Jenni a big smile.

"Look at you," he said, proudly. "I mean, just look at you. Three chicken dinners and not even a bead of sweat."

She smiled for the first time since service started and gestured at the row of tickets. "And everyone has an allergy," she said, wiggling her fingers on either side of her besieged head. "Aaaaahhhh!"

Another server came back with a second bulletin from the dissatisfied two-top. One of the women had announced that they did not want to be interrupted by passed pintxos. They wanted their food to come out in courses, as it was supposed to.

Jenni put a new paper roll in the printer and stared, in horror, as a handful of backed-up order tickets spit at her. She glanced up and saw a man standing in the aisle looking lost and impatient, holding a credit card aloft, and dispatched a server to get him his check. She got the orders under control—food was flying out of the kitchen—and started to feel that she had found her rhythm, but satisfaction didn't last long. Nate returned with the two-top's final complaint of the evening: Their churros with chocolate dipping sauce were late.

She watched as one of them walked past the kitchen to the restroom and passed judgment: She did not like the woman's face, her expression, or her clothes, neither the top nor the pants. While she hated to reward the two women for what she considered to be excessive demands, they hadn't spent that much, and the easiest solution might be to comp the whole check and send them home happy at least about that. Nate agreed, but only up to a point: He dropped a check that showed no charge for several items, to let the women know that he'd registered and acknowledged their dissatisfaction, and perhaps to send a subtle message: We didn't comp the whole thing because we know, and you know, that you overdid the complaints. It might make them feel too guilty to badmouth the restaurant.

The birthday party buyout had its own syncopated rhythm, which had nothing to do with a standard meal—there were toasts and more toasts, speeches and random interruptions, requests to hold a course or serve a course or drop the volume of the music or turn it up again. Everyone pitched in to keep the kitchen moving, including one of the bartenders, who between drink orders ferried a few stacks of dishes to the shelves under the pass, so that the dishwasher could stay at his station and catch up. Nate ran plates to waiting tables.

Still, carrots went to a table lukewarm. Fish came out less than done. Eight chicken dinners came out for an order of seven. The kitchen was so crowded with people trying to help that the dishwasher couldn't get from the back of the kitchen to the front with the next stack of clean dishes. He had to circle outside the kitchen and weave past customers to get to the shelves under the pass.

In the midst of it all, one of the hosts stationed at the front door approached Nate and Jenni: A woman was on the phone wanting to know if she could turn her party of seven into a party of nine. She knew it was late, she knew it was a squeeze, but please?

Nate pulled his hand sideways across his throat.

"No. We can't do it."

"What do I say to her?"

"Tell her we can't do it. No. She's calling too late to ask for that."

A server rushed up to interrupt: A customer with a crustacean allergy worried that whatever she had ordered might be cooked in the same oil as the octopus, and she didn't want to get sick. Jenni was in the midst of decorating a display birthday cake and answered without looking up.

Octopus isn't a crustacean, she told the server. It's a cephalopod. It doesn't matter what oil we cook things in. She won't get sick.

Then she countermanded Nate and told the host to accommodate the table of seven that had become a table of nine. Jenni was in charge of the kitchen, and if they could handle this much activity, they could handle more. She was not going to turn away business.

Things threatened to get out of hand at every turn. The dishwasher's arms barely came into focus, he was moving so fast, but clean cutlery wasn't the last step—before it hit the table it was supposed to be polished to eliminate any water spots. Nate had a box full of clean flatware that he couldn't polish fast enough to keep up with demand, so he grabbed a passing bartender by the elbow as he walked past and hissed, *"We don't have any silverware"* in an urgent whisper. The bartender broke away because he had orders for bottles of wine that in his estimation mattered more than spotless knives and forks. One of the servers stepped over to help Nate, in between running plates of food, and as soon as the bartender dropped off the bottles he joined them at a crowded corner of the pass.

Jenni madly portioned almond cake for the back room and stared at the plates; the cake might be delicious, but it was pretty plain to look at. She tried adding whipped cream around the slices, wasn't satisfied, added more sugar to the aerosol canister full of already-sweetened cream, and tried again. She spooned a dollop of Max's homemade bitter orange marmalade onto each plate, which added color and kept the whole thing from being too sweet, and sent out the cake just as the strains of "Happy Birthday" floated up from the dining room, at which point she went back to hacking up whole chickens for the large-format orders.

She reached over to grab the next ticket from the order printer, which she'd ignored while she decorated the cakes, and three tickets came out in one long snake. Jenni recoiled.

"My god," she said, "I didn't think it was going to be that long."

Nate took small revenge on the last-minute table of nine by seating them as a party of five and a party of four and requiring that they order two large-format dinners, not one. The dinners were designed to serve a maximum of six, so even seven was a stretch. Nine people didn't get to hold down all that real estate to divide a large-format meal into appetizer portions.

They presented Nate with nine credit cards at the end of the meal.

"I'll take four," he said, trying to remain polite. "Four. You figure it out."

A few days later, Jonah showed up for work with a side part in his hair, which was still not long enough to have a sense of direction but long enough to hold a part. In three weeks Huertas would be a year old. Eater had decided to do a long story on the big changes in store for Huertas's second year; the one-year minimum wait on a full liquor license was almost up; and Jonah and Nate were about to spend $20,000 of Huertas's post-review profits not only on new front windows but on new tables to replace the standing counter in front, a smaller counter to replace the table between the windows and the bar, and glass doors for the back wall of the dining room, to bring in more light. It was time to present a more mature profile.

"I figure it was a haircut for a very young kid," he said, referring to the old $15 brush cut. "And now that I'm older I should have a part."

16

FUN

There was something sobering about an anniversary. It forced a summary, a fill-in-the-blank finish to the sentence that began, Our first year was _____, and too many of the options tipped toward the negative. Our first year was unresolved, uncertain, unlicensed. Jonah was good at fending off day-to-day problems, but it was hard to evaluate a whole year. Could it have been better? Sure. That much better? Probably not, but that was small consolation. The high points that a more detached observer might have tallied—the *Times* review, the overall improvement ever since, the upcoming Eater story where he and Nate could control the spin on the menu change—looked too small, from Jonah's point of view.

He could quantify his success in all kinds of ways—he'd survived a scary first summer, the new menu seemed like a smart hedge against a repeat of that slump in a couple of months, and he had great reviews and lots of coverage for someone who didn't already have a brand to promote. By any objective measure, Jonah was about to celebrate a first year that had exceeded expectations—but he was having a hard time accessing any sense of accomplishment. All the good news existed on a happy distant plain that he could barely make out from a kitchen that refused to align, no matter how hard he tried.

At ten o'clock in the morning, a week before Huertas's one-year anniversary, Jonah was alone in the kitchen, chopping carrots and celery for stock, which he had sworn he would not be doing by now but found hard to hand over to anyone else. His mood was in free fall. He was as unhappy as he had been since he started looking for a space—which didn't mean that he had been unhappy then, because he wasn't, but rather that none of the disappointments since then had made him as blue as he felt now. He confessed as much to Jenni when she got in and she pushed back, insisting that she'd seen him unhappier at various points along the way. He wouldn't be argued out of it. This was the low point of his short tenure as a chef-owner, and if she looked at the newly revised schedule for April 22, anniversary night, she'd understand why. Jonah was at the pass, Jenni was working the roast and sauté station, and Max had stepped down to fry because it was Alberto's night off and the regular fry cook had left unexpectedly, after some vague mutterings about how he needed to leave the country immediately. A year in, and he still didn't have the kitchen set up the way he wanted it.

Anyone driven enough to want his own restaurant by the time he was twenty-three was probably never going to be satisfied—and Nate was Jonah's front-of-house equal in terms of the age-success equation, so he walked around with a similar cloud over his head as the anniversary approached. They lost their compensatory rhythm, in which the happier one at any given moment talked his partner out of a darker mood. They agreed only on their shared dissatisfaction. Whatever their specific goals had been on the day Huertas opened, they had redefined success: It was more than they had at any given moment.

The unspoken tension finally bubbled over into an inevitable fight about nothing, in the middle of service, at the pass, where anyone could hear them. Jonah forgot to fire a cauliflower puree, so the entrée went out without it. When he realized that a customer's dinner was missing its side dish, he yelled at one of the new servers, "Why didn't you take the cauliflower puree?"

Before she could say anything, Nate stepped in. "Because you didn't *tell* us," he said. "I haven't even *seen* this dish."

"I put it up on Monday," said Jonah.

"We have four people here on Monday," said Nate. The rest of the front-of-house staff needed to know about new dishes, because otherwise they couldn't tell if one of them was missing. That was a simmering gripe: Sometimes Jonah added a new item without letting all the front-of-house people know about it—and even if they did know, they didn't always get to taste it first, which meant that they couldn't sound as smart as Nate wanted them to.

"Should I have put it up *twice*?" Jonah shot back, struck by the impracticality of consulting the schedule to make sure that everyone got to taste a cauliflower puree. It was a side dish, not a new entrée they wanted to promote. "What about food costs?"

Nate didn't know what to say. From his perspective, how could they not spend whatever it cost to make another batch of cauliflower puree for the staff? He wasn't suggesting a steak for every server.

They weren't really arguing about cauliflower, but about partnership and direction and pace and mutual respect. Nate's head swam with unresolved concerns: The octopus portions were too small, Jonah spent too much time in the kitchen and not enough establishing himself as a chef people recognized—and Nate still worried that the food wasn't sufficiently smart and cool. Worse, Jonah had dismissed Nate's suggestion that they start the new à la carte menu after Memorial Day because he,

Jonah, thought it better to start in early May, and he'd done so in front of staffers, which to Nate skated close to insult.

On top of that, Nate had started up a conversation with a manager at a new place he'd tried out, and the guy had never heard of Huertas. The Eater reporter was coming in the day after the restaurant's anniversary to do a long interview for the stand-alone piece on the first year and the new plan, and yet people in the industry didn't even know it existed. There was no insider buzz, despite all the stories that had preceded this one. So what good was more coverage, after all? It wasn't as though a year's worth of stories had raised their profile.

That was Nate's all-encompassing gripe: Huertas was not yet on anyone's short list.

There was no place to go with that during service, and they could hardly keep bickering about cauliflower. Nate turned his back, charged downstairs, grabbed his bicycle, and headed out the front door to take a ride, too upset to do his job.

Jonah couldn't decide to storm out of the kitchen, so he kept calling orders until Nate got back, and then he took a quick break so that they could go downstairs to the office and talk things out before they got any worse. Yes, the new menu was going to make a difference, and yes, they had to sit down together to make sure they agreed on what they wanted to tell the writer from Eater. Yes, they would make sure, together, that the servers knew everything they needed to know about the new food. They agreed that anniversaries, by their nature, were tough, because such a milestone raised a second, more difficult question: Where did you think you'd be by now?

That was the one thing they agreed on: Further was where they thought they'd be. The idea that they'd be ready to open a second place in the fall of 2015 now seemed a naive joke, and any talk of paying off investors in even four years seemed more wistful than likely. Weekly figures were back to exceeding their projections, but that was part of what frustrated them. They were in pretty good shape—very good, when compared to their first summer, and yet nowhere near Nate's list of the restaurant groups everyone talked about and followed. There was an obvious explanation—the groups on that list were years older, so it was an unfair comparison—but in truth, many of them had drawn crowds from the beginning. It was hard not to wonder if explosive success had a best-by date stamped on it, if after a while a decent profile became a permanent condition, and it was too late to aspire to more.

That skated too close to surrender. By the time they were done sorting out their grievances, they were back to questions of what to do next. The shorthand goal was simple: They wanted to be on what Jonah called people's "'Oh, I really want to go there' lists," and all of their coming decisions had to be based on that.

The sign went up on the front door on Wednesday afternoon: CLOSING AT 8 FOR FIRST ANNIVERSARY.

All soul-searching was put on temporary hold at the afternoon lineup meeting, when Nate showed up toting a porrón that was full to the brim with cava. He'd instructed everyone to show up for the meeting prepared to share a favorite memory from the past year—and as their reward, he held the porrón aloft, a good two feet above a kneeling staffer's head, and poured a slow stream of wine until the recipient made some indication that it was time to stop.

One server recalled the night when Jonah and the bartender had attempted to eject a drunken participant in the city's annual SantaCon bar crawl after he'd stumbled in to use the bathroom—only to get tangled up in the vestibule they'd bought to enclose the entryway during the winter months, as Jenni fretted that the Santa was undoubtedly from a wealthy and powerful family and would sue, putting Huertas out of business. The server tipped her head back; Nate poured.

Max remembered worrying that Jenni hated him because the first batches of churros he tried to make kept exploding in the deep fryer, which was not only messy but dangerous. He smiled at Nate. "Porrón me," he said.

One fairly new server was happy that people liked the playlists he put together; an even newer guy offered a memory from his previous job because he didn't yet have any from Huertas. Laura, a server who'd been at Huertas since the beginning, remembered how grateful she was to learn that she wouldn't have to work brunch service.

Nate's dominant memory was of his anxiety level in the moments before the *Times* review hit; on a happier note, he recalled dancing at the holiday party with Lance, the dishwasher, who was more than a full head taller than Nate. He fell to his knees, tilted his chin, and said "Porrón me," as Stew cheered him on and someone started humming the theme from the movie *2001: A Space Odyssey*.

When it was Jonah's turn, he thanked Nate first, sarcastically, for not giving him a heads-up about the assignment so that he could have been prepared. But he had an answer: One of his favorite memories was the first day of training, when he tried to show Jenni how to make churros and couldn't get the fryer to light. By then, with opening day so close, every glitch felt like an apocalypse, and his first reaction was to worry that the gas connection was the problem. He was already on the phone with the plumber when Jenni checked the connection on a tube that led from the main gas line to the fryer. It wasn't properly locked into a metal holder at the fryer end, so she simply clicked it into place— a minor but essential move from a sous who had helped her dad fix things around the house. They could start making churros.

"I had an idea of what I wanted, but no idea of how to get there," he said. "I guess I've learned that things like the fryer happen every day. So Day One of training, that's it for me."

A server approached him with the porrón and he gave her the boss's stare. "I am not kneeling," he said, with a small smile. "You can get on a chair."

They consulted the reservation list, which they'd cut off early to get the party started. The final table was booked for eight o'clock. The plan was to be celebrating no later than ten.

The restaurant was full of balloons, including an enormous pink pig balloon and an even larger white octopus that floated over the service station. Jonah was there but not there, at least at first: Jenni would run the kitchen while he devoted himself to party food, "so people don't drink so much they get sloppy." He was making pressed sandwiches on baguettes the length of a sheet pan—pulled pork, cheese, piquillo peppers "to make it more Spanish," and, he said sheepishly, "because it's what we have." He separated the loaves of bread with rolled cylinders of aluminum foil, an old catering trick he'd learned to keep the filling from squishing out the sides when he pressed the sandwiches.

It wasn't a busy night, not with the early closure, so Jonah and Nate stood at the pass discussing the packaging for the hot dog window, which Nick intended to install in the coming week. Shake Shack put its hot dogs in cardboard containers inside rectangular paper bags with handles cut into them, but Nate knew a designer who said he could come up with something that looked more like a popcorn bag—just pop the hot dog in the bag—and they could save money by stamping the outside with their logo rather than pay for it to be printed. Jonah wondered if they might need some cardboard reinforcement in the bottom of the bag to keep the hot dog sitting right. Jenni, eager to have input, suggested traditional pleated-paper hot dog holders.

They talked about the new menu, too—Nate's victory, because it didn't include chicken. There were sweetbreads, and shrimp dumplings, and the pulpo orders would be three big pieces of octopus. The new duck entrée was on tonight's menu for a test run. Having vented all of their distress in the fight over a plate of cauliflower puree, Jonah and Nate focused on what came next and cheered themselves up with one eye on the clock. When Stew came by to ask what he ought to say to latecomers, Nate was adamant: Tell them we're closing early.

The last call at the bar was at nine fifteen. Five minutes later, Jonah raised his arm in a cutoff gesture and announced, "Two hot dogs, two duck, and I am done cooking for the night." He took off his apron with a flourish and headed downstairs to change out of his chef's shirt.

Nate and a couple of servers ferried tubs of drinks and iced beer upstairs, and Nate filled the porrón with something he slyly called punch. Jonah set hotel pans on top of his trays of sandwiches, weighted the pans with cast-iron skillets, and loaded everything into the oven. Servers ran downstairs in drab work clothes and emerged in party clothes that ranged from bright dresses to a clean shirt over dark pants, followed by the kitchen staff once cleanup was done.

It was not quite as manic a party as the *Times* review celebration had been, as there was no suspense or relief attached to a day on the calendar. People drank too much and tried to remember to have a sandwich—and Jonah and Nate, mindful of the visit from the Eater writer the very next day, tried to modulate their behavior to ensure that they'd be at their clearheaded best for the interview.

17

NEXT

It was just past six o'clock on an indecisive night in early June: The clean afternoon sunlight had congealed into a flat sky and thick air, and the humidity made people linger outside because they figured they might get caught in the rain later on. They sat on stoops, or meandered toward home with none of the urgency that marked the centers of finance and business to the north and south; even if locals worked there, their pace seemed to slow once they hit the neighborhood. Clots of longtime residents stood in front of the corner produce market or the Laundromat. Dogs dreamed of autumn.

Nate and Jonah sliced across East Fourth Street like visitors from an alien planet, dressed as though it were, in fact, September, which was as close as they got to business attire—dark cotton pants and darker-still shirts, Nate's a deep maroon, Jonah's navy verging on black. On an easygoing block, they vibrated with anxiety.

They were item 27 on the community board licensing subcommittee's agenda for Monday, June 8, the last on a roster of eight applicants for liquor licenses, except that they'd been told to be ready at the start of the six thirty meeting. The numerical agenda, it seemed, had little to do with reality.

This was the first step in a two-step strategy that Levey had devised to get them approved without further delay, one way or another, even though it required a short wait past the one-year mark for the local and state schedules to align. If the community board approved the application, the SLA would rubber-stamp it. If the community board balked again, which they shouldn't, he had Huertas on the SLA agenda a week later and was ready to inform the new director that the previous one had as much as promised a license at the one-year mark, which had already passed.

Jonah and Nate had been courting regulars for weeks, encouraging them to show up to speak on behalf of the full license—and this time they had cherry-picked supporters who lived or worked in the area, or both, mindful that last April they'd imported speakers from the Upper West Side, which only reinforced their carpetbagger status. They had collected petition signatures, letters of support, and an information packet that ran close to one hundred pages, one copy for each committee member.

All of which either meant something or nothing, depending on how they felt at any given moment. They had been turned down by this committee and by the SLA, ambushed both times by resistance they hadn't seen coming. What if it happened again? The rational part of Nate's brain was sure it wouldn't, because they'd passed the one-year mark. The irrational part kept him from making so much as a list of what he might order, let alone a list of specific cocktails. He didn't want to jinx things.

Nate stood outside the community board office and chewed on his thumbnail while Jonah took advantage of his height and focused straight ahead, which made it easy to avoid eye contact. Nate confessed to one Huertas regular that he wished they had some sense of what was about to happen, and she reassured him that surely their lawyer would have a take on things before the meeting began.

Nate was hardly going to ask Levey what it was. He remembered how angry he'd been after the SLA meeting and tried to focus instead on the simple logic of today's meeting. It was six weeks past the year they'd been told they had to wait, and that ought to be that.

When Peter Hoffman arrived, Jonah broke away to talk to him, comforted by the surprise presence of his ex-employer, who was there not because of Huertas but to support another applicant—the restaurant that was moving into the space previously occupied by Back Forty.

"You here for the upgrade again?" asked Hoffman. Jonah nodded, and the two men engaged in a quiet conversation while around them Huertas supporters introduced themselves to each other and Nate instructed them on how to sign in so that they were registered to speak. Once the doors opened the short rows of seats filled quickly, but Jonah and Nate hung back in the doorway, too antsy to sit down. They were last in a trio of applicants scheduled for six thirty on the revised agenda. It wouldn't be long.

The first applicants were back with a sidewalk café application a month after a stymied first appearance, having addressed all of the committee's concerns, and they got their permit quickly. The next applicant didn't show up on time, so suddenly Huertas was the second item on the agenda, not the third.

Jonah, Nate, and their lawyer hustled up the aisle and stood to one side of the long table where the committee members sat. They listened while the chairwoman synopsized their liquor license history: beer and wine granted in the fall of 2013, full liquor license turned down by Community Board 3 in September of 2014 "because they'd only been open for six months," turned down again by the SLA in December of that year. The committee had the packet the lawyer had distributed, a petition with over 120 names, and the letters of support. Was there anything else the applicants wanted to add?

Before Jonah and Nate could find their voices, Levey spoke up: Yes, the board had turned down Huertas's first request for an upgrade because it was too early. He wanted board members to appreciate that Huertas was back here, not at the SLA, because "it seemed like the right thing to do," to come back to the community for approval. He pointed out that there was no opposition. He mentioned that the *New York Times* had given Huertas a rave review.

That shook Jonah loose. "Press is great," he said. "But what's most gratifying is the response from the neighborhood."

The chair consulted the sheaf of speaker requests and started to read off names. One by one, regular customers stood up to testify.

The first speaker, a young man in rumpled survive-the-heat clothes, said that a full liquor license would help Huertas survive.

The second, a man in a suit, announced that he had taken his sister to Huertas to celebrate her engagement. "It's really an asset to the community."

A young woman said, "The beverage program even now is impressive, but I'd like to see what more they can do."

A young man said that he went to Huertas all the time with his girlfriend. "It's good for the community."

A woman from Northern Spain who had lived in the East Village for forty years praised the restaurant's authenticity. "It represents a happy, jovial people. The mix is wonderful," she said, glancing at the previous speakers, all of whom were young enough to be her children. "Seniors like me. Young people."

A soft-spoken twenty-four-year-old resident took a more practical stance: "They've shown success so far," she said, "but the atmosphere is competitive. A liquor license is a tool. I'd like to see them here for the long haul."

At that, the committee chair asked her colleagues if anyone had a motion. The lawyer broke in, nervously. There were more speakers. Didn't the board want to hear all of them?

"I think that you've made your point," said another committee member. Her colleagues laughed. Jonah and Nate allowed themselves a short, nervous chuckle and the lawyer, a hopeful smile.

Just like that, it was over: A motion that included language about Huertas having "established itself as a high-quality restaurant," a fast second, a unanimous vote to approve. Jonah and Nate and the lawyer and the group of supporters, who made up almost half of the audience, rushed out the door in a scrum of congratulatory hugs. The others scattered quickly, leaving Nate and Jonah alone on the sidewalk, staring at each other. Levey handed them a form to sign and peeled off as well, and in a mutual daze they started across East Fourth Street toward Huertas.

Nate grabbed his cell phone to call his father. Jonah winced, balled up his fist, and pressed it against his torso. "Kind of a knot in my stomach," he muttered. More than a year after he'd first hoped for it, he had a full liquor license, the one thing that could yield a substantial, consistent improvement in Huertas's profits.

In their excitement—and relief—Jonah and Nate had forgotten to ask when they could start serving liquor. They would figure it out tomorrow. Today was Jonah and Marina's one-year wedding anniversary, and Jonah wanted to leave work early and meet her at Maialino to combine past, present, and future in one celebratory meal: spaghetti alle vongole and a side order of the tripe.

The walk back to Huertas was much quicker than the walk over to the board meeting had been, now that there was no longer a reason to be worried, and when they burst in the door Jonah hurried to the kitchen to tell Jenni, while Nate hugged the host and gave Stew the good news. It was an unusually busy Monday night, so there was no time to bask. An hour after the community board meeting, Jonah was back at the pass in his apron, instructing a new server on which plates were to be taken to whom, surveying an impressive row of tickets, and watching the door. He'd talked to a line cook at Per Se who seemed to want to make a change, a woman he'd love to hire as a sous chef down the line, a notion—down the line—that he was again prepared to entertain. She was supposed to come in to eat tonight; nice timing, as it turned out, and he wanted to be sure to spot her the moment she arrived.

Nate appeared at the pass with three short glasses and a bottle of Woodford Reserve whiskey that he'd stashed somewhere, and poured a half inch for himself, and for Jonah and Jenni. They sipped, but he drank it down in one gulp, yelled "Whoo," and giggled.

"I am doing this illegally," he said, and headed off to hide the temporarily contraband bottle.

18

HUERTAS

Pete Wells had laid in a coded message at the end of his *Times* review, back in October, although he doubted that Jonah would have wanted to hear it flat out at that point. He wrote, "Once the familiar conventions of the modern tasting menu kicked in, I did steal a few looks at the front room, where a tray of hot croquetas always seemed to be going around. Maybe I wanted more spontaneity. Or maybe I just wanted a croqueta." The front room felt like more fun—but he understood that a young chef with his first place wanted to show that he could do more than great pintxos and memorable potato chips; more than charred octopus or his version of papas bravas.

And he could. Almost a year after his first visit, Wells still savored the memory of his two dinners at Huertas. What had impressed him about the menu del dia, he said, was Jonah's ability to create "thought-out meals, rather than a barrage of separate recipes. I thought he was really good at that." Good enough to remind Wells of Alice Waters's Chez Panisse, which, "has always had menus that were supposed to make sense and give you some variety, not become redundant and not fatigue you." Jonah did that, too.

But the food wasn't rarefied enough to warrant its own room—which was a practical assessment, not a criticism. "My impression was that this was a chef wanting to make a statement," said Wells, "and not quite getting that he had made a statement in the front room."

"It was clear to me that he thought the back room was really what the restaurant was all about. I thought that the front room was what the restaurant was all about. But I didn't hammer that point. I kind of left it between the lines."

Three days after the liquor license hearing, Jonah and Nate got the story they wanted, a long Q and A on Eater that ran under the headline, "For Huertas Owners Jonah Miller and Nate Adler, Change Is Nothing to Be Afraid Of." They packed up the past in a box labeled "then," and dismissed it: "We just had a cold, long winter," said Jonah, "and our first summer was trying, but then we got our *Times* review, and I've never looked back."

Nate seconded the message. "Being young, both of us are very eager to make changes," he said. "Stagnation, complacency is not something that is in our bloodlines at all."

They came off as two talented and ambitious partners who had figured out a better way to show people a good time, and were willing to upend the very concept they'd opened with, only a year earlier, in order to do so. They claimed the intersection of heritage and innovation for themselves—invoked their USHG legacy to prove that they were more substantial than their ages might suggest, and talked about making the bold move in case someone saw a similarity to David Chang or Major Food Group, both of them masters of the smart and profitable revamp.

They gave themselves credit for surviving in an unexpectedly difficult—sometimes hostile—environment.

"If you asked me two years ago, What would it feel like to have been open a year, I would have been like, 'No big deal, we should be open a year, otherwise we're huge failures,'" said Jonah. "But having been open a year, I understand now what the accomplishment is, and it's tough."

The first year's success required that they set new goals for the second, because a static restaurant was as good as out of business.

"We've been on people's lists," said Jonah, in the hope that Eater's readers would appreciate the brave overhaul and help propel Huertas forward, "but we want to inch closer to the top, and make sure we can't miss."

The new menu was a mix of front-room standards and dishes that might have appeared in the dining room in the old days: Jonah added a whole fish in a salt crust, a steak, and a foie gras pintxo; he created a dish of kimchi made with Spanish spices and served with chunks of jamón, and it sold as well as the fried rice had. He built a salad on his favorite seasonal green, which happened to be Italian, and stopped worrying quite so much about the provenance of what was on the menu. He made sure he had a chance to show what he could do—Huertas was not the pintxo bar that a worried investor had suggested a year earlier—this time with a nod to the way the current generation of restaurant-goers wanted to eat, a whole fish for the table to split, a bunch of pintxos, maybe one order of that kimchi rice, why not, to pass around. The permutations were up to the customer now; there were fewer rules, more ways to assemble a meal, and enough of a creative challenge to inspire the chef. Jonah might someday have the restaurant he dreamed of, where he got to show off exactly what he could do with a more challenging menu. Not yet.

There was no arguing with the daily numbers. The new menu did exactly what it was supposed to do—lured more people to Huertas and made this June the antithesis of the first June, a smooth and profitable transition past the dreaded Memorial Day marker and into a better second summer. This time around, the people who stayed in town came by to eat, and to have a cocktail. When Jenni complained about a slow weekend afternoon, it was because one table was empty, not because one table was full.

Jonah and Nate would never know if what made the difference was the new menu, or the simple passage of time, or Eater's big story, or the hot dog. It could be a combination of all those things. They didn't care. However they had gotten here, it was better, and it was more consistent day to day. They allowed themselves to assume that it would stick.

They sidled up to a renewed conversation about the future. Investors had stopped poring over the monthly reports and inquired, some of them, about what Jonah had in mind for his second project, because they were ready to write checks. Nate took Jonah at his word about wanting to do something different next time, and they started to consider a dramatic departure—not Spanish, not necessarily a traditional restaurant format, but one that combined a seated space with takeout and a delivery service. New Yorkers relied on takeout, which they wanted at breakfast and lunch as well as dinner, and while they could find it at every corner bodega or grocery store, the opposite end of the business, high-quality portable food, wasn't as crowded. It was smart from a business standpoint because it saved labor costs; there were no servers for the take-out side, only counter help. Nate had seen the kind of operation they had in mind on his trips to the West Coast—homemade everything, sold by well-informed staffers who could engage millennials in the sort of microanalysis they enjoyed, about where the smoked fish used to swim or who grew the peppers. There wasn't yet enough of it in New York to preclude what he and Jonah had in mind.

A great big space with seasonal American dishes, a market-restaurant that applied Jonah's standards to takeout if a diner didn't have the time to hang around, or brought it to the door when the weather was bad. New dishes all the time, based on a stronger relationship with the farmers at the market. They could do that.

They could probably afford Williamsburg this time, with its wall-to-wall clientele. If they put together a smart proposal, raising enough capital to buy a building would not be out of the question. They might as well start to look.

EPILOGUE: RIGHT-SIZED

Huertas's first twelve months were the business equivalent of mood swings, and the first anniversary brought with it a sense of relief. Bleak memories had been eclipsed by life since the *Times*'s review. Now the dips were shallower and shorter, and they yielded more readily to the solutions that Jonah and Nate engineered. Less apocalypse, more daily challenges they felt able to address. It seemed as though the worst was over.

People who'd been around longer knew better. "The restaurant cycle is such that the real years that you need to focus on, the ones that either make it or break it, it's two through five," said USHG's Richard Coraine, who in 1995 had opened a four-star restaurant in San Francisco that closed when it failed to sustain its early promise. "You're always going to be the new person in year one, and people always want to write about what's new and exciting. Years two through five it's 'Have you planted enough roots that are now starting to take?' If you're really good in year one and you're very popular and you're solid in years two through five, you're probably built for a longer race. If after year three it starts to dip, whatever was getting people in the door in the first place hasn't

completely stuck, so there's something that's off about what you're offering and what people want."

A chef-owner always had to keep an eye out for a dip that threatened
to become a trough, so that he could adjust on his terms and not in
panic mode. He had to be able to "right-size," as Coraine put it, "to make
sure that the expenditures are commensurate with the amount of revenue you have coming in."

"The trick in this business is reading the tea leaves," he said, "to
make sure it's not like a cold shower. You don't want to come in someday
and go, 'Wow, we need to not have four employees here.' Maybe you say,
'We're going to right-size it with one fewer employee for the next three
months and see where we get. Then we might have to lose another one,
but everybody's still busy doing what they do in the kitchen.'"

He thought that the decision to abandon Huertas's menu del dia was
a good one, because a fixed-price meal ran counter to basic notions of
hospitality: "This is all metaphorical," he said, "but it takes your wallet,
because you have no stake in how much you spend; it's what my menu
costs. And it takes your watch, because dinner's going to take as long
as it takes me to serve the courses I've defined. I could be wrong, but I
don't think that people want to eat minus those two things on a regular
basis."

The new a la carte menu was a smart move, as was the accompanying Eater article about the partners' willingness to embrace change.
A restaurant's identity lingered forever, online and in social media.
Change it without controlling the message and some customers might
feel betrayed.

"In year one, you go, 'Here's who I am, here's who I am, here's who I
am,' and then it's 'Guess what? Never mind,'" said Coraine.

Jonah and Nate had anticipated that reaction, though, and managed
to get their story out. If they saw more trouble ahead, they had to find

what Coraine called the "sweet spot" and continue to adjust, knowing that what was right-sized during the fall was probably not going to be right-sized after New Year's unless they catapulted to the ranks they aspired to join, the short list of restaurants everyone had to go to all the time.

Striking the right balance concerned Elizabeth Briggs as well, far earlier in the process. The Culinary Institute of America launched a new batch of students every three weeks at its main campus in Hyde Park, New York, and Chef Briggs was one of the first instructors they met: She taught Product Knowledge, where students like Jenni and Alyssa learned what Jonah had learned in David Waltuck's kitchen at Chanterelle, the basic vocabulary they had to master if they hoped someday to write their own menu. She taught her class how to identify high-quality ingredients, to distinguish a good onion from one whose appearance warned of rot, of mold, of age, of having been frozen, or to recognize different kinds of potatoes and understand how to cook each one. She taught them to transform a past-its-prime red onion into a marmalade to serve with a smoked beef tenderloin, because a smart chef didn't throw anything out.

Of late, she had added another lesson to the curriculum: She talked about doing "damage control," because a chef's life bore little resemblance to what her students saw on television or read about in profiles of the famous, wealthy few. Briggs liked food television because it made a food career more accessible to more people, but the narrow focus on becoming a restaurant chef concerned her. Notions of empire worried her even more because the odds were so great against it. "I try to teach reality, because if you don't, you set them up to fail," she said. "They think it's all going to be glory, and they go on an externship, no glory, and they're disappointed. Not glory, not high energy, not big money. They can be disenchanted."

Briggs wanted her students to appreciate at the outset that there were alternatives to the goal that drove so many of them to enroll—to own and run their own restaurants someday—and that the road to success was not an easy one. "Think about it," she said. "You're going to leave school with debt, do you really want to be a line cook? Maybe for a few years, but then you have to see."

In addition to its two- and four-year programs, CIA had added degrees in food science and food studies, both of which were more popular than the school had anticipated they might be, as people who loved to cook looked for more stable environments in which to do so. A graduate whom Briggs referred to as "a phenomenal cook" added nutrition studies to the mix and went to work for a healthcare company. Others might choose to work for a hotel chain or open a butcher shop or be drawn to kitchens at companies like Google, whose employee food service operation prized quality and innovation. Cooks might not get rich and famous in a corporate kitchen, but they wouldn't go out of business, either.

And yet she understood how difficult it was to abandon the notion of being a chef and owning a place. Somebody had to succeed, and a young cook who believed in himself would likely assume that he was going to be one of the chosen few who made it—and hardly be discouraged by the cautionary advice of someone who had been in the classroom for thirty years.

Briggs, a compact woman who wore wire-rimmed glasses and had her hair tucked tight behind her ears, looked back on her own life and saw "markers, little flags" of her early interest in food. She recalled her parents' vegetable garden, the tin of sardines she liked for breakfast when she was seven, her grandfather's homemade fudge—and her early appreciation of hot peppers, which she considered a sign of a sophisticated palate. She spent her college summer vacations working in a New England tea kitchen making tea sandwiches and hors d'oeuvres, although she was not allowed to work in the full kitchen, which was limited to men. She'd worked at golf and tennis clubs and as a personal chef who aspired to turn out meals "as good as Escoffier's."

She was a mainstay of the CIA faculty, but she wanted to be clear about what might have been. Then and now: No one had encouraged her to pursue a career as a chef when she was growing up, but today she might have been one of the students who ignored the more practical alternatives and made a name for herself.

"I'm science-minded," she said. "If I had been nurtured as a child I could have been Grant Achatz," the Chicago chef who had been her student, graduated in 1986, and went on to open Alinea, one of only two restaurants in Chicago to have been awarded three Michelin stars.

David Waltuck never found his equilibrium at Élan, though not for want of trying. The post-review holiday season did not live up to his expectations, but the start of 2015 did—it was as slow as those winter months usually were. He had to use profits to cover costs. "We'd stashed money in the fall," he said, "but we went through that pretty quickly." He started to build up debt.

So Waltuck cut back on staff, watched food costs even more closely, and waited for things to get better in the spring—which they did, but not at a sufficient level to reverse things. Élan still wasn't right-sized. He went back to his investors to ask for funds to get through what he hoped was a finite slump, but he raised only "some," and the turnaround was not substantial enough to make up the difference.

Business was "really not great," he said, and by July that had devolved into "not viable." He had a great chef de cuisine and sous chef, but he didn't have the money to support both of them and himself, nor enough confidence to promise them any kind of job security. The chef de cuisine, who had a pregnant wife, gave notice. The sous chef did as well.

At sixty-one, Waltuck was back on the line, running up and down stairs carrying five-gallon containers. "I was killing myself physically and stress-wise," he said. He and his partner cut their paychecks in half.

He figured he could continue like this until the fall, when things usually picked up, and once they did he could staff up again and catch his breath. He went back to his investors a second time to see if they would help him get that far—and then his second fall season let him down. "It was fine, good, okay but not what we needed it to be, not wonderful," in Waltuck's estimation. He was exhausted, and he saw the specter of another grim January just months ahead. He had to admit it: The contemporary restaurant scene was a foreign country that he was unable to navigate successfully.

"It's very difficult right now," he said. "Too many restaurants, costs are high, including labor, rents are high, margins are minuscule. And there's a different kind of restaurant-goer than there used to be; it's changed in ways I didn't see before I got back. It's hard to get beyond 'Let's go check this place out.' They go, they're done, they check you off the list."

In February 2016, Waltuck and his partner announced their decision to close Élan. They would serve a fixed menu of favorite dishes for a few weeks, and that was that. By then Waltuck was in the midst of a very different kind of business challenge, as he tried to extricate himself from the space without further financial loss. If someone was willing to assume the lease or could negotiate a new one—and if Waltuck stayed current on rent payments through that process—he would recoup both his security deposit, four months of his $30,000 rent, and the $400,000 key money. But he'd already missed his February rent, which meant that one month of the security deposit was gone. If they burned through three more months of non-payment before another tenant appeared, he'd lose both the four months' rent, $120,000, and the $400,000 key money.

He anticipated that renting out the West Village apartment where he and his wife had raised their family was not going to suffice to get him out of this hole. Once everything at Élan was wrapped up, he'd almost surely have to put it on the market. At the moment, it was his biggest asset.

February turned into June and the space sat, empty. Waltuck lost the four months' rent and the key money and prepared to embark on the next phase of his life, as director of culinary affairs for the Institute of Culinary Education in Manhattan, which offered six- to twelve-month programs as well as continuing education classes for professionals. In late June he started to audit classes, as any new instructor did. Eventually, he said, "I'll be teaching, and some special events, mentoring, probably going to work on creating electives, optional classes."

He considered the magnitude of the shift, which had its appeal. "It's a very different life in terms of hours and stress," he said, "and it enables me to do some other things. It's not as all-encompassing as having a restaurant—certainly not as having one that's not doing well."

Waltuck was optimistic, if not quite ready to entertain the notion that he was done running a restaurant kitchen. "It could be good," he said of his new job, "for a while."

Gavin Kaysen got offers every week from all over the country, New York, Los Angeles, San Francisco, Chicago, from hotels and independent restaurateurs, offers to open whatever he wanted or to run a project that someone already had in mind. In January 2015, the U.S.A. Bocuse d'Or team took the silver medal, second behind Norway, and the story of the years-long effort behind the victory made prospective partners all the more determined to go into business with him.

Rather than feel excited or inspired by all the possibilities, he complained about "how cloudy all of these things make me feel in my head." It was too much random input for a man who did not like to jump into things. He needed to develop a filter, an efficient way to evaluate opportunities, so that he could get back to the business of feeding people.

His company was called Soigne Hospitality, but what were its priorities? He called a meeting of his chef de cuisine and some of his investors to discuss what they were about. "'Community, culture and cuisine' is our rallying cry," said Kaysen, when they were done. Out of that came a set of basic questions that he and his group would ask about any potential project, including, Is it true to who we are? and, Is it financially responsible? If they couldn't answer every question in the affirmative they would pass, because there was no reason to consider compromise. He was in the kind of position other chefs dreamed of: The restaurant was jammed, reservations were still two months out, and customers drove to Minneapolis with no agenda other than to dine at Spoon & Stable. At the outset Kaysen had endured a single "scathing" review, but he counseled his people not to change what they were doing. He figured it had to happen, in part because of the attendant noise when the restaurant opened. Expectations were so high; backlash was inevitable.

"We were on every list you could be on," he said. "We could have served gold on a plate and it wouldn't have been good enough. We could have given all the food away for free, and for some people it just was not going to be good enough. That's okay."

Kaysen missed New York and refused to join the chorus of ex-pats who occasionally suggested that the future was elsewhere. "Nothing will change how I feel about in terms of where I made my culinary chops," he said. "It's always New York City. I made my name in New

York City, and there's no way of getting around that. Sure, we may receive more press in Minneapolis, but the truth of the matter is that all of my relationships stem from New York City. It is still the most powerful food city in the world, for me." Opening a restaurant there someday wasn't out of the question, but for now he saw opportunity pretty much wherever he wanted to be.

"I think in America we're going through this phase that Europe went through many, many years ago," he said, "having all these great restaurants that are not just in these big cities, but that you have to drive to and go to."

When he thought about expanding, he kept coming back to the notion of legacy. He took pride in being able to provide careers for the people who worked at Spoon & Stable—and if he opened more places he would be able to do that for more of them. "What inspires me is that eighty-two people work at this restaurant," he said. "That's eighty-two families that rely on our fiscal responsibility. It's eighty-two families that rely on us to be busy, to be successful, to be responsible.

"I want to open up another restaurant, and I want to open more than just two and three and four and five—not because of my ego, and not because I want to be busier, and I can promise you it's not because I want to make a lot of money," he said. "It's because I see a lot of really talented, hungry, passionate driven people who have helped, given up a portion of their lives to help me achieve goals in my life—and now it's my responsibility to figure out a way to give it back to them in the same way."

The one thing he refused to do was to pick up the pace, regardless of how fast other chefs opened one place after another. He'd found a potential second location in Minneapolis and had what he felt were great ideas for what to do with it. His team produced a presentation board that he happily judged to be amazing—and yet he couldn't quite commit to moving forward because the floor plan wasn't quite right.

That observation led to a flurry of e-mails the night after a meeting about the plan, and the next day Kaysen sent out an e-mail of his own. "I said, I want everybody to just walk away from it," he said. "I want everybody to just stop looking at it right now, and I want us to come back to it in two weeks. Just step back. Let's look at it from a different perspective after our break. After we've all had time to reflect."

People who wanted to work at the current revved-up pace were welcome to do so. Kaysen, who had opened Spoon & Stable later than he had thought he should, in a city he turned to after months of looking in likelier locations, was more than pleased with the results of his own personal slow food movement. If he wasn't convinced about the floor plan when everyone got back after break, and if no one came up with a new solution, they'd move on to the next prospect.

Which they did.

"The business we are in is not easy, everyone knows, but it is even more difficult when you lack or forget to be disciplined about things," he said. "Ask a chef and he will tell you never to cut corners when roasting a perfect chicken. Why do anything different when it comes to your lease?"

A pregnant Stephanie Izard barreled toward the 2016 opening of Duck Duck Goat and pending motherhood with the determination that had defined her forward march ever since she picked herself up off the floor at Scylla. The restaurant opening was delayed more than once, not that it put a dent in her confidence. She was happy to open a few months late, she told Eater Chicago, because it gave her the chance to "tweak" the food, to invite industry insiders for a trial run and then incorporate their suggestions. The soup dumplings had more soup in them because she had time to reconsider, so waiting had worked to her advantage.

The restaurant was packed from the moment it opened and got a rave review from the *Chicago Tribune* before a month had passed. "I'm starting to wonder," wrote the *Tribune*'s Phil Vettel, "if Stephanie Izard remembers what a slow night looks like."

Izard was about to forget that even on her nights off, with her due date fewer than two months after the restaurant's opening, but three restaurants and a cookbook and a new baby and whatever project came next felt as right to her as a more stately pace did to Kaysen. This time she was doing it right, with business partners who supported the expansion effort and conversations with her husband about what constituted a reasonable agenda. Success bred success, and she intended to enjoy it on all fronts.

She told Eater's reporter that she hoped to be a role model as more women found work in restaurant kitchens and wondered how to achieve a balance between work and family. Izard couldn't provide practical advice yet, but she could inspire them to assume that they could pull it off. Attitude might be all they needed, and on that level she was clear.

"I think you can do it all."

Alberto reset his one-year clock for early 2016 when he started to work the roast and sauté station at Huertas, but months before that he started to wonder if he ought to make plans to leave. He got used to the station quickly and could stare down one hundred covers without flinching—and if he still aspired to Alyssa's finesse, he knew how to get through a rough night without falling apart. The longer he worked with Jonah, the more he admired his boss's calm, which in Alberto's mind was synonymous with professionalism. He was going to be that good.

He was barely twenty-two; he could afford to hang around, but the voice in his head was impatient. A year was a year. It might be time to take the next step—a higher-volume place or a different cuisine, a learning opportunity in either case. Alberto had to stick to his plan or he'd end up idling. He had to work the station long enough to prove that he'd mastered it but not for so long that it began to seem as though that was all he could do.

And then, in October, Max confided to Alberto that he was going to leave, told him before he told Jonah or Nate, which left Alberto wondering how they would react. Could he be in line for yet another promotion, this time to sous chef? Jonah had sent him over to Marta to trail to give him a sense of what else was out there, and Alberto came back reeling at the sheer volume. A Tuesday night at Marta beat a Saturday night at Huertas, lapped it and kept going, and when he first arrived he'd looked in bewilderment at fifteen cooks prepping their stations, unable to figure out who the sous was or how many of them there might be. He came back humbled, wondering if it was too soon for a move like that; he'd never seen anything like it. It might be smarter to hang on— to take one more step up at Huertas and see what happened when the second place materialized. Jonah had already started to let Alberto handle some of the ordering, which might be a sign that he knew he could lose his senior line cook if he didn't make life more interesting. A promotion wasn't out of the question.

The offer came quickly, because Jonah was not interested in another protracted round of failed trails. He wanted Alberto to appreciate what the job of sous chef meant, not only as a promotion but as part of the team that would build the next restaurant, the people he could trust to maintain high standards once he and Nate were ready to move ahead. Jonah pointed out that he had been twenty-four when Nick Anderer promoted him to sous chef at Maialino. Alberto was twenty-two. He ought to be proud; he ought to say yes.

He did. He was intimidated, as he had been when he stepped up to the roast and sauté station, but this time it was different. Running the pass was a mental challenge more than a physical one. He'd have to manage the cooks, make sure that they were on top of all the orders, accommodate special requests from the servers, and figure out how to take care of diners who ate faster or slower than the average. He'd place orders and often be the one to close the restaurant. If the line cooks didn't work fast enough or clean enough he'd have to figure out how to inspire them. He'd be in charge some nights, and he vowed to do it the way Jonah did—firm instead of frantic—no matter how nervous he felt inside.

Jenni was not frantic, but by her own estimation she was too often frazzled. The promotion she got at the end of March 2015, was it—no further mention of equity or partnership over the summer or into the fall. When she and Jonah finally started to circle around the notion of a promotion to chef de cuisine it was a tense conversation. The leadership qualities he wanted to see in her had not emerged at a level that satisfied him, and the person who ran the Huertas kitchen during the expansion had to have those skills. A promotion was no longer a warm inevitability but contingent on improved behavior. He couldn't be worried that she might blame someone, front or back of house, when she should instead be looking for a way to correct and inspire. For her part, Jenni felt undercut by a lack of support from the partners; the more they criticized the more she doubted herself, until she got to the point where she began to wonder if in fact she was not ready for this much responsibility.

The strain showed. Jonah offered to send her to a leadership class and wondered privately if it would suffice. Jenni vowed to set more of an example even as she began to think that it was simply time to make a change. She had never seriously considered anything but a future with Jonah—and yet the best thing might be to take one of those sideways steps and continue her education.

Fall kept them too busy to make a decision, and Jonah suggested that they regroup in January to see how they felt about the chef de cuisine job. Jenni knew the answer before she got there. "It was taking too much effort to convince myself that I wanted it, which meant that I didn't want it," she said. "I kept trying to talk myself into it—find the motivation—and I couldn't. I could see: I'm not ready."

"If I'd felt more included in the partnership it might have been different," she said. "Even though it was the four of us from the start—Jonah, Nate, Luke, and me—it slowly became Jonah and Nate. I needed growth. I needed to move on." She wanted to cook more and manage less.

Jenni started to look for a new job and found one as a sous chef with Missy Robbins, a highly regarded chef who had run the kitchens at the Michelin-starred A Voce and A Voce Columbus and was about to open her own place, Lilia, in a warehouse space in Brooklyn. While it was a step down in the kitchen hierarchy, it was a chance to go back to Italian food under the tutelage of a chef known for her pasta. The other sous and the chef de cuisine were both men, so Jenni was the highest-ranking woman in the kitchen after Robbins herself.

Jenni explained the move in the same way both to her new employer and to Jonah: "I want to learn from another new chef," she said. "It's time for a transition." But it was a difficult decision, and she told herself that this might merely be a profitable detour, not a permanent separation. She might come back around to her dream of a food truck as part of what would by then be Jonah's far larger restaurant group.

That left Jonah with yet another kitchen vacancy, and he rolled up to Huertas's second anniversary facing the kind of hiring dilemma that had plagued him for more than a year, though for a far more important position. He had to find a chef de cuisine who could step in and take over, and the longer that took the longer they would have to wait to do anything else.

It was time to revise his definition of success again, to get it to align with reality. The second place they'd talked about opening late in 2015 had eluded them, and his immediate short-term goal was to make sure they had a second profitable summer. He started to wonder if they would even be able to put a project together by the end of 2016. They still didn't have a business plan, though they continued to talk about the concept they'd discussed and to look for a name that conveyed either their regional roots or a local-and-homemade philosophy. Jonah suggested Sunchoke because they grew in the region and were more interesting than other tubers. Nate thought that Croft would work, because it meant a small plot of arable land on which a farmer lived, and would convey all the attributes they wanted to sell.

Jonah was fine with the pace for now; he and his wife were about to have their first child, and he had no interest in ramping up a new project in the first months of his daughter's life. Nate, who despaired of ever having time for a social life, was in more of a hurry—if he was going to miss out on a chunk of his twenties he'd like to have more to show for it. Their natural rhythms diverged even further than normal. Jonah knew that multiple restaurants were a necessity when the time was right. Nate figured the time was right now, and they needed to get going.

Chris McDade showed up on Jonah's doorstep to say that he was thinking about leaving his latest job, so Jonah pitched an idea that benefited both of them: Chris could be the new chef de cuisine at Huertas, which would free Jonah, finally, to get serious about a second place. Chris would have to tolerate a pay cut to align with Jonah's budget, but that was a short-term problem. The promise of having his own kitchen to run made up for it.

Chris had left Marta at the end of 2015 to be the executive sous chef at Café Altro Paradiso, the second restaurant from the team behind Estela, a small place not too far from Huertas that counted President and Michelle Obama among its guests. It was the kind of high-profile job that would get him that much closer to opening his own place, and while it meant an obvious delay in Jonah's plan to work alongside his Maialino colleague, he tried to be philosophical when he heard the news. This would only enhance their eventual collaboration, even if he had to wait a bit longer for it to materialize.

And then Chris decided to quit, only weeks into the perfect gig, because he didn't like the way the kitchen ran. Suddenly Jonah's future was right in front of him, complete with an alternate concept for a new place, one that Jonah had to admit he preferred—not a bigger space that emphasized takeout but a cozier, smaller one where he and Chris could serve their versions of whatever New York classics they felt like cooking, anything from the city's culinary past that inspired a reboot. Nate could probably raise money for a forty-seat place without breaking a sweat, and Jonah was ready for a place that was packed all the time. The often empty back room at Huertas did not earn its keep; he wouldn't mind having to turn people away.

Nate loved the idea of having Chris around because he injected new energy into the kitchen and made a second restaurant more of an imperative. He did not love the idea of a smaller second place unless it made his as-yet undisclosed agenda easier to implement. Nate was almost done with a business plan he'd been working on for six months, whenever he had a day off, for a concept that would not necessarily include Jonah. If Jonah and Chris preferred their idea, as Nate expected they would, he would have less trouble striking out on his own. He could hire another chef to work for him, and if Jonah wanted to consult, that might work out fine.

Nate had convinced himself that they'd taken Huertas as far as they could, and being a minority partner in a small business was not enough for him. He wanted to own a business. He had even started to look for a space, not in the bustling center of Williamsburg but "on the outskirts of the main strip," where rents might be a bit lower and he'd have a better chance of leasing a space he could build out to his specifications. He looked closer to downtown Brooklyn and near the area that Jonah had dismissed years before, which seemed to have developed more of a street life since then. Nate hoped to raise $1 million, find a warehouse space, and design a combination of retail and restaurant with an emphasis on the former; he figured 400 square feet for take-out and 1,400 square feet for seated service, but no servers, only food runners who delivered orders that customers made at the counter. He hoped to translate the places he loved in Los Angeles—Gjusta in Venice and Sqirl in Silver Lake—into a version that worked in his hometown.

It had to be fast. In a glowing review of High Street on Hudson, a Philadelphia import, Pete Wells had pointed out a shortcoming of the New York restaurant scene: "Restaurants that aim to be useful and interesting all day long are becoming more common in Los Angeles and other cities; New York could use more of them." That single sentence was the food equivalent of the call to post for the Kentucky Derby, as talk spread on the restaurant circuit about this chef or that front-of-house person who was ready to step into the void. Travis Lett, chef and co-owner of Gjusta and its sister restaurant, Gjelina, had just announced that he was coming to Manhattan to take over a big downtown space with restaurateur Ken Friedman of The Spotted Pig, The Breslin, and John Dory, a plan that had been rumored for months.

"You better hurry," a colleague warned Nate. "You're going to miss the boat."

Jonah assumed that Nate was working on the idea they had talked about, the one he called Sunchoke and Nate called Croft, and had begun to wonder why it was taking him so long to share it. But he didn't push; if Nate had a reason for holding back there was probably nothing Jonah could do about it. Still, he was a money-raising machine, and while Chris and Jonah were capable of finding investors they weren't as good at it as Nate was. It would take longer without him, if that was what was about to happen. Jonah knew that Nate would expect an equal partnership on the next place, so he decided to show his good intentions: He offered Nate some of his own equity in Huertas to confirm that they were in this together.

Nate thought, That's not much money and it could be years down the line. The 2016 budget anticipated $100,000 in profits, less than the 2015 figure and a nod to what they called a "sad truth" in a letter to investors: It was harder for established restaurants to maintain volume. They'd sent out the first distribution checks to investors in the third quarter of 2015, much earlier than anyone anticipated, but then postponed a second distribution until after the first quarter of 2016, in the hope of being able to cut larger checks later in the year. And money wasn't the real issue: Once Nate started to think about running his own place he couldn't stop thinking about it, and while Jonah's offer was very generous it wasn't enough to distract him. Nate was in the same place Jonah had been when he quit Maialino: He was ready to venture out on his own.

Jonah and Nate and Chris circled one another, trying to figure out what would get them farthest, fastest, wondering if the best answer would require a new configuration. Jonah could partner again with Nate and figure out how to involve Chris, but Nate had started to drop hints about what he was working on and it sounded less like a creative partnership and more like a chef-for-hire, which hardly interested Jonah. Nate could try to convince Chris to decamp with him, a long shot given the chefs' friendship but a pitch he was prepared to make if Chris seemed at all interested. Or he could pursue his project without either Jonah or Chris. He could hire a chef to run the back of house and not have to take on another partner at all.

Jonah could move forward on the smaller place with Chris and Nate, or with Chris and without Nate, which meant that he would have to hire a general manager. Restaurants ran that way, so it wasn't out of the question, and Jonah had resources of his own, Huertas investors who were ready to invest in a new project. For that matter, Chris could take the menu he was working on and find a place—he was looking as well—either with Jonah or on his own.

Chris floated the idea of the three of them working together on a set of overlapping projects: Huertas, Nate's idea, whatever it was, and Jonah's and Chris's idea, all of them tied together in a loose framework that played to everyone's strengths. But that didn't give Nate autonomy or get Jonah out of Huertas, so clearly it was not going to be their first choice.

Nick Thatos, the contractor and designer who built Huertas, said that the answer was simple: Go bigger. He wanted Jonah to consider not 40 seats but 100 or even 120. That's what made money these days

When Gavin Kaysen was Jonah's age, he was Daniel Boulud's employee. When Stephanie Izard was Jonah's age, she was passed out on the floor. David Chang was battling to keep his second place, Momofuku Ssäm Bar, afloat, and April Bloomfield had not yet started cooking at The Spotted Pig. Jonah had plenty of options, when he thought about it; maybe too many. For the first time since he quit Maialino and got ready to open Huertas, he took a breath and looked around.

He knew what he didn't want: the big place Nick was talking about or Nate's chef-for-hire notion, whatever the actual business arrangement might be. If Chris wanted to pursue the smaller restaurant project together, Jonah would be happy to do so, because having him around

Huertas only reminded Jonah of how much fun it was to be in the kitchen together—but in truth the notion of a second restaurant overwhelmed him at the moment. He'd done it. Nate and Chris hadn't, yet. The key, for him, was to keep his head and not rush into anything. There was a next chapter for a talented chef, he knew it. To his surprise, given the hell-bent pace of the last few years, he wasn't quite sure what it was.

His first responsibility was to keep Huertas healthy, so he decided to make some changes of the sort that Coraine prescribed. In the summer of 2016 Jonah right-sized the back-of-house staff—eliminated one cook and got ready to cut a second one during slow weeks. The kitchen could handle the current volume with four people, not five, which gave him at least a salary's worth of savings. To make it easier for the remaining cooks, he intended to make another round of what he called "menu edits," not as sweeping as when he gave up the menu del dia but designed to accommodate both the smaller kitchen staff and Huertas's regular customers.

As the restaurant entered its third year, Jonah took "a hard look at who comes here, and they're not necessarily foodies. They're people who want Spanish food, so maybe we give them what they come to expect rather than put as much of a spin on it." Customers were not as interested in creative preparations as he or Nate had thought they would be—so he decided to offer charred shishito peppers year-round rather than when they were in season, even if it meant buying Mexican ones when the local supply ran out. He added albondigas because meatballs were popular, and figured that at least his would be far better than average. Diners could still order a meat or cheese plate but not choose the individual components, because a standard assortment was faster for the kitchen to prepare. He put the saffron fried rice on the menu.

"More surefire crowd pleasers," he said. "Stuff we're still proud of, but maybe not that exciting for us to cook day in and day out." He had a business to run, and this, he believed, was the formula for a profitable 2016.

With those adjustments in place he could afford to focus on the smart next move. Nate finally showed him the business plan for Gertie, named for his grandmother and now closer in concept, he said, to the Washington, DC, salad chain sweetgreen than to Gjusta or the idea that he and Jonah had originally discussed. Sweetgreen had raised $18.5 million to expand beyond its twenty-seven East Coast locations, including money from both Danny Meyer and Daniel Boulud, and Nate wanted a concept he could replicate down the line.

It was an easy call for Jonah. He reiterated that he didn't want to be in the kitchen unless he had "pushback" on the menu, which clearly wasn't part of the plan, so he'd be happy to help out or give advice but didn't want to participate more actively than that. He had not worked this hard—and achieved this much—to cook someone else's food. Privately, he wondered how much trouble Nate might have finding the chef he was sure was out there, because to Jonah the menu fell in the tricky space between great, challenging food and no-brainer cuisine.

"It's not the food I want to cook," he said. "And in a way it's very ambitious, but in another sense it's like Blue Smoke," referring to the USHG barbecue restaurants. "You're going to have a hard time attracting talented cooks because it's not that interesting food, but it takes a lot of people to keep it moving. It's hard to find that in-between person, because it doesn't sound like fun cooking." And that was only one of the challenges Nate faced; he confessed that what looked easy often wasn't. One landlord wanted him to bring a committed investor along to prove that someone involved with the project had deep pockets, the Brooklyn neighborhood that at first looked promising was dead when Nate bicycled through at eleven at night, and a sure-thing investor who Nate had counted on for $50,000 had just bought a new house and had a baby on the way, so maybe next time.

It all sounded very familiar to Jonah, and it raised an immediate logistical question, because he knew how much energy and time it would take to get Gertie off the ground. He could let Nate keep his equity but replace him on the floor, but he didn't, and wouldn't until he saw how this played out. "The hardest thing will be trying to figure out his continued role and salary here, and make sure things aren't falling through the cracks," said Jonah. "But he wants to do it. It's in his system to pursue it." If doing so meant that Nate let his Huertas responsibilities slip, Jonah would have to hire a new general manager.

Jonah was unsettled at first by Nate's news, although it wasn't unexpected. It was disorienting. All their talk of what they might do next was about to come unraveled, at least until they saw whether Gertie's got off the ground. The possibility of having to take on a new partner or hire a replacement hardened into a probability, a substantial variable added to the list of unknowns that defined the immediate future. But Jonah was good at turning disappointment into motivation—and after all, his relationship with Nate was not yet three years old. He had wanted to be a chef for far longer than that, and it had never been a conditional dream. He'd never thought, I want to be a chef and own my place but only if I can raise a million dollars, or find a spot in Williamsburg, or hire an already-accomplished team, or have a full liquor license on opening day. He had always intended to be a chef and have a restaurant, no matter what obstacle he had to dodge to do so, and he'd find a way to step around Nate's ambition and move forward. This might turn out to be a good thing in the end if it restored his sense of urgency.

He righted himself quickly and set a personal deadline: He would find something new to do within the next year. Jonah got a half-dozen unsolicited realty listings every week, and while he wasn't actively looking he always checked them out, just in case one of them "charmed" him in a way that the Huertas location hadn't. He still blamed his space for Huertas's solid but not runaway performance—and while he might not welcome the stress of opening another full-scale restaurant he did wonder what would happen when the address was not a drawback. No reason not to look; he might stumble onto a great place just as Chris got enough investors lined up.

In the meantime, there was the hot dog. *New York* magazine had run an item in its summer 2015 Cheap Eats edition that posed the question, "The East Village pintxos bar's new Basque-hot-dog takeout window might not be the Coney Island boardwalk, but isn't this more or less how Shake Shack got its start?" which fairly guaranteed that readers would take notice. The hot dog window was open again in 2016, even as Jonah started to branch out: He accepted an invitation to have a stall at the Grub Street Beats & Eats event at the weekly Hester Street fair, which promised as many as four thousand hungry guests, and if it went well he'd go back for the regular Saturday fairs through the end of the summer. The organizers of the HBO Bryant Park Summer Film Festival invited him to join a select group of vendors and he said yes to them as well. The hot dog bags had HUERTAS BASQUE DOG stamped on them, so he was building the brand with every sale.

He started to wonder if the hot dog could lead to something more. Like Nate, he was interested in the replicable concept—the Shake Shack connection was a compliment but also a reminder that there was safety in numbers and in easy food. Jonah found himself circling back to the idea of a vermút and pintxo bar, which could be a vermút and hot dog bar, no, why stop there, a beer and wine and cocktails hot dog bar, or wait: Part of what made the hot dog great was the Martin's potato roll, so it made sense to expand from there, and besides, Basque Dog was a pretty cool name for a bar.

Basque Dog: a full bar menu with maybe eight sandwiches and a couple of salads, daytime grab-and-go and a bar at night. The hot dog along with anything else that tasted good on a Martin's roll—and in Jonah's estimation, everything tasted good on a Martin's roll, so there were lots of possibilities. The next few months would be full of unknowns, as Nate did or didn't get Gertie started, and Chris kept looking, and real estate listings hit Jonah's inbox. It wasn't where he thought he'd be by now, but something would fall into place because it had to. Basque Dog: It might be good business, and it could be fun.

ACKNOWLEDGMENTS

I was nine when my father introduced me to the backstage world of restaurants—I drank Shirley Temples while he sold stockpots—and I have loved it ever since. At its best, a restaurant kitchen is full of people who simply want to make us happy at mealtime and are willing to work crazy hours under difficult conditions to do so.

Chef Jonah Miller took a big chance on a stranger; one minute we were sitting in Union Square Park as he pulled sketches out of his backpack and described his dream, and the next I was his shadow whether things were going well or not. He never flinched, not even on the gloomier days. I thank him for his nerve and integrity.

The partners and staff inherited a fly on the wall and got used to it, so thanks to Nate Adler, Luke Momo, Jenni Cianci, Alyssa Campos, Alberto Obando, Max Lotlin, Stew Parlo, Laura Valla, Caleb Cutchin, and Lance Hester-Bay.

Chefs around the country provided a historical perspective or a complementary narrative or both. I'm grateful to David Waltuck, Gavin Kaysen, and Stephanie Izard for taking the time to share their stories, and to Nick Anderer, Joyce Goldstein, Peter Hoffman, Tom Colicchio, and Nancy Silverton for providing their perspective. Restaurateurs Danny Meyer of Union Square Hospitality Group and Michael McCarty of Michael's restaurants on both coasts put everything in context; and Pete Wells, restaurant critic at the *New York Times*, took the time to elaborate on his experience at Huertas. Richard Coraine at USHG contributed his analysis of the current scene and then cast a veteran's eye over the pages; his help was invaluable. Joseph Levey made sure I understood the liquor licensing process.

At the Culinary Institute of America, communications manager Jeff Levine provided an overview of the program, and Chef Elizabeth Briggs allowed me to sit in on her class. At the Culinary Institute of New York Monroe College, Dean Frank Constantino let me watch his competitive team rehearse and discussed access for minority students. I thank all of them for their help, as well as C-CAP founder Richard Grausman, who talked to me about diversity in the professional kitchen.

Eric Lupfer at WME looked after this book as though we'd known each other for years, not months, before we started. An auspicious beginning; I appreciate his attentive support.

At Avery Books, editor Lucia Watson is insightful, precise, and funny; I was the fortunate beneficiary of her enthusiasm. Thanks as well to Megan Newman, Lindsay Gordon, Louisa Farrar, Roshe Anderson, Farin Schlussel, and Anne Kosmoski.

William Whitworth read the manuscript even though he didn't have the time to do so, and I am as grateful as always for the opportunity to discuss my work with him. My thanks to Lisa Belkin for her careful read.

Friend-colleague is an awkward hyphenate, but I am lucky to have several of them at the Columbia University Graduate School of Journalism: Paula Span, Laura Muha, Amy Singer, Alexis Clark, and Merrill Perlman are great friends and supportive colleagues at the Columbia University Graduate School of Journalism, as is alum and fellow food writer Kate Cox. I thank ex-students Alex Hubbard and Thomas Brennan for teaching me a thing or two about resilience.

Jesse Kahn upped my coffee game and confirmed the value of a dry sense of humor.

I have friends without borders back on the West Coast who refuse to let geography do us in, and I'm grateful when we land in the same time zone: Vicky Mann, Lori Rifkin, Patty Williams and Kenneth Turan, Laura Moskowitz, Cassidy Freeman, and Clark and Megan Freeman. Thanks to Ginger Curwen, who is easier to access.

Carolyn See is with me no matter where we are.

My thanks to my sister, Lori, to Lesly and Trey, Josh and Lani, and the next generation of diners—and to my mother, Norma, who probably would have preferred plain chicken but was always a good sport about dining out. And always, to my father, Ira.

Which brings me to the person who rounds off these acknowledgments more often than not. Sarah Dietz first appeared in this space as a four-year-old who loved words. She's had some birthdays since, but I thank her for being that girl in spirit, still.

AUTHOR'S NOTE

Complete access is a lot to ask of a young chef about to open his first restaurant, but that is what I needed, and that is what Jonah Miller provided. I stood in the kitchen during service and in the hours that preceded and followed it, attended lineup and partners' meetings, and observed everything from recipe prep to the tense moments before a big review hit. To fill out the story, I spent hours interviewing the principals—so when I describe how they were feeling or their private thoughts, it's not because I can read minds. It's because I asked and they told me. If I wasn't present at a particular moment, I talked to multiple sources who were, to make sure that I had consensus on what happened. I also sought out sources whose stories complemented the central narrative at Huertas, from chef David Waltuck, Jonah's first mentor, to chefs Stephanie Izard and Gavin Kaysen, whose paths are very different from Jonah's.

For part of the time my daughter worked at Huertas. If she were a cook we would have had a conflict to resolve. Since she worked front-of-house, she remained out of my professional line of sight.

I made a decision about names that splits the difference between informality and tradition. I refer to the Huertas staffers by their first names because last names—the way journalists usually do it—felt too removed. They're a family, and I was in the midst of it. Everyone else gets the usual last-name treatment.

One last note on parameters: I stick to third-person narrative because I had no role in the story except to watch and listen as it unfolded. I stepped into the story on only two small occasions: I changed the names of a couple of job applicants who came and went, fast—and I changed the fake name that restaurant critic Pete Wells used to make one of his reservations at Huertas, in case he still uses it.